Promoting Transboundary Water Security in the Aral Sea Basin through International Law

International Water Law Series

VOLUME 3

The titles published in this series are listed at *brill.com/iwl*

Promoting Transboundary Water Security in the Aral Sea Basin through International Law

By

Dinara Ziganshina

BRILL
NIJHOFF

LEIDEN | BOSTON

Ziganshina, Dinara, author.
Promoting transboundary water security in the Aral Sea basin through international law / By Dinara Ziganshina.
p. cm. -- (International water law series)
Includes bibliographical references and index.
ISBN 978-90-04-27423-5 (hardback : alk. paper) -- ISBN 978-90-04-27426-6 (e-book) 1. Water--Law and legislation,--Asia, Central. 2. Water rights (International law) 3. Water--Law and legislation--Aral Sea Region (Uzbekistan and Kazakstan) 4. Water resources development--Law and legislation--Aral Sea Region (Uzbekistan and Kazakstan) I. Title.

KLA477.Z57 2014
346.5804'691--dc23

2014029900

This publication has been typeset in the multilingual "Brill" typeface. With over 5,100 characters covering Latin, IPA, Greek, and Cyrillic, this typeface is especially suitable for use in the humanities.
For more information, please see www.brill.com/brill-typeface.

ISSN 2351-9606
ISBN 978-90-04-27423-5 (hardback)
ISBN 978-90-04-27426-6 (e-book)

This book is printed on acid-free paper.

Contents

Foreword

Addressing the world's imminent water crisis requires new thinking, new approaches, and innovation across the board. We are fortunate to have this new scholarship which explores how international law contributes to transboundary water cooperation. As one of the most pressing issues of contemporary society, how we manage our diminishing quantities and quality of freshwater resources will determine the health and wealth of communities all around the world.

Dr. Dinara Ziganshina in this monograph, *Promoting Transboundary Water Security in the Aral Sea Basin through International Law,* tackles a number of critical challenges with thoughtful insights and ambitious aims. How to 'make international water law work' in the context of the Aral Sea, taking into account the extra-legal aspects of international law – well, this is a mammoth and courageous undertaking! If only to appreciate how such a complex set of problems can be identified, analysed and presented in a coherent manner, readers are strongly encouraged to deeply consider Dr. Ziganshina's study.

The Aral Sea basin, shared by Afghanistan and five post-Soviet republics of Central Asia – Kazakhstan, Kyrgyzstan, Tajikistan, Turkmenistan and Uzbekistan, presents one of the most challenging case studies for exploring water security. Its geo-political situation, combined with water quality and quantity issues, and the upstream-downstream challenges in this region present a complex matrix of problems. Dr. Ziganshina grapples with these, introducing an innovative legal analytical framework for rigorously considering the issues arising in the Aral Sea – offering 'a more dynamic and systemic picture of international water law in the Arial Sea basin'. Her work, however, has broader application, offering a multi-dimensional legal lens through which we can assess transboundary water-related problems around the world and it is this contribution that is the most significant.

One of the persistent criticisms of international law, generally, is its (alleged) lack of effectiveness. Dr. Ziganshina tackles this challenge through locating the analysis beyond the 'compliance' dimension of international law. Instead, she locates the analysis of the effectiveness of international water law within a nested framework that evaluates norms and processes, which she considers together determine how international law works in practice.

It is Dr. Ziganshina's interface of legal and socio-legal research that marks this work as a unique contribution in this field. Introducing two strands of analysis through legal norms (determinacy and stringency) and through legal processes (inclusiveness, transparency, discursiveness, and coherence), this study presents a framework for analysis that forces us to look beyond the static structures of treaties. Focussing on this combination of norms and processes crystallises the essence of international law; applying such an approach to the complex case study of the Aral Sea provides a unique opportunity to test her analytic approach. It is a difficult test, but this makes it all the more fascinating. Analysing legally relevant behaviour and legal consciousness provides a substantive context for considering how *legal relationships* are developed – a core theme of this study. Without functional international relationships, the global community is left bereft of effective avenues for meaningful engagement. Dr. Ziganshina posits that the true purpose of international law is to build these relationships and it is in this context that legally relevant behaviour and legal consciousness – the *process* elements – are so important. Indeed, the role of law in water diplomacy efforts must consider more than the collective body of treaty and customary norms – how States and key actors act and engage are a necessary part of the picture and may determine the quality of the final outcomes.

This comprehensive study closes with recommendations for policy-makers and practitioners in an attempt to provide guidance on 'how to make international water law work'. This pragmatic orientation aligns with the key purpose of the study and draws together the key findings of the scholarship. Importantly, these observations are then considered in a more generic sense in a convincing way. Clearly this study has broader application and it would be interesting to see how this applies in other parts of the world where transboundary water cooperation remains elusive.

On another note, I would like to raise a specific issue, which has been highlighted for me recently through a novel workshop convened by the Asian Development Bank (Manila, February 2014), that focused on a topic that fails to receive the attention it merits – the role of women in the water sector. Dr. Ziganshina, as a young woman has demonstrated the perseverance, commitment and diligence required for high scholastic achievement. This is a significant accomplishment in *many* respects that requires full recognition and high commendation. I have completed this foreword around the time of International Women's Day (8 March) and would like to formally congratulate Dr. Dinara Ziganshina on her considerable and most important contribution to the field of water – she is making the world a better place for us all. Women in water – something we need to applaud, support and encourage.

It has been my sincere pleasure and honour to be provide this foreword – Dr. Dinara Ziganshina provides us all with inspiration for the future. I already look forward to her next major work in this field.

Dr. Patricia Wouters
Xiamen Law School – China International Water Law Programme
University of Dundee Centre of Water Law, Policy and Science, under the auspices of UNESCO

Preface

I have been engaged in transboundary water interactions in Central Asia since 2003. As a lawyer I was in the minority and most of the time had to explain to people with technical background the basics of international law and its relevance to addressing transboundary water issues in the region. The most frequently asked questions had to deal with practical relevance and effectiveness of international water law. Intention to answer these hard practical questions in a systematic and comprehensive way brought me to the best possible place – to the IHP-HELP Centre for Water Law, Policy and Science under the auspice of UNESCO, University of Dundee (UK) – where, thanks to a grant from the Scottish Government, I pursued my PhD research. I examined international water law in the Aral Sea basin shared by Afghanistan and five post-Soviet countries of Central Asia (Kazakhstan, Kyrgyzstan, Tajikistan, Turkmenistan and Uzbekistan) by posing the question, 'How does international law work in addressing transboundary water challenges in the Aral Sea basin?' This book presents the results of this study.

I would like to thank all those who gave me the opportunity to pursue PhD research in Dundee and those who accompanied me on this journey. I warmly thank all staff, past and present, at the IHP-HELP Centre for Water Law, Policy and Science, and especially my supervisors Professor Patricia Wouters and Dr. Alistair Rieu-Clarke for being supportive and encouraging throughout the process, and also Dr Sarah Hendry for her irreplaceable heartiness and understanding. My special thanks go to fellow PhDs – Bjørn-Oliver Magsig, Hugo Tremblay, Musa Abseno, Mohamad Al Afghani, Ana Maria Daza Vargas, Tran Tran, Jing Lee and Yumiko Yasuda – whose company I enjoyed for three years and whose friendship will cherish even though we are separated by distance now.

I owe a very particular debt of gratitude to members of my thesis examination committee composed of Professor Stephen McCaffrey, Dr. Sergei Vinogradov and Dr. Melaku Geboye Desta. It was a great honor and an enormous pleasure to be examined by such a panel.

Most especially, I thank my family for being with me, for being mine, for being so special and supportive. Still, my deepest thanks go to Professor Victor A. Dukhovny – my mentor and critic – for giving me, among many other things, confidence in myself.

List of Tables and Figures

Table

Figure

List of Abbreviations

ADB	Asian Development Bank
ASBP	Aral Sea Basin Programme
BWO	Basin Water Organisation
CA	Central Asia
CAREC	Central Asia Regional Economic Cooperation
CARs	Central Asian Republics
CAREWIB	Central Asia Regional Water Information Base
CIS	Commonwealth of Independent States (or Commonwealth)
COP	Conference of the Parties
EC IFAS	Executive Committee of the International Fund for Saving the Aral Sea
ECO	Economic Cooperation Organisation
EIA	Environmental Impact Assessment
ESIA	Environmental and Social Impact Assessment
EU	European Union
EurAsEC	Eurasian Economic Community
GIZ	German Technical Cooperation
HPP	Hydroelectric Power Plant
IFAS	International Fund for Saving the Aral Sea
ICJ	International Court of Justice
ICWC	Interstate Commission for Water Coordination in Central Asia
ICSD	Interstate Commission for Sustainable Development
IFIs	International financial institutions
ILA	International Law Association
ILC	International Law Commission of the United Nations
ILM	International Law Materials
IWRM	Integrated Water Resources Management
GW	Gigawatt
GWh	Gigawatt-hour
KWh	Kilowatt-hour
MEA	Multilateral Environmental Agreement
MDG	Millennium Development Goals
MOP	Meeting of the Parties
MW	Megawatt
NGO	Non-governmental Organisation
OECD	Organisation for Economic Cooperation and Development
OM	Operations Manual

PCIJ	Permanent Court of International Justice
RETA	Regional Technical Assistance
SCO	Shanghai Cooperation Organisation
SEA	Strategic Environmental Assessment
SIC	Scientific Information Centre
TEAS	Techno-Economic Assessment Study
UN	United Nations
UNDP	United Nations Development Programme
UNECE	United Nations Economic Commission for Europe
UNEP	United Nations Environmental Programme
UNESCO	United Nations Educational, Scientific and Cultural Organisation
UNTS	United Nations Treaty Series
USSR	Union of Soviet Socialist Republics
WHO	World Health Organisation

Table of International Treaties and Other Instruments

1909

Treaty between Great Britain and the United States Relating to Boundary Waters, and Questions Arising between the United States and Canada, Washington (adopted 11 January 1909, entered into force 5 May 1910) 36 Stat 2448.

1931

Treaty between the Union of Soviet Socialist Republics and Afghanistan of Neutrality and Non-Aggression (signed 24 June 1931) 157 UNTS 371.

1944

Treaty between the United States of America and Mexico Relating to the Utilization of the Waters of the Colorado and Tijuana Rivers, and of the Rio Grande (Rio Bravo) from Fort Quitman, Texas, to the Gulf of Mexico, Washington (adopted 3 February 1944, entered into Force 8 November 1945) 3 Unts 314.

1946

Statute of the International Court of Justice (18 April 1946) annexed to the Charter of the United Nations.

Frontier Agreement between Afghanistan and the Union of Soviet Socialist Republics (Including Exchange of Notes), Moscow (signed 13 June 1946, entered into force 17 January 1947) 31 UNTS 158.

1958

Treaty between the Government of the Union of Soviet Socialist Republics and the Royal Government of Afghanistan Concerning the Regime of the

Soviet-Afghan State Frontier (with Annexes and Protocols), Moscow (signed 18 January 1958) 321 UNTS 166 (1959).

Protocol between the Union of Soviet Socialist Republics and Afghanistan on the Joint Execution of Works for the Integrated Utilization of the Water Resources in the Frontier Section of the Amudarya, Kabul (signed 25 June 1958).

1960

Treaty between India and Pakistan Regarding the Use of the Waters of the Indus (adopted 19 September 1960, entered into force 1 April 1960) 419 UNTS 125 (1960).

1964

Convention and Statutes relating to the Development of the Chad Basin (signed 22 May 1964, entered into force 15 September 1964).

Agreement concerning the River Niger Commission and the navigation and transport on the River Niger (signed 25 November 1964, entered into force 12 April 1966) 587 UNTS 19.

1966

Agreement (with final protocol) regulating the withdrawal of water from Lake Constance (signed 30 April 1966, entered into force 25 November 1967) 620 UNTS 191.

1968

Agreement between the Union of Soviet Socialist Republics and Afghanistan on Economic and Technical Co-Operation During the Period 1967–1972 (with Annexes) (signed 6 February 1968) 31 UNTS 124 (1970).

1969

Convention on the Law of Treaties, Vienna (adopted 23 May 1969, entered into force 27 January 1980) 8 ILM 679.

1971

Agreement between Finland and Sweden Concerning Frontier Waters (signed 15 December 1971, entered into force 1 January 1972).

Convention on Wetlands of International Importance Especially as Waterfowl Habitat, Ramsar (adopted 2 February 1971, entered into force 21 December 1975) 996 UNTS 245.

1976

Agreement for the Protection of the Rhine Against Chemical Pollution (signed 3 December 1976) 1979 UNTS 406.

1978

Convention on Succession of States in Respect of Treaties Vienna (adopted 23 August 1978, entered into force 6 November 1996) 1946 UNTS 3 (1978).

Agreement between Bangladesh and India on Sharing of the Ganges Waters at Farakka (signed 5 November 1977) 17 ILM 103 (1978).

Treaty of Friendship, Good-Neighbourliness and Co-Operation, Moscow (signed 5 December 1978) 1145 UNTS 133 (1979).

1980

Convention Creating the Niger Basin Authority, Faranah (signed 21 November 1980).

1982

UN Convention on the Law of the Sea (adopted 18 December 1982, entered into force 16 November 1994) 21 ILM 1261(1982).

1991

UNECE Convention on Environmental Impact Assessment in a Transboundary Context, Espoo (adopted 25 February 1991, entered into force 10 September 1997) 30 ILM 800 (1991).

1990

Agreement between Niger and Nigeria concerning the Equitable Sharing in the Development, Conservation, and Use of their Common Water Resources (signed 18 July 1990) <http://www.fao.org>.

1992

Agreement on Interaction in the Field of Ecology and Environmental Protection, Moscow (signed 8 February 1992; all CARs are parties).

Agreement between the Republic of Kazakhstan, the Kyrgyz Republic, the Republic of Tajikistan, Turkmenistan, and the Republic of Uzbekistan on Cooperation in the Field of Joint Management of the Use and Conservation of Water Resources of Interstate Sources, Almaty (signed 18 February 1992).

UNECE Convention on the Protection and Use of Transboundary Watercourses and International Lakes, Helsinki (adopted 17 March 1992, in force 6 October 1996) 31 ILM 1312.

UNECE Convention on the Transboundary Effects of Industrial Accidents, Helsinki (adopted 17 March 1992, entered into force 19 April 2000) 31 ILM 1330 (1992).

UN Framework Convention on Climate Change, New York (adopted 9 May 1992, entered into force 21 March 1994) 31 ILM 849.

UN Convention on Biological Diversity, Rio de Janeiro (adopted 5 June 1992, in force 29 December 1993) 31 ILM 818.

Declaration of the UN Conference on Environment and Development (Rio De Janeiro, 13 June 1992) *in Report of the United Nations Conference on Environment and Development*, Annex I, UN Doc a/Conf.151/26 (Vol. I) Reprinted in 31 Ilm 876 (1992).

Agenda 21: A Programme for Action for Sustainable Development (Rio De Janeiro 13 June 1992) *in Report of the United Nations Conference on Environment and Development* Annex Ii UN Doc a/Conf.151/26 (Vol Ii) (1992), Rio de Janeiro.

Convention for the Protection of the Marine Environment of the North-East Atlantic, 32 ILM 1069 (1992).

Statute of the Interstate Commission for Water Coordination in Central Asia (ICWC), Tashkent (approved 5 December 1992 by ICWC members).

1993

Agreement between the Republic of Kazakhstan, the Kyrgyz Republic, the Republic of Tajikistan, Turkmenistan, and the Republic of Uzbekistan on

Joint Actions for Addressing the Problems of the Aral Sea and Its Coastal Area, Improving the Environment, and Ensuring the Social and Economic Development of the Aral Sea Region, Kzyl-Orda (signed 26 March 1993).

Charter of the Commonwealth of Independent States, Moscow (adopted 22 June 1993) 34 ILM 1279 (1995).

North American Agreement on Environmental Cooperation (signed 14 September 1993, entered into force 1 January 1994) 32 ILM 1480 (1993).

1994

UN Convention to Combat Desertification in Those Countries Experiencing Serious Drought and/or Desertification, Particularly in Africa, Paris (adopted 14 October 1994, entered into force 26 December 1996) 33 ILM 1328.

1995

Issik-Kul Declaration on Regional Cooperation between the Central Asian States, Issik-Kul (adopted 1995).

Nukus Declaration of the Central Asian States and International Organisations on the Problems of Sustainable Development in the Aral Sea Basin, Nukus (adopted 5 September 1995).

Agreement on the Cooperation for the Sustainable Development of the Mekong River Basin (signed 5 April 1995) 34 ILM 864 (1995).

1996

Agreement between Turkmenistan and the Republic of Uzbekistan on Cooperation over Water Management Issues Chardjev (signed 16 January 1996).

Agreement between the Government of the Republic of Kazakhstan, the Government of the Kyrgyz Republic and the Government of the Republic of Uzbekistan on the Use of Fuel and Water Resources, Construction and Operation of Gas Pipelines in Central Asian Region, Tashkent (signed 5 April 1996).

Agreement between the Government of the Republic of Kazakhstan, the Government of the Kyrgyz Republic, the Government of the Republic of Tajikistan and the Government the Republic of Uzbekistan on Joint Activities on the Rehabilitation of the Tailings and Rock Dump That Have Transboundary Effect, Tashkent (signed 5 April 1996).

1997

Statute of the Executive Committee of the International Fund for Saving the Aral Sea (EC IFAS), Tashkent (approved 20 March 1997 by the Decision of the IFAS President № 2Р-ИК, The President of the Republic of Uzbekistan I. Karimov).

Statement of Understanding Accompanying the UN Convention on the Law of the Non-Navigational Uses of International Watercourses, New York (11 April 1997) UN Doc A/51/869.

UN Convention on the Law of the Non-Navigational Uses of International Watercourses, New York (adopted 21 May 1997, not in force yet) 36 ILM 700.

Almaty Declaration of the Heads of States of the Republic of Kazakhstan, the Kyrgyz Republic, the Republic of Tajikistan, Turkmenistan and the Republic of Uzbekistan, Almaty (adopted 28 September 1997).

1998

Agreement between the Government of the Republic of Kazakhstan, the Government of the Kyrgyz Republic and the Government of the Republic of Uzbekistan on Cooperation in the Area of Environment and Rational Nature Use, Bishkek (signed 17 March 1998).

Agreement between the Governments of the Republic of Kazakhstan, the Kyrgyz Republic, and the Republic of Uzbekistan on the Use of Water and Energy Resources of the Syrdarya Basin, Bishkek (signed 17 March 1998, Republic of Tajikistan joined in 1999).

UNECE Convention on Access to Information, Public Participation in Decision-Making and Access to Justice in Environmental Matters, Aarhus (adopted 25 June 1998, entered into force 30 October 2001) 38 ILM 517 (1999).

Agreement between Government of the Republic of Belarus, the Government of the Russian Federation, the Government of the Republic of Kazakhstan and the Government of the Republic of Tajikistan on the Main Principles of Interaction in the Field of Rational Use and Protection of the Transboundary Water Bodies Moscow (adopted 11 September 1998, in force for Belarus, Russian Federation and Tajikistan 6 June 2002).

Agreement on Informational Cooperation in the Field of Ecology and the Environmental Protection, Moscow (11 September 1998; among others ratified by Kazakhstan, the Kyrgyz Republic and Tajikistan).

1999

Agreement between the Republic of Kazakhstan, the Kyrgyz Republic, the Republic of Tajikistan, Turkmenistan, and the Republic of Uzbekistan on the Status of IFAS and Its Organizations Ashgabad (signed 9 April 1999).

Ashgabad Declaration of the Heads of States of the Republic of Kazakhstan, the Kyrgyz Republic, the Republic of Tajikistan, Turkmenistan and the Republic of Uzbekistan, Ashgabad (adopted 9 April 1999).

Joint Statement Made by the Heads of States of the Republic of Kazakhstan, the Kyrgyz Republic, the Republic of Tajikistan, Turkmenistan and the Republic of Uzbekistan, Ashgabad (adopted 9 April 1999).

Statute of the International Fund for Saving the Aral Sea (IFAS), Ashgabad (adopted 9 April 1999 by the Decision of the Heads of the CARs).

Agreement between the Government of the Republic of Kazakhstan, the Government of the Kyrgyz Republic, the Government of the Republic of Tajikistan and the Government of the Republic of Uzbekistan on the Parallel Operation of the Energy Systems of Central Asian States, Bishkek (signed 17 June 1999).

Agreement between the Government of the Republic of Kazakhstan, the Government of the Kyrgyz Republic, the Government of the Republic of Tajikistan and the Government the Republic of Uzbekistan on Cooperation in the Sphere of Hydromet, Bishkek (signed 17 June 1999).

2000

Agreement between the Government of the Republic of Kazakhstan and the Government of the Kyrgyz Republic on the Use of Water Management Facilities of Intergovernmental Status on the Rivers Chu and Talas, Astana (signed 21 January 2000).

Statute of the Interstate Commission for Sustainable Development (ICSD), Ashgabad (aproved 18 October 2000 by the Decision of ICSD).

2001

Protocol between the Governments of the Republic of Kazakhstan, the Kyrgyz Republic, and the Republic of Uzbekistan on the Use of Water and Energy Resources of the Naryn-Syrdarya Cascade in 2001, Bishkek (signed 20 May 2001).

Tashkent Statement Made by the Heads of States of the Republic of Kazakhstan, the Kyrgyz Republic, the Republic of Tajikistan and the Republic of Uzbekistan, Tashkent (adopted 28 December 2001).

2002

Statute of the Executive Committee of the International Fund for Saving the Aral Sea (EC IFAS), Dushanbe (approved June 2002 by the Decision of the IFAS President, The President of the Republic of Tajikistan E. Rahmonov).

Dushanbe Declaration of the Heads of States of the Republic of Kazakhstan, the Kyrgyz Republic, the Republic of Tajikistan, Turkmenistan and the Republic of Uzbekistan, Dushanbe (adopted 6 October 2002).

UN Economic and Social Council, Committee on Economic, Social and Cultural Rights *General Comment 15 (2002) the Right to Water (Arts 11 and 12 of the International Covenant on Economic, Social and Cultural Rights)* 20 January 2003 UN Doc E/C.12/2002/11.

2003

Protocol on Strategic Environmental Assessment to the Convention on Environmental Impact Assessment in a Transboundary Context, Kyiv (adopted 21 May 2003, entered into force 11 July 2010).

Amendment to Articles 25 and 26 of the Convention on the Protection and Use of Transboundary Watercourses and International Lakes (adopted by decision III/1 of the Meeting of the Parties to the Convention of 28 November 2003, not in force).

2006

Framework Convention on Environmental Protection for Sustainable Development in Central Asia, Ashgabad (signed 22 November 2006 by the Kyrgyz Republic, Tajikistan and Turkmenistan, not yet in force).

2008

Statute of the Interstate Commission for Water Coordination in Central Asia (ICWC), Almaty (approved 18 September 2008 by ICWC members).

2009

Statute of the Executive Committee of the International Fund for Saving the Aral Sea (EC IFAS), Almaty (approved 21 March 2009 by the Decision of the IFAS President, The President of the Republic of Kazakhstan N. Nazarbaev).

Joint Statement Made by the Heads of States Founders of the International Fund for Saving the Aral Sea, Almaty (adopted 28 April 2009).

2010

UN General Assembly Resolution *the Human Right to Water and Sanitation* (28 July 2010 UN Doc a/Res/64/292).

Table of Cases and Arbitrations

CHAPTER 1

Introduction

1.1 Problematique and Research Question

Ensuring the fair and effective management of transboundary water resources is one of the most pressing contemporary challenges. As a UN Millennium Development Goals Report indicates, more than 1.2 billion people in the world live under conditions of physical water scarcity, and another 1.6 billion people live in areas of economic/political water scarcity, where human, institutional and financial issues limit access to water.[1] Since the world's 263 international river basins and 275 transboundary aquifers[2] are home to almost half the global population, most states rely heavily on transboundary watercourses for at least some of their water, and the rest import goods – 'virtual' or 'embedded' water[3] – from shared river basins. The impact of climate change on transboundary waters is increasing the level of uncertainty and risk, so the need for effective management is becoming more urgent.[4] The 2009 UNECE Guidance on Water and Adaptation to Climate Change states: '[...] in addition to the uncertainty over climate change impacts, countries are faced with uncertainty about their neighbours' reactions'.[5] Critical freshwater ecosystems are also under increasing stress.[6] Despite these common problems, transboundary

1 *The Millennium Development Goals Report 2008* (United Nations (UN) Department of Economic and Social Affairs (DESA), 2008) at 40.

2 See the provisional findings of an inventory of transboundary aquifers implemented by Internationally Shared Aquifers Resources Management Programme (ISARM). Online: <http://www.isarm.net/>accessed 29 February 2012. ISARM has so far inventoried 275 transboundary aquifers: 68 on the American continent, 40 in Africa, 65 in South Eastern Europe, and 12 in Asia where the inventory is still in progress.

3 The concept of 'virtual' water was established by Tony Allan in 1997 and relates to the water used in the production of any commodity. John Anthony Allan, *Virtual water: A long term solution for water short Middle Eastern economies?* (SOAS Water Issues Study Group, School of Oriental and African Studies/King's College-London Occasional Paper 3, 1997).

4 Bryson C. Bates and others (eds), *Climate Change and Water. Technical Paper of the Intergovernmental Panel on Climate Change* (IPCC Secretariat 2008).

5 UNECE, *Guidance on water and adaptation to climate change to Convention on the Protection and Use of Transboundary Watercourses and International Lakes* (UN Economic Commission for Europe (UNECE), UN Doc ECE/MPWAT/30, 2009).

6 *Millennium Ecosystem Assessment Ecosystems and Human Well-Being: Wetlands and Water* (World Resources Institute, 2005). See also Hugo Tremblay, 'An analytical framework

 | DOI 10.1163/9789004274266_002

water management is context-specific. Differences in the characteristics and uses of the watercourse, geopolitical factors, socio-economic conditions and so on, mean that each transboundary basin has its own issues and peculiarities.

The Aral Sea basin, shared by Afghanistan and five post-Soviet republics of Central Asia – Kazakhstan, Kyrgyzstan, Tajikistan, Turkmenistan and Uzbekistan, is one of those basins where water security issues are the most pressing. The Amudarya and Syrdarya, the two largest rivers of the Aral Sea basin, sustain the basin countries' economies, the livelihoods of their populations, and the health and integrity of freshwater ecosystems. High dependency on the availability and quality of the Aral Sea basin's waters has already compromised a delicate ecological balance in the region and put under stress its environmental integrity. One of the most telling examples of this is the devastating degradation of the Aral Sea, its ecosystem, and surrounding areas. It has also aggravated the competition for resources between sectors, such as irrigated agriculture and hydropower production; and ultimately between upstream and downstream countries trying to reach energy and food self-sufficiency. The large-scale hydropower development in the upper reaches of the Amudarya and Syrdarya may complicate the issues further – unless countries find peaceful and mutually acceptable ways to deal with the conflicts of interests over the planned measures and the regimes of water resources use. Pressure on water resources aggravates even more in the face of the increasing demand for water due to population growth and expected decrease in river flow influenced by climate change. Additionally, demand for water in the basin is most likely to increase as a result of the expansion of irrigated lands in Northern Afghanistan.

Thus, a shortlist of the region's water-related problems includes controversies over water allocation, competition between irrigation and hydropower, worries over water quality deterioration, environmental degradation, loss of biodiversity, and climate change. This complicated web of water, food, energy and environmental problems can be addressed in a holistic, mutually beneficial and peaceful manner only through collaborative actions, whether that is cooperation to increase economic and social benefits or cooperation to mitigate the negative effects of resource dependency.

Over the past two decades, the Central Asian Republics (CARs) have entered into a variety of sub-regional, regional and global water-related agreements and reaffirmed their adherence to the principles of international law. Despite

---

for legal regimes applicable to freshwater ecosystems' (2009) 20 Journal of Water Law 152–164.

the intensity of legal development, the role of international law as it relates to transboundary waters (international water law)[7] has met a mixed response in the sub-region. The states themselves acknowledge the positive implications of the legal framework for transboundary water cooperation and stress the need for strengthening compliance with existing agreements and developing more effective legal and institutional mechanisms.[8] Some external observers consider these legal developments an important step in promoting cooperation over transboundary waters in the Aral Sea basin while pointing out their low efficacy in dealing with environmental, economic, and social challenges.[9] Others appear even less optimistic and note that existing sub-regional agreements and institutions are weak and that the level of cooperation over shared waters is unsatisfactory.[10] Some commentators further claim that one of the difficulties in establishing an effective regulatory regime for transboundary waters in Central Asia is that international water law lacks clarity in guiding the states' course of action.[11] Finally, the 2003 United Nations Development Programme's Mission Report considers the irresponsible intervention of donors to be 'a dramatic example of legal malpractice'.[12]

---

7 International law dealing with transboundary watercourses is referred in academic writings and policy documents in a number of different ways, such as international water law, international law of water resources, the law of international watercourses or the law of transboundary watercourses. For the sake of consistency, the present study uses the term 'international water law' throughout.

8 Joint Statement made by the Heads of States Founders of the International Fund for saving the Aral Sea, Almaty (adopted 28 April 2009). Online: <http://cawater-info.net/bk/waterlaw/pdf/ifasalmaty2009e.pdfS> accessed 22 December 2013; Findings of the Central Asian Countries Reports on the Effectiveness of Existing Basin Agreements from the Standpoint of National Interests prepared by the national working groups for the Asian Development Bank (ADB) TA 6163-REG: Improved Management of Shared Water Resources in Central Asia (2005) (on file with author).

9 Sergei Vinogradov, 'Background paper on the legal basis for transboundary water cooperation (in Russian)' (2004) CWC project workshop on Legal Basis for Transboundary Water Cooperation.

10 Urs Luterbacher and Ellen Wiegandt, 'Cooperation or confrontation: Sustainable water use in an international context' in Edith Brown Weiss, Laurence Boisson de Chazournes and Nathalie Bernasconi-Osterwalder (eds), *Fresh water and international economic law* (Oxford University Press 2005).

11 Victor Dukhovny and Vadim Sokolov, *Lessons on cooperation building to manage water conflicts in the Aral Sea Basin* (Paris, UNESCO-IHP 2003).

12 United Nations Development Programme (UNDP) Central Asian Water Mission, 'Final Report and Recommendations', 15 August 2003 (on file with author). In particular, the Report states that 'the various treaties that have been drafted or even adopted under

Clearly, evaluating the validity of these sentiments requires more careful scholarly attention: a variety of factors may undermine the success of international water law in the Aral Sea basin; similarly, 'success' itself can be treated differently, depending on actors or observers' perspectives or interests. But any discussion of *how well* international water law works in the Aral Sea basin would be premature without some prior understanding of what international water law is and how it works. These questions have not been the subject of any comprehensive academic research in the context of international water law in the Aral Sea basin. This book therefore seeks to fill this gap by posing the question of 'How does international law work in addressing transboundary water challenges in the Aral Sea basin?'.

1.2 Contribution to Existing Research

Legal and social science scholarship has examined international water law in the Aral Sea basin in a number of important ways. Various legal studies have sought to ascertain the normative content of existing treaties in the basin with a view to identifying its deficits and suggesting the ways of possible improvement.[13] As a result, existing treaty law in the basin and its normative prescriptions are relatively well documented. Nonetheless, there exist areas where further research is needed to gain a deeper understanding of the role and workings of international water law in the Aral Sea basin.

First, the main focus of the existing legal studies has been on treaties adopted amongst the five CARs, the examination of treaties at the regional and global levels, and complementary ways in which they potentially reinforce

---

various USAID, UNDP, and TACIS projects threaten to radically change, or possibly have radically changed, existing state rights without adequate explanation to the states involved. These interventions are a dramatic example of legal malpractice (and therefore foreign assistance disaster) in the development context'.

13 Sergei Vinogradov, 'Transboundary water resources in the Former Soviet Union: Between conflict and cooperation' (1996) 36 Natural Resources Journal 393–416, Sergei Vinogradov and Vance Langford, 'Managing transboundary water resources in the Aral Sea basin: in search of a solution' (2001) 1 International Journal of Global Environmental Issues 345–362, Vinogradov, 'Background paper on the legal basis for transboundary water cooperation (in Russian)', Bakhtiyor Mukhamadiev, 'Evolution of a treaty-based law in the Aral Sea basin: Relevance, application and impact of international water law' (2006) unpublished LLM thesis University of Dundee, Marcella Nanni, 'The Aral Sea basin: Legal and institutional issues' (1996) 5 Review of European Community & International Environmental Law 130–137.

basin instruments would add to current knowledge. Hence, this book seeks to extend the scope of the law under consideration and examine within a multi-level governance context. Basin or sub-regional treaties covered in this study encompass agreements signed between the CARs, but also water-related agreements concluded between the Union of Soviet Socialist Republics (USSR) and Afghanistan. Regional agreements relevant to the case include treaties adopted under umbrella of Commonwealth of Independent States (CIS or Commonwealth) and United Nations Economic Commission for Europe (UNECE). Among the global treaties are United Nations Convention on the Law of the Non-Navigational Uses of International Watercourses (1997 UN Watercourses Convention)[14] and multilateral environmental agreements such as the Convention on Wetlands of International Importance Especially as Waterfowl Habitat (Ramsar Convention),[15] Convention on Biological Diversity (Convention on Biodiversity),[16] UN Convention to Combat Desertification in Countries Experiencing Serious Drought and/or Desertification, Particularly in Africa (Convention on Desertification),[17] and UN Framework Convention on Climate Change (Convention on Climate Change).[18]

Second, legal studies undertaken in the Aral Sea region have by and large offered a formalistic and positivist analysis of law that fails to discuss the role of legal processes in international relations. The CARs have been working on strengthening the legal and institutional frameworks for transboundary water cooperation under two Aral Sea Basin Programmes (ASBPs) since 1994,[19] but to date there has not been any rigorous examination of the process of law making

14 UN Convention on the Law of the Non-Navigational Uses of International Watercourses, New York (adopted 21 May 1997, not in force yet) 36 ILM 700.

15 Convention on Wetlands of International Importance Especially as Waterfowl Habitat, Ramsar (adopted 2 February 1971, entered into force 21 December 1975) 996 UNTS 245.

16 UN Convention on Biological Diversity, Rio de Janeiro (adopted 5 June 1992, in force 29 December 1993) 31 ILM 818.

17 UN Convention to Combat Desertification in those Countries Experiencing Serious Drought and/or Desertification, particularly in Africa, Paris (adopted 14 October 1994, entered into force 26 December 1996) 33 ILM 1328.

18 UN Framework Convention on Climate Change, New York (adopted 9 May 1992, entered into force 21 March 1994) 31 ILM 849.

19 In 1994 the heads of CARs decided to adopt the Programme of concrete actions for environmental improvement in the Aral Sea basin over the next 3–5 years (ASBP-1) and to approve the main provisions of the strategy for addressing problems of Aral, Priaralie and the Aral Sea basin in light of regional socio-economic development. In 2002 they approved the Programme of concrete actions on environmental and socio-economic improvement in the Aral Sea basin for 2003–2010 (ASBP-2). In 2009 they mandated relevant agencies to develop ASBP-3 that was approved in 2013. See 2009 Almaty Joint Statement.

in that context. Equally, the possible influence of law development *processes* at the global and regional levels, particularly the 1997 UN Watercourses Convention and the UNECE Convention on the Protection and Use of Transboundary Watercourses and International Lakes (1992 UNECE Water Convention),[20] on state practice in the Aral Sea basin has not been fully analysed. An inquiry that draws attention to law making and law implementation is timely when considering that there are still unresolved issues between the basin countries regarding their shared water use and management and negotiation in a progress. For example, such research might be valuable in guiding the countries' efforts to implement the Third ASBP for 2011–2015, which primarily seeks to improve social, economic and environmental conditions in the sub-region through the implementation of integrated water resources management and the development of mutually acceptable mechanisms for complex water resources use and protection in Central Asia.[21] To address these deficiencies, this book examines legal processes as an integral element of the analysis of international law and its operation.

The third line of critique is concerned with the research on the actual operation of international water law in the Aral Sea region. So far, legal appraisals of international law workings have largely tended to use compliance, understood as 'a state of conformity or identity between an actor's behavior and specified rule',[22] as a measurement of its operation and efficacy. From this perspective, observers have raised concerns about non-compliance with treaty provisions in the sub-region.[23] However, this approach provides only a part of the story. An exclusive focus on compliance leaves several important aspects of

20 UNECE Convention on the Protection and Use of Transboundary Watercourses and International Lakes, Helsinki (adopted 17 March 1992, in force 6 October 1996) 31 ILM 1312.

21 See 2009 Almaty Joint Statement and ASBP-3. Online: <http://www.ec-ifas.org> accessed 29 February 2012.

22 Kal Raustiala, 'Compliance and effectiveness in international regulatory cooperation' (2000) 32 Case Western Reserve Journal of International Law 387–440, at 391. See also Harold Jacobson and Edith Brown Weiss, 'A Framework for analysis' in Edith Brown Weiss and Harold Jacobson (eds), *Engaging countries: Strengthening compliance with international environmental accords* (MIT Press 1998) at 4, (differentiating non-compliance with substantive and procedural obligations or with 'the spirit of the treaty') and Ronald B. Mitchell, *International oil pollution at sea: Environmental policy and treaty compliance* (Cambridge, MIT Press 1994) (defining 'compliance' as 'behaviour that conforms to a treaty's explicit rules').

23 Iain Watt and Sergei Vinogradov, *Transboundary water security in Central Asia: Addressing the crisis* (Cairneagle Associates LLP, July 2011).

the workings of international law unaddressed. First, a focus on compliance does not answer the question of whether the law has a role to play in the pre-commitment period. Brunnée points out that '[e]ven a regime that does not arrive at a binding standard may be effective if it develops a process of norm generation that is perceived as legitimate by all those involved'.[24] Secondly, compliance does not clarify how law strikes a balance between the *status quo* and the need for change. Koskenniemi warns from a normative perspective that 'focus on compliance silently assumes that the political question – what the objectives are – has already been resolved'.[25] In the Aral Sea basin, the 1992 Almaty Agreement illustrates the latter point. Taken in isolation this agreement fixes the Soviet-time *status quo* and requires 'strict observance' of then-established rules,[26] but the need for change is justifiable when considered in a wider landscape of the principle of equitable and reasonable use, which adopts a flexible all-encompassing approach to reconciling a broad range of existing and new economic, social and environmental issues. Thirdly, a rigid concern with compliance alone appears to leave no room for appreciation of the communicative and constitutive role of international law. Thus, Hathaway argues that human rights treaties might fulfill both instrumental ('create binding law that is intended to have particular effects') and expressive ('express the position of those countries than join them') functions.[27] She also illuminates the constitutive effect of the treaties in the sense that they change 'perception of what constitutes acceptable behaviour'.[28] From an expressive perspective, each of the signed agreements in Central Asia can be considered as remarkable demonstrations of willingness to engage with the international community and actively deploy the rules and principles of international law to deal with the pressing water problems. The constitutive value of the agreements can be traced in terms of their contribution to a 'shared conception of appropriate behaviour' in building and maintaining transboundary water

---

24 Jutta Brunnée, 'Wrap-up plenary: What's next in implementation, compliance and effectiveness?' (1997) 91 American Society of International Law Proceedings 504–511 at 506.

25 Martti Koskenniemi, *The gentle civilizer of nations. The rise and fall of international law 1870–1960* (Cambridge, Cambridge University Press 2001) at 485.

26 Agreement between the Republic of Kazakhstan, the Kyrgyz Republic, the Republic of Tajikistan, Turkmenistan, and the Republic of Uzbekistan on Cooperation in the Field of Joint Management of the Use and Conservation of Water Resources of Interstate Sources, Almaty (signed 18 February 1992). Online: <http://cawater-info.net/library/eng/l/ca_cooperation.pdf> (an unofficial English translation).

27 Oona A. Hathaway, 'Do human rights treaties make a difference?' (2001–2002) 111 Yale Law Journal 1935–2042.

28 Ibid.

cooperation.[29] Finally, the recent work of Howse and Teitel points out that '[l]ooking at the aspirations of international law through the lens of rule-compliance [...] obfuscates the character of international legal normativity, tending to ignore the centrality of interpretation to the generation of legal meaning, as well as the horizontal relation between diverse norms and regimes ("fragmentation")'.[30] Therefore, research that considers the role and workings of international law beyond compliance is of crucial importance.

From a different angle, social science scholarship has focused on *performance* of legal arrangements – or depth of cooperation – in individual river basins of the region. Most notably, Bernauer and Siegfried have analysed the Syrdarya river case from a problem-solving standpoint, following the Downs and others' argument that cooperation as measured by the existence of treaties and compliance with international commitments may sometimes be more 'shallow' than it appears.[31] These researchers found that the implementation of the 1998 Syrdarya Agreement[32] has been characterised by a high level of compliance as assessed on the basis of ratios of actual water releases from the Toktogul reservoir and the targets for the respective months as defined in the agreement.[33] At the same time, the performance of the 1998 Agreement, measured in terms of optimal performance ('the outcome that should ideally be reached') and counterfactual performance ('the outcome that would have occurred in the absence of this policy'), was seen to be very low and highly variable.[34] These findings lead the authors to conclude that cooperation in the basin is rather 'shallow' and existing water governance system needs urgent reforms.

29 See eg Martha Finnemore and Kathryn Sikkink, 'International norm dynamics and political change' (1998) 52 International Organization 887–917 and Jutta Brunnée and Stephen J. Toope, 'The changing Nile Basin regime: Does law matter?' (2002) 43 Harvard International Law Journal 105–159.

30 Robert Howse and Ruti Teitel, 'Beyond compliance: Rethinking why international law really matters' (2010) New York University School of Law Public Law & Legal Theory Research Paper Series Working Paper No 10-08.

31 Thomas Bernauer and Tobias Siegfried, 'Compliance and performance in international water agreements: The case of the Naryn/Syr Darya basin' (2008) 14 Global Governance 479–501.

32 Agreement between the Governments of the Republic of Kazakhstan, the Kyrgyz Republic, and the Republic of Uzbekistan on the Use of Water and Energy Resources of the Syrdarya Basin, Bishkek (signed 17 March 1998, Republic of Tajikistan joined in 1999). Online: <http://cawater-info.net/library/eng/l/syrdarya_water_energy.pdf> (an unofficial English translation).

33 Bernauer and Siegfried, 'Compliance and performance' at 482.

34 Ibid, 495.

Uzbekistan's accession to the 1997 UN Watercourses Convention has triggered another social science research, which sought to analyse whether the norms of international water law, namely the equitable and reasonable use and the no harm rule, are neutral or biased towards early or late developers. Wegerich and Olsson consider these norms to be biased towards the first developer, which, in their opinion, is a result of 'the games of the rule' – that institutionalise or freeze power relationships prevailing at a particular period in time.[35] While highlighting the role of state power in international law making, the study overlooks the point that law's normativity – or its obligation-creating feature – is rooted in its internal sources rather than in material power or coercion. The role and workings of international law cannot be understood fully, unless law's normativity is demystified, an issue discussed in considerable detail throughout this book.

Despite the fact that these social science studies focus only on a specific treaty or individual norms, they are a welcome contribution to the debate about the role and practical relevance of international water law in the Aral Sea region. Such critical appraisals are helpful in illuminating the possible ways that legal arrangements might be improved, and also revealing caveats in understanding international law and its operation. There exists a great potential to enrich social science scholarship through the awareness of how international law operates as a system (as opposed to a set of scattered norms) to impose constraints on actors, but also to facilitate interactions between them and build legal relationships.

It is against this backdrop that the present book seeks to draw a more dynamic and systemic picture of international water law in the Aral Sea basin that would help understand and enable its potential to address transboundary water challenges in the basin more fully. Moving beyond the static identification of treaties and norms, this book asks how to make these treaties or norms work in practice. It is argued that the work of international law is the work of building and maintaining legal relationships through a system of norms and processes that allows for adaptability, flexibility and learning, while also anchored by the requirements of clarity, predictability and stability. In framing the thesis in such a way, the real test for the peaceful and sustainable regulation of transboundary watercourses and their ecosystems in the Aral Sea basin consists not only in the quantitative and qualitative aspects of treaties, protocols, and declarations, but in building legal relationships across the spectrum of actors. Such legal relationships emerge and mature through practicing the

---

35 Kai Wegerich and Oliver Olsson, 'Late developers and the inequity of "equitable utilization" and the harm of "do no harm"' (2010) 35 Water International 707–717.

law comprised of legal norms, legally relevant behaviour and legal consciousness. As such, international law cannot be conceived in passive and static terms: it demands meaningful activities and interactions among various actors and it implies a sustained intensity and reciprocity of relationships. Therefore, this study focuses on both legal norms *and* processes through which norms emerge, evolve, change and decline. By looking at international law in such a way, it is possible to better understand – and ultimately improve – its workings.

The intent of this book is not to provide a recipe for resolving transboundary water issues in the Aral Sea basin through the means of international law. Rather, it offers *a* perspective that can guide actors in addressing these problems within the frame of international law. The motivation of the book is to clear up misunderstandings about international water law and its operation in the sub-region and provide insights for policy-makers, diplomats, water managers, scientists, lawyers and the general public to make use of its potential in their daily practice. It is also hoped that this study findings may be useful in the efforts to ensure water security in other transboundary basins around the globe.

Moreover, this book aims to make a theoretical contribution to a broader debate on the role and workings of international law. The last few decades have seen research in both international law and international relations disciplines that has begun to focus more rigorously on the influence of law in international affairs. This interest has emerged and formed part of a broader discussion regarding factors that influence actors' behaviour in international relations. The scholarly literature related to the influence on actor behaviour can broadly be divided along two analytical accounts – rationalist (often referred to as following a 'logic of consequences') and normative (often referred to as following a 'logic of appropriateness').[36] Rationalist theories posit a state as a unitary, rational, self-interested actor that calculates the costs and benefits of its actions vis-à-vis the rules in order to maximise payoffs.[37] Realism, institutionalism, and liberalism are modifications of the rationalist school.

36 March and Olsen define the logic of consequences as a perspective that sees actor's action as 'driven by calculation of its consequences as measured against prior preferences' and the logic of appropriateness as a perspective that sees actor's action as 'driven by rules of appropriate or exemplary behaviour'. See James G. March and Johan P. Olsen, 'The institutional dynamics of international political orders' (1998) 52 International Organization 943–969 James G. March and Johan P. Olsen, 'The Logic of appropriateness' (2004) ARENA – Centre for European Studies, University of Oslo Working Papers WP 04/09 28.

37 Durwood Zaelke, Donald Kaniaru and Eva Kružíková (eds), *Making law work: Environmental compliance and sustainable development*, vol I (Cameron May Ltd 2005).

An alternative worldview of international law's influence on state behaviour emphasises the normative power of rules, the persuasive power of ideas, and the importance of shared discourse and knowledge in shaping actors' behaviour in the international arena.[38] Constructivism, legitimacy and fairness theories, managerialism, and transnational legal process theory are the main analytical strands of the normative school of thought. From these diverse approaches, a host of interrelated factors, such as self-interest, identity, community or regime membership, certain properties of norms and processes, or capacity of states, has been put forward as factors that influence actors behaviour and thus drive international relations towards or away from stated goals.[39] While certain progress has been made in identifying some driving forces behind these factors, such as power, knowledge, legitimacy, persuasion, or socialisation, a complete and integrated understanding of the factors influencing actor behaviour is still to be reached.

The present study seeks to add to this scholarship by focusing on the distinct role of international law in international affairs. Broadly, legal scholars contributed to the debate with the extensive description and analysis of international law, its evolution and content, whereas students of international relations achieved considerable progress in pursuing explanatory and evaluative assessments of the law. More precisely, distinct international legal compliance scholarship has emerged out of theorisation across international law and international relations divide.[40] The limitations of legal methodology in addressing the questions of whether, and if so, why and under what circumstances states comply with international law pushed legal scholars to search for the insights from international relations theory and to employ the methodologies of social science.[41] These attempts have been combined with a growing

38 Ibid.

39 Abram Chayes and Antonia Handler Chayes, *The new sovereignty: Compliance with international regulatory agreements* (Cambridge, Harvard University Press 1995), Thomas Franck, *The power of legitimacy among nations* (Oxford, Oxford University Press 1990), Ryan Goodman and Derek Jinks, 'How to influence states: Socialization and international human rights law' (2004–2005) 54 Duke law journal 621–703, Harold Koh, 'Why do nations obey international law?' (1997) 106 Yale Law Journal 2599–2659, Hans J. Morgenthau, 'Positivism, functionalism, and international law' (1940) 34 American Journal of International Law 260–284, Alexander Wendt, 'Anarchy is what states make of it: The social construction of power politics' (1992) 46 International Organization 391.

40 See William C. Bradford, *International legal compliance: Surveying the field* (SSRN 2004).

41 Benedict Kingsbury, 'The concept of compliance as a function of competing conceptions of international law' (1998) 19 Michigan Journal of International Law 345–372 (stating that "Compliance" is one of the central concepts in current and proposed research projects

recognition that not all international relations approaches are skeptical of the role of law in international affairs. Therefore, this book intends to bring together insights from international legal studies and the normative thoughts of international relations scholarship, such as constructivism, legitimacy and fairness theories, managerialism, and transnational legal process theory, to develop a deeper account of the role and workings of international law. More specifically, a framework by which to examine the role and workings of international law in a more sophisticated way is suggested. Doing such an analysis through the 'case study' of international water law in the Aral Sea basin is especially valuable because it provides dynamic social context, characterised by a recently changed political structure (emergence of newly independent countries in early 1990s) and urgent need for legal regulation to address water security challenges in a peaceful way.

1.3 Methodology and Outline of the Book

To answer the main question posed in this book, namely 'How does international law work in addressing transboundary water challenges in the Aral Sea basin?', a legal and analytical methodology is employed. The analysis relies on the primary legal sources and state practice at the sub-regional, regional and global levels and of secondary sources as to theories of international law and international relations to explain the role and workings of international law.

Chapter 2 sets out a theoretical and analytical foundation of the research. The first section asks, 'What is international law and how does it work?'. The underlying argument of the section is that the problems with the operation of international law are not so much in the law itself, but in the misconception of international law, its potential and limits. A broad conceptual framework mapping the terrain of international law as comprised of legal norms (normative facet), legally relevant behaviour (sociological facet), and legal consciousness (psychological facet) is offered to facilitate understanding of this phenomenon. It is argued that international law works and gains its authority and power through the internal complexity and interconnection of its normative, sociological and psychological facets. Built on this conceptual understanding, the

---

using social science methods to study the effects and significance of international law). See also Gregory Shaffer and Tom Ginsburg, 'The empirical turn in international legal scholarship' (2011) University of Minnesota Law School Legal Studies Research Paper No 12-09 at 2 (stating that 'a central question becomes the conditions under which international law is produced and has effects, as well as the actors and mechanisms involved').

second section proposes an analytical framework of norm and process properties by which to examine international law with due regard to its normative, sociological and psychological facets. Two properties of legal norms (determinacy and stringency) and four properties of legal processes (inclusiveness, transparency, discursiveness, and coherence) are proposed as an entry point for such an inquiry.

The subsequent four chapters use an analytical framework of norm and process properties to study international water law in the Aral Sea basin. In order to provide the context of the study, Chapter 3 outlines the characteristics of the basin, its major transboundary water issues and the legal architecture of transboundary water cooperation.

Chapters 4 and 5 examine the determinacy and stringency of the norms that govern transboundary waters in the Aral Sea basin around the issues of scope, substantive and procedural norms, compliance and dispute settlement. The main question explored in these two chapters is whether relevant provisions establish a required standard of conduct for the Aral Sea basin states in a determinant and stringent language. As argued in Chapter 2, the norms expressed in precise and stringent terms influence the ability of law to generate behavioural expectation as the very sense of the legal function.

Chapter 6 studies international water law in the Aral Sea region through the lenses of four process properties – inclusiveness, transparency, discursiveness and coherence. It examines whether international water law in the basin constitutes and enables inclusive, transparent, discursive and integrative process of interactions to generate, elaborate and refine shared understandings and collective expectations about the meaning and implementation of the norms.

Chapter 7 draws together the main findings of the study to conclude that international law does not work as a sound system of norms and processes in addressing transboundary water challenges in the Aral Sea basin. This is so because international law is conceived only as comprised of legal norms, whereas legally relevant behaviour and legal consciousness are left aside. This omission makes it difficult to build legal relationships, which emerge and mature through practicing the law within normative communities. Further, the chapter offers insights and recommendations for policy-makers and practitioners that may help to enable more fully the potential of international water law in the basin and beyond; discusses the broader implications of the research for on-going debate on the role and workings of international (water) law; and suggests areas for further research that have emerged as a result of this study. Finally, the concluding chapter summarises the main findings of the book.

PART 1

Conceptual and Analytical Frameworks

CHAPTER 2

International Law

Conceptual and Analytical Frameworks

Before proceeding to a detailed analysis of international water law in the Aral Sea basin in the following chapters, this chapter provides an overview of international law and its operation in order to lay down a theoretical and analytical foundation of the study. The first section offers *a* perspective on international law and its operation that brings together insights from international legal studies and the normative thoughts of international relations scholarship, such as legitimacy and fairness theories, managerialism, transnational legal process theory, and constructivism, which emphasises the workings of international law through the means of persuasion and socialisation.[42] Based on this conceptual understanding, the second section sets up an analytical framework by which to examine the role and workings of international water law in the Aral Sea basin and beyond in a more sophisticated way.

2.1 International Law: Norms, Behaviour, Consciousness

This section disaggregates international law into three facets, which help to disclose its essence and nature. In so doing, it builds on Peczenik's take on law as a complex phenomenon that is comprised of three classes of entities called 'legal': valid legal norms (normative aspect), legally relevant behaviour (sociological aspect), and the legal consciousness (psychological aspect).[43] Peczenik made this observation back in 1968, seeking to provide 'juristic definition of law'. Likewise, normative, sociological and psychological accounts are helpful to understanding international law and its operation.

2.1.1 *Normative Facet: Legal Norms*

According to Peczenik, the normative category of law deals with 'valid legal norms', understood as norms to which 'the juristic method' is continually applied, or in other words, 'those norms which are continually elaborated according to the principle of strict interpretation and, simultaneously, according

42 The trend to look beyond sanctions and think of law without any sanctions was started by Henkin in his seminal book How Nations Behave. See Louis Henkin, *How nations behave: Law and foreign policy* (2nd edn, Columbia University Press 1979).

43 Aleksander Peczenik, 'Juristic definition of law' (1968) 78 Ethics 255–268.

 | DOI 10.1163/9789004274266_003

to the principle of justice'.[44] He maintains that the results of the elaboration are always put in writing, which constitutes 'the peculiar internormative relation, that is, the relation of coexistence between norms and the above-indicated principles'.[45]

In the most general terms, law is about 'the rules of the game' to be applied consistently and uniformly.[46] International law provides a framework for establishing norms that define required conduct, outline the parameters of interactions and ensure that disputes, if these arise, are resolved in a peaceful manner. International norms can be found in the traditional sources of international law, such as treaties, custom, general principles, as reflected in Article 38(1) of the Statute of the International Court of Justice.[47] The normative account also reveals international law as a system, rather than a set of scattered norms. Most prominently, Hart maintained that a legal system – in contrast to a set of unrelated norms – consists of a union of primary rules of obligation rooted in secondary rules of recognition, change and adjudication.[48] International legal scholars too built their analysis around the conception of international law as a system, which signifies the idea of interconnectedness and mutual support of legal norms, among other things.[49] Recently, normative expansion of international law raised concerns of fragmentation,[50] which was suggested to address through the process of legal interpretation that 'performs an integrating tasks within the legal system'.[51] For this purpose, Article 31(3)(c) of the Vienna Convention on the Law of Treaties, requiring that 'There shall be

44 Ibid, 260.

45 Ibid.

46 Malcolm N. Shaw, *International law* (Cambridge, 6th edn, Cambridge University Press 2008).

47 Statute of the International Court of Justice, (18 April 1946) annexed to the Charter of the United Nations art 38(1).

48 Herbert Lionel Adolphus Hart, *The concept of law* (Oxford 2nd ed./ with a postscript edited by Penelope A. Bulloch and Joseph Raz edn, Clarendon Press 1994).

49 See eg Hersch Lauterpacht, *The function of law in the international community* (Hamden, Conn., Archon Books 1966), Rosalyn Higgins, *Problems and process: International law and how we use it* (Oxford Clarendon Press 1994) at 1.

50 Gerhard Hafner, *Risk ensuing from fragmentation of international law* (General Assembly, Official Records, 55th Session, Supplement No. 10 (A/55/10), Report of the International Law Commission on the work of its fifty-second session 2010). *Fragmentation of international law: Difficulties arising from the diversification and expansion of international law* (Report of the Study Group of the International Law Commission Finalized by Martti Koskenniemi UN Doc GAOR A/CN4/L682, 2006) at 20.

51 Campbell McLachlan, 'The principle of systemic integration and Article 31(3)(c) of the Vienna Convention' (2005) 54 International & Comparative Law Quarterly 279–320 at 286.

taken into account, together with the context: [...] (c) any relevant rules of international law applicable in the relations between the parties', has been suggested to provide for the systemic integration within the international legal system.[52] The fact that the meaning of norms is established through the acts of interpretation facilitates a partial opening towards a sociological dimension of international law considered below.

Traditional legal scholarship has made a significant contribution to explaining normative facet of international law, mainly through analysis of the law, focusing on its sources, form and normative content to answer the questions such as whether there is an obligation, what are the sources of this obligation, what is its content, who are the parties to this obligation, and what are the consequences of the non-performance of the obligation. In turn, international relations scholars too have looked at the legal norms and their properties, but mostly with the interest on their functional content and the behavioural and societal roles of individual norms, often taken out of a wider legal context and ignoring complex interrelations between one norm and another.[53] International relations research generally adopts a broad definition of norms that does not distinguish between the legal and non-legal and 'does not align perfectly with the concept of a norm established through custom'.[54] Hafner-Burton and others explain the lack of interest in custom from political scientists, especially those preoccupied with the issue of power, by the fact that customary norms 'do not necessarily derive from the interests of powerful states' and are therefore unimportant.[55] Despite these discrepancies, international relations scholars also mark the quality of norms and their fit within a whole regime as especially relevant to understanding their potential operation.[56]

---

52 Ibid, 280.

53 For notable exception see Friedrich Kratochwil, *Rules, norms, and decisions: On the conditions of practical and legal reasoning in international relations and domestic affairs* (Cambridge, Cambridge University Press 1995) and Nicholas Onuf, 'Do rules say what they do? From ordinary language to international law' (1985) 26 Harvard International Law Journal 385–410.

54 Emilie M. Hafner-Burton, David G. Victor and Yonatan Lupu, 'Political science research on international law: The state of the field' (2011) Laboratory on International Law and Regulation Working Paper No 1 at 11. See however Friedrich Kratochwil, 'Thrasymmachos revisited: On the relevance of norms and the study of law for international relations' (1984) 37 Journal of International Affairs 343.

55 Hafner-Burton, Victor and Lupu, 'Political science research on IL' at 72.

56 Antje Wiener, 'The dual quality of norms and governance beyond the state: Sociological and normative approaches to "interaction"' (2007) 10 Critical Review of International Social and Political Philosophy 47–69.

2.1.2 *Sociological Facet: Legally Relevant Behaviour*

Sociological understanding of international law brings into play legally relevant behaviour of actors and their interrelationships with each other. According to Peczenik, legally relevant behaviour includes acts of formulation of the text in which the basic legal relation occurs, acts of creation of the norms which later become legal and valid, and acts of observance or violation of the legal norms.[57] As such, issues related to international law making and implementation, the law of state responsibility, and compliance and effectiveness studies are the most relevant for this account.

Although treaty making in which the traditional requirement of formal state consent is deeply rooted has become the basic means for regulating relations between nation states,[58] other forms of international law making increasingly emerge.[59] Collective consensus-based law making has become more often the norm, emphasising participation of unprecedentedly broad range of non-state actors along with representatives of states in international law making process, particularly within the UN system, in other international organisations, diplomatic conferences, codification bodies, NGOs and courts.[60] Contemporary international law making has come to be more deliberative and continuous.[61]

Today, normative development seems to appear not only through traditional sources of international law, but also through simplified amendment procedures and through secondary decision-making.[62] In these situations, the formal notion of state consent is relaxed in requiring state consent to a process

57 Peczenik, 'Juristic definition of law' at 265.

58 Jan Klabbers, *The concept of treaty in international law* (Leiden/Boston, Martinus Nijhoff Publishers 2006).

59 See generally Rüdiger Wolfrum and Volker Röben (eds), *Developments of international law in treaty making* (Springer 2005), Alan Boyle and Christine Chinkin, *The making of international law* (Oxford, Oxford University Press 2007) and Jan Klabbers, 'Constitutionalism and the making of international law: Fuller's procedural natural law' (April 2008) 5 NoFo 84–112.

60 See eg the functions of the Meeting of the Parties under the Montreal Protocol on Substances that Deplete the Ozone Layer, art 11. See also Boyle and Chinkin, *The making of international law*.

61 Thomas Gehring, 'Treaty-making and treaty evolution' in Daniel Bodansky, Jutta Brunnée and Ellen Hey (eds), *The Oxford Handbook of International Environmental Law* (Oxford University Press 2007) at 477. Jutta Brunnée, 'COPing with consent: Law-making under multilateral environmental agreements' (2002) 15 Leiden Journal of International Law 1–52.

62 Gehring, 'Treaty-making and treaty evolution' at 469. Jason Morrison and Naomi Roht-Ariaza, 'Private and quasi-private standrad setting' in Daniel Bodansky, Jutta Brunnée and Ellen Hey (eds), *The Oxford Handbook of International Environmental Law* (Oxford University Press 2007).

of normative development, the outcome of which is frequently unknown when consent is given.[63] Based on an example of multilateral environmental treaty systems, Gehring demonstrates how treaties evolve to treaty regimes, with scientific and technological apparatus undertaking assessments to reinforce and accelerate normative development; and with political and administrative decision-making 'broadening and tightening commitments over time as well as elaborating upon, and in some cases, redefining existing obligations'.[64] The advantages of such systems are seen in allowing for adaptability, flexibility, and learning in response to new scientific and social information and claims that resolutions and decisions of the consensus-based Conference of the Parties activity enrich original legal obligations by thickening them;[65] while disadvantages include the dangers of incoherence, forum shopping, and loss of overall political control over decision-making arising from the multiplication of such functional treaty regimes, dominated by technical experts and semi-formal procedures.[66]

Despite doctrinal disagreements over the value and appropriateness of this phenomenon, the shift in the making of international law is undisputed. Hence, contemporary international law making requires focus on various actors and processes by whom and through which international law is generated. It also clearly unites norm creation with the interpretation, application and development of international law.[67] As such, sociological account helps to capture the dynamic and fluid nature of international law, in which norms emerge, develop, change, and demise in response to society's common needs through legally relevant behaviour.[68]

---

63 Ellen Hey, 'International institutions' in Daniel Bodansky, Jutta Brunnée and Ellen Hey (eds), *The Oxford Handbook of International Environmental Law* (Oxford University Press 2007) at 758–759.

64 Gehring, 'Treaty-making and treaty evolution' at 495.

65 Annecoos Wiersema, 'The new international law-makers? Conferences of the Parties to multilateral environmental agreements' (2009–2010) 31 Michigan Journal of International Law 231–288 at 234.

66 See eg Martti Koskenniemi, 'The fate of public international law: Between technique and politics' (2007) 70 Modern Law Review 1–30, Prosper Weil, 'Towards relative normativity in international law?' (1983) 77 American Journal of International Law 413–442, Michael W. Reisman, 'The democratization of contemporary international law-making processes and the differentiation of their application' in Rüdiger Wolfrum and Volker Röben (eds), *Developments of international law in treaty making* (Springer 2005) at 26, 28, and Hey, 'International institutions' at 758–759.

67 The Series Editor's Preface in Boyle and Chinkin, *The making of international law* at v.

68 Gehring, 'Treaty-making and treaty evolution' at 477.

A similar trend of moving beyond traditional public international law approaches is noticeable on matters related to acts of observance or violation of the legal norms. Various forms of reporting, verification, monitoring, and non-compliance procedures[69] have been developed to supplement the traditional law of state responsibility and dispute settlement systems such as courts and arbitration.[70] This new phenomenon considers that compliance is more often a function of the state's capacity and commitment[71] and therefore punishing non-compliance and invoking responsibility are often counter-productive, especially on environmental matters.[72] Such a managerial approach

69 For examples in international environmental law see Kal Raustiala, *Reporting and review Institutions in 10 Multilateral Environmental Agreements* (UNEP, 2001), Jørgen Wettestad, 'Monitoring and verification' in Daniel Bodansky, Jutta Brunnée and Ellen Hey (eds), *The Oxford Handbook of International Environmental Law* (Oxford University Press 2007), Tullio Treves and others (eds), *Non-compliance procedures and mechanisms and the effectiveness of international environmental agreements* (T.M.C. Asser Press 2009).

70 Charter of the United Nations (26 June 1945) Can TS 1945 No 7 (entered into force 24 October 1945) art 2(3). See also United Nations General Assembly Draft Articles on the Responsibility of States for Internationally Wrongful Acts in 'Report of the International Law Commission on the Work of its Fifty-third Session' UN GAOR, Supp (No 10) UN Doc A/56/10 (2001).

71 Chayes and Chayes, *The new sovereignty* at 10.

72 Non-compliance procedures can be found, *inter alia*, in Convention on Climate Change UNECE Convention on Access to Information, Public Participation in Decision-Making and Access to Justice in Environmental Matters, Aarhus (adopted 25 June 1998, entered into force 30 October 2001) 38 ILM 517 (1999), UNECE Convention on Environmental Impact Assessment in a Transboundary Context, Espoo (adopted 25 February 1991, entered into force 10 September 1997) 30 ILM 800 (1991). See eg Edith Brown Weiss and Harold Jacobson (eds), *Engaging countries: Strengthening compliance with international environmental accords* (MIT Press 1998), Chayes and Chayes, *The new sovereignty*, David G. Victor, Kal Raustiala and Eugene B. Skolnikoff (eds), *The implementation and effectiveness of international environmental commitments: Theory and practice* (MIT Press 1998), Ulrich Beyerlin, Peter-Tobias Stoll and Rudiger Wolfrum (eds), *Ensuring compliance with multilateral environmental agreements: A dialogue between practitioners and academia*, vol 2 (Martinus Nijhoff Publishers 2006), Treves and others, *Non-compliance procedures and mechanisms* and LeRoy Paddock and others (eds), *Compliance and enforcement in international law: Towards more effective implementation* (Edward Elgar 2011). See also 'Guidelines on compliance with and enforcement of multilateral environmental agreements' Doc UNEP (DEPI)/MEAs/WG1/3 Annex II; 'Guidelines for Strengthening Compliance with and Implementation of Multilateral Environmental Agreements in the ECE Region' Doc ECE/CEP/107. Wouter G. Werner, 'Responding to the undesired. State responsibility, risk management and precaution' (2005) 30 Netherlands Yearbook of International Law 57–82.

to securing compliance, including exchange of information, financial and technological assistance and capacity building, is said to be crucial and is especially valuable for building transboundary water regimes that seek to enhance and enable long-standing governance arrangements to accommodate diverse interests and needs of riparian countries, the issue discussed in more detail in Chapters 5 and 6.

To describe the changes in the international legal system related to observance and violation of its norms, scholars also invoke the broader term 'accountability' which is used to imply that 'some actors have the right to hold other actors to a set of standards, to judge whether they have fulfilled their responsibilities in light of these standards, and to impose sanctions if they determine that these responsibilities have not been met'.[73] Although this concept originated in the domestic domain in relation to democracy[74] has not acquired a clearly defined legal meaning in international settings;[75] citizen and non-governmental organisations-triggered mechanisms are gaining greater strength in keeping states accountable for their actions in domestic and international domains.[76] Again, this shift is especially noticeable in the field of environment protection and natural resources management.

---

73 Ruth W. Grant and Robert O. Keohane, 'Accountability and abuses of power in world politics' (2005) 99 American Political Science Review 29–43, Nico Krisch and Benedict Kingsbury, 'Introduction: Global governance and global administrative law in the international legal order' (2006) 17 European Journal of International Law 1–13, and ILA, Accountability of International Organisations, Final Report of the Committee, Report of the Seventy-First Conference (Berlin), 2004.

74 Helmut Philipp Aust, 'The normative environment for peace – On the contribution of the ILC's articles on State Responsibility' in George Nolte (ed), *Peace through international law: The role of the International Law Commission A colloquium at the occasion of its Sixtieth Anniversary* (Springer 2009) at 31.

75 Jutta Brunnée, 'International legal accountability through the lens of the law of state responsibility' (2005) 36 Netherlands Yearbook of International Law 3–38 and Aust, 'The normative environment for peace' at 30.

76 Examples include the system of the International Labour Organisation, the North American Agreement on Environmental Cooperation, the World Bank and many human rights treaties. See eg David B. Hunter, *The emergence of citizen enforcement in international organizations* (INECE 2005), Raustiala, Reporting and Review Institutions in 10 Multilateral Environmental Agreements, Svitlana Kravchenko, 'The Aarhus Convention and innovations in compliance with multilateral environmental agreements' (2007) 18 Colorado Journal of International Environmental Law and Policy 1, and Mari Koyano, 'Effective implementation of international environmental agreements: Learning lessons from the Danube Delta conflict' in Teruo Komori and Karel Wellens (eds), *Public interest rules of international law: Towards effective implementation* (Ashgate 2009).

Finally, socio-legal studies and research on the effectiveness of law and regimes have contributed to a better understanding of the sociological facet of international law. Starting from the interest to explaining the gaps between 'law in books' and 'law in action',[77] socio-legal studies expanded to include inquiries about the law as embedded in the larger society.[78] In turn, effectiveness studies[79] brought about a number of different perspectives on defining and assessing effectiveness, ranging from the goal achievement and problem-solving capacity of a regime or institution,[80] to the more modest – but not less valuable – assessment of compliance with treaty rules.[81] However, in the majority of these inquiries, international law is understood in a too narrow and formal way[82] and perceived only as imposing constraints on states and therefore its effectiveness is assessed on the basis of 'enforcement' whereas the facilitative and enabling role of law is broadly overlooked.[83] These shortcomings are still present, despite the fact that the inappropriateness of viewing law merely as a system of sanctions and constraints as well as of its

77 Gap studies grow out and reflect an instrumentalists conception of law. See eg Robert Summers, *Instrumentalism and American legal thought* (Ithaca, Cornell University Press 1982), Brian Z. Tamanaha, 'The perils of pervasive legal instrumentalism' (2005) 1 Montesquieu Lecture Series, Tilburg University.

78 Malcolm Feeley, 'The concept of laws in social science: A critique and notes on an expanded view' (1976) 10 Law and Society Review 501–528 and Malcolm Feeley, 'Three voices of socio-legal studies' (2001) 35 Israel Law Review 175.

79 See eg on the effectiveness of international environmental law and institutions. Brown Weiss and Jacobson, *Engaging countries*, Victor, Raustiala and Skolnikoff, *Implementation and effectiveness*, E L Miles et al. *Environmental regime effectiveness: Confronting theory with evidence* (Cambridge MIT Press 2002), Olav Schram Stokke and Davor Vidas (eds), *Governing the Antarctic: The effectiveness and legitimacy of the Antarctic Treaty System* (Cambridge University Press 1996), Oran R. Young (ed) *The effectiveness of international environmental regimes: causal connections and behavioral mechanisms* (MIT Press 1999).

80 Krasner defines 'regime' as 'principle, norms, rules, and decision-making procedures around which actor expectations converge in a given issue-area', see Stephen D. Krasner, 'Structural causes and regime consequences: regimes as intervening variables' (1982) 36 International Organization 185–205 at 185. See also Oran R. Young, Leslie A. King and Heike Schroeder (eds), *Institutions and environmental change: Principal findings, applications, and research frontiers* (MIT Press 2008).

81 Ronald B. Mitchell, 'Regime design matters: Intentional oil pollution and treaty compliance' (1994) 48 International Organization 425–458.

82 Martha Finnemore and Stephen J. Toope, 'Alternatives to "legalization": Richer views of law and politics' (2001) 55 International Organization 743–758 at 746.

83 Ibid. See also Dinara Ziganshina, 'International water law in Central Asia: Commitments, compliance and beyond' (2009) 20 Journal of Water Law 96–107.

assessment in terms of compliance/non-compliance and measurable behaviour was noted in the international relations and socio-legal literature long time ago. As far back as 1984, Kratochwil argued that 'to focus exclusively on the constraining aspects of [legal] prescriptions – as opposed to a fuller account which includes the justificatory, enabling and communicative aspect of norms – leads to serious distortions concerning the efficacy of law in social life'.[84] In her critical review of legal effectiveness and social studies of law, Sarat also encouraged scholars to abandon the distinction between law in action and law on the books, claiming that 'they are but one type of legal practice' and ask instead 'how does one practice influence another'.[85] She went on to maintain, 'Law doesn't govern society in either an instrumental or ideological fashion; it is part of social life not above or outside it'.[86] This sentiment confirms that although law seeks to influence behaviour of actors in fulfilling certain social functions, it seems to be misguiding to simply set the law in opposition to actors' behaviour in measuring its implementation, compliance and effectiveness, or study law as if it were a separate realm from society. On this account, state behaviour is not only a benchmark for compliance or non-compliance, but also an essential part of international law itself. In other words, behaviour is not outside the law, but a building block of law. This is not to be confused, however, with merely equating international law with state conduct, stating that law mirrors behaviour, as realists would do.[87] Similarly, compliance should be seen not only as a result of the fulfilment of obligations, but as a constitutive part of the process by which the law is formed (state practice).[88]

The formation of custom is a vivid example of the embeddedness of state behaviour and compliance – under conditions of generality and consistency of state practice – in the very fabric of international law. State practice is a material factor in creating customary law and therefore may reflect 'power

84 Friedrich Kratochwil, 'Thrasymmachos revisited: On the revelevance on norms and the study of law for international relations' (1984) 37 Journal of International Affairs 343–356 at 344.

85 Austin Sarat, 'Legal effectiveness and social studies of law: On the unfortunate persistance of a research tradition' (1985) 9 Legal Studies Forum 23–32 at 30.

86 Ibid, 31.

87 Paul R. Viotti and Mark V. Kauppi, *International relations theory: Realism, pluralism, globalism and beyond* (Boston, MA/London, 3rd edn, Allyn and Bacon 1999) and Robert Jervis, 'Realism and the study of world politics' (Autumn 1998) 52 International Organization 971–992.

88 Dinah Shelton, 'Soft law' in David Armstrong (ed), *Routledge handbook to international law* (Routledge 2009) at 72.

equilibrium',[89] but it must be accompanied with *opinio juris*, the second essential prerequisite for a customary norm to emerge, which requires a 'belief that practice is rendered obligatory by the existence of a rule of law requiring it'.[90] This brings us to the third (psychological) facet of international law.

2.1.3 *Psychological Facet: Legal Consciousness*

Psychological considerations in law are conceptualised by Peczenik through the notion of 'the legal consciousness'. In its literal meaning, 'consciousness' refers to the state of being aware of and responsive to surroundings and has to deal with awareness, understanding, and perceptions.[91] For Peczenik, the legal consciousness consists of (a) the acts of understanding of the legal and valid norms and (b) other feelings caused by those acts.[92] As applied to the international legal context, this sub-section first considers the role of consciousness in the formation and 'empowerment' of legal norms and in 'legalization' of behaviour in international law. Then, it turns to discussion of how to build legal consciousness in the international domain.

The notion of consciousness in international law essentially relates to the concepts of natural law, with its emphasis on commonly shared values,[93] and to the long-standing debates on the sources of obligations.[94] In her analysis of the roots and power of international law, O'Connell provides a good summary on the matter,

> As Grotious, Kelsen, Lauterpacht, Henkin, Franck and others indicate, there is much about international law that transcends the material, positive acts such as consent. International law's claim to be law is based on belief. It contains peremptory norms, *jus cogens* principles, that cannot be altered by positive acts, including the norms against genocide,

89 Oscar Schachter, *International law in theory and practice* (Dordrecht, Martinus Nijhoff Publishers 1991) at 9.

90 *North Sea Continental Shelf (Germany/Denmark; Germany/Netherlands)* Judgment, ICJ Reports (1969) para 77. See also Koh, 'Why do nations obey international law?' at 2608.

91 Oxford Dictionaries, *'consciousness'. Oxford Dictionaries. April 2010* (Oxford University Press) ('consciousness', noun: (i) the state of being aware of and responsive to one's surroundings, (ii) a person's awareness or perception of something, the fact of awareness by the mind of itself and the world).

92 Peczenik, 'Juristic definition of law' at 265.

93 See eg Dennis Lloyd, *Introduction to jurisprudence* (4th edn, Stevens and Sons 1979) at 79–169.

94 Oscar Schachter, 'Towards a theory of international obligation' in Stephen M. Schewbel (ed), *The effectiveness of international decisions* (Sijthoff 1971).

> apartheid, extra-judicial killings, slavery, and torture. The third primary source of international law rules after customary international law and treaties is the general principles of law – which have counterparts in principles articulated by the great jurists of classical Roman law. They understood them as requirements or implications of reason, inspired by the natural order of things. General principles from this category, such as necessity, proportionality, and good faith, play an important role in regulating enforcement measures. While most of international law is based on positive acts of consent, ultimately the ontology and legitimacy of international law is based on more than consent, just as it is more than sanctions.[95]

Thus, 'perception', 'sense' and 'belief' are not alien to international law, but rather central to the creation and operation of international obligations. Franck's scholarship is illustrative in this respect. The scholar grounds his understanding of legitimacy on 'the perception of those addressed by a rule or a rule-making institution that the rule or institution has come into being and operates in accordance with generally accepted principles of right process'.[96] It is not a right process itself, but the *perception* of right process matters most. Similarly, *a sense* of community laid a foundation for his fairness discourse.[97]

The well-established concepts of good faith and *opinio juris* are further examples. Good faith is in part to be determined perceptually.[98] For instance, the principle of good faith as applied to negotiation 'consists in *a sincere and honest desire*, as evidenced by genuine efforts, to fulfil the substance of the mutual agreement' [emphasis added].[99] As was noted above, *opinio juris*, often referred to as the psychological element in the creation of custom, suggests that state practice alone does not suffice, the practice must be followed out of

95 Mary Ellen O'Connell, *The power and purpose of international law: Insights from the theory and practice of enforcement* (Oxford, New York, Oxford University Press 2008) at 9.

96 Franck, *The power of legitimacy among nations*.

97 Thomas Franck, *Fairness in international law and institutions* (Oxford, Clarendon Press 1995). See also Edith Brown Weiss, 'International law in a kaleidoscopic world' (2010) Asian Journal of International Law 1–13 at 5 and Brunnée and Toope, *Legitimacy and legality* at 40, 42.

98 In psychology, and cognitive science the term 'perception' refers to the process of attaining awareness or understanding of sensory information. James R. Pomerantz, 'Perception: Overview' in *Encyclopedia of Cognitive Science* (MacMillan/Nature Publishing Group 2002).

99 Bin Cheng, *General principles of law as applied by international courts and tribunals* (London Stevens and Sons 1953) at 118.

a *belief* that it is required by a legal obligation for a customary norm to emerge.[100]

Besides the self-perception of a state's conduct, the perceptions or reaction of others are also attributive to legally relevant behaviour. Explaining that not any behaviour is constitutive to international law, Georges Abi-Saab observes,

> [T]here is a great confusion, particularly in US literature, between 'action' and 'practice'. The general tendency there is to consider that anything a government does, and for which it gives a legal justification, whether genuine or specious (and however specious), is 'practice' liable to become the law. But mere 'action' does not necessarily constitute 'practice'. It can also be a mere violation of law. The legally significant action which constitute legal 'practice', is the action that is perceived, not by the actor (and his self-interpretation), but by the international community, as being compatible with law, even if it implies a new interpretation or a further elucidation of that law. It is only in this way that 'practice' can contribute to the development of law, by responding to the legal expectations of the international community as a whole. It is not the action by one or some States, but the legal perception and reception of that action by the others that gives legitimacy as law or proscribes it as a violation of that law.[101]

In addition to the legal perception and reception of the conduct by others, the above passage highlights the importance of expectations, which are beliefs centred on the future.[102] Such beliefs and expectations serve as an invisible thread in building legal relations in the international arena. Reflecting on this feature of law, Philip Allott maintains that 'Law is not, as so often supposed, a system of legal rules. Law is a system of legal relations'.[103]

---

100 Shaw, *International law* at 74–75 and Peter Malanczuk, *Akehurst's modern introduction to international law* (London, Routledge 1997) at 44–45.

101 Georges Abi-Saab, 'Comment to M. Reisman "The democratization of contemporary international law-making processes and the differentiation of their application"' in Rüdiger Wolfrum and Volker Röben (eds), *Developments of international law in treaty making* (Springer 2005) at 34.

102 See also Robert Summers, *Lon L. Fuller: Jurists: Profiles in legal theory* (William Twining ed, Stanford University Press 1984) at 78, Michael W. Reisman, 'The enforcement of international judgments' (1969) 63 American Journal of International Law 1 at 7 and Shaw, *International law* at 67.

103 Philip Allott, 'The concept of international law' (1999) 10 European Journal of International Law 31 at 36.

The final example to illustrate the significant role of legal consciousness in the international legal domain is the existence and viability of the notion 'public conscience' in positive international law. Reference to 'public conscience' first appeared in the field of international humanitarian law in the so-called Martens Clause.[104] The Martens Clause was introduced to the Preamble of the 1899 Hague Convention II containing the Regulations on the Laws and Customs of War on Land as a compromise to break a deadlock over the definition of combatants and generally provided that international humanitarian law, in case of doubt, must be interpreted consistently with 'the laws of humanity and the requirements of public conscience', looking beyond treaty law and custom.[105] Despite divergent views on its legal significance, commentators agree that the Martens Clause provides a link between positive law relating to armed conflicts and natural law.[106] In the view of Rupert Ticehurst, the dictates of the public conscience referred in the Clause serves as 'an objective means of determining natural law' and allows the participation of all States in its development.[107] Since its formulation in the Martens Clause, the idea of public conscience has been reiterated in other humanitarian law treaties and human rights instruments and articulated by the International Court of Justice (ICJ).[108] The related notions of 'conscience of nations', 'the conscience of mankind' and 'the conscience of humanity' have also emerged.

104 This Clause took its name after the Russian lawyer, publicist and diplomat, Fiodr Fiodorovich Martens (Frederick de Martens), who suggested its text in 1899 at the First International Peace Conference. See Rupert Ticehurst, 'The Martens Clause and the laws of armed conflict' (1997) 137 International Review of the Red Cross.

105 Preamble to the 1899 Hague Convention II containing the Regulations on the Laws and Customs of War on Land.

106 See eg Antonio Cassese, 'The Martens Clause: Half a loaf or simply pie in the sky?' (2000) 11 European Journal of International Law 187–216 at 189 and Ticehurst, 'The Martens Clause and the laws of armed conflict'.

107 Ticehurst, 'The Martens Clause and the laws of armed conflict'.

108 See eg Protocol for the Prohibition of the Use of Asphyxiating, Poisonous or Other Gases, and of Bacteriological Methods of Warfare, Geneva, 17 June 1925, preamble ('conscience of nations'); Universal Declaration of Human Rights, Paris, 10 December 1948, preamble ('the conscience of mankind'); four 1949 Geneva Conventions on the protection of war victims, paragraph 4 of art 63/62/142/158 and two 1977 Additional Protocols relating to the protection of victims of international armed conflicts to the 1949 Geneva Conventions, Additional Protocol I, art 1, and Additional Protocol II, preamble, ('the dictates of the public conscience'); UN Convention on Prohibitions or Restrictions on the Use of Certain Conventional Weapons which may be deemed to be Excessively Injurious or to have Indiscriminate Effects, Geneva, 10 October 1980, preamble ('the dictates of public conscience'); Convention on the Prohibition of the Use, Stockpiling, Production and Transfer

Useful analogies can be drawn from the evolved meaning of the public conscience in the humanitarian field to our broader discussion on the legal consciousness. Meron speculates that the dictates of public conscience can be seen, firstly, as public opinion that shapes the conduct of the parties to a conflict and promotes the development of international humanitarian law and, secondly, as a reflection of *opinio juris*.[109] He argues that *the vox populi* (public opinion) helps to form *opinio juris* by influencing the opinion of governments.[110] International public opinion also has a role to play in building the public consciousness. For example, Judge Weeramantry, in his dissenting opinion in the *Nuclear Weapons* case, emphasised the significant role of the human rights movement in shaping the dictates of public conscience.[111] It is therefore safe to conclude that the public opinion has a role to play in the development of international law and, as was discussed in the section on sociological facet, its influence is increasing. The question remains, however, how to mould public opinion to make it worthy public conscience and how to transform perceptions and awareness to legally relevant practice. Understanding legal consciousness as participation in the construction of legality that comes from socio-legal research, constructivist theory of international relations and the theory of communicative action can facilitate such transformations.

Legal consciousness understood as participation in the construction of legality requires examination of the forms of participation and interpretation through which actors construct, sustain, reproduce or amend the circulating

---

of Anti-Personnel Mines and on their Destruction, 18 September 1997, preamble ('public conscience'); Rome Statute of the International Criminal Court, 17 July 1998, preamble [as corrected by the procès-verbaux of 10 November 1998, 12 July 1999, 30 November 1999, 8 May 2000, 17 January 2001 and 16 January 2002] ('the conscience of humanity'). In the Corfu Channel case, the ICJ stated that Albania's 'obligations [were] based, not on the Hague Convention of 1907, No. VIII, which is applicable in time of war, but on certain general and well-recognized principles, namely: elementary considerations of humanity, even more exacting in peace than in war'. *Corfu Channel case (United Kingdom of Great Britain and Northern Ireland v. Albania)* (Merits) ICJ Reports 4 (1949) 22. In his dissenting opinion in the Nuclear Weapons case, Judge Shababudden pushed the view that nuclear weapons are outlawed because of 'repugnance to the conscience of the international community'. Dissenting Opinion of Judge Shahabuddeen, *Legality of the Threat or Use of Nuclear Weapons* General List No 95 [1996] ICJ Reports 226 at 386.

109 Theodor Meron, 'The Martens Clause, principles of humanity, and dictates of public conscience' (2000) 94 American Journal of International Law 78–89.

110 Ibid. See also Abi-Saab, 'Comment to M. Reisman "The democratization of contemporary international law-making processes and the differentiation of their application"' at 36.

111 See Dissenting Opinion of Judge Weeramantry, *Nuclear Weapons* at 490.

structures of meanings concerning law.[112] The significance of legal consciousness in this conception is to provide norm's addressees with interpretative and discursive frameworks to guide their interactions with the means of law. As such, 'legal thought', 'epistemic communities', 'interpretive communities', 'communities of practice' and treaty bodies can be seen as a particular form of legal consciousness, helping to focus on the legal subjects' contribution to legal understanding and certain ways of interactions in and through the law.[113]

Legal consciousness cannot emerge from and does not imply one-way transfer of legal knowledge, rather it requires all actors' on-going participation in the process of constructing legality. As Berman maintains, 'legal consciousness includes the ways in which individuals themselves deploy, transform, or subvert official legal understandings and thereby "construct" law on the ground'.[114] Not only does on-going interaction help to build 'individual' understandings, but also to transform subjective experience with and understanding of law to intersubjective – commonly shared within a group of actors – meanings and understandings, essential for effective law making and application.[115]

In this sense, legal consciousness seems to serve as a bridge between formal norms and state behaviour. A recent study of legality and legitimacy in international law from an interactional account undertaken by Brunnée and Toope brings together these three elements to demonstrate *how* international law matters.[116] The latter scholars maintain that '[t]he form of law is not enough to generate behavioural change'; what is need is 'to work to construct shared understanding'.[117] Drawing upon Fuller's work and the insights from

---

112 For an extensive summary of various definitions of the term 'legal consciousness' see Susan S. Silbey, 'After legal consciousness' (2005) 1 Annual Review of Law and Social Science 328–368 at 334. See also 'Legal culture and legal consciousness' International Encyclopedia of Social and Behavioral Sciences New York: Elsevier, Pergamon Press (2001) at 8624. Patricia Ewick and Susan S. Silbey, *The common place of law: Stories from everyday life* (Chicago, University Chicago Press 1998) at 39. Paul Schiff Berman, 'From international law to law and globalization' (2005) 43 Columbia Journal of Transnational Law 485 at 497.

113 See eg Balkin, 'Understanding legal understanding', Duncan Kennedy, 'Toward an historical understanding of legal consciousness: The case of classical legal thought in America, 1850–1940' (1980) 3 Research in Law and Sociology 3–24.

114 Berman, 'From international law to law and globalization' at 497.

115 Oxford Dictionaries, *'intersubjective'. Oxford Dictionaries. April 2010* (Oxford University Press) (*'intersubjective'*, adjective: existing between conscious minds; shared by more than one conscious mind).

116 Brunnée and Toope, *Legitimacy and legality* at 119.

117 Ibid, 33.

constructivism and cognitive anthropology, they explain that legal norms that meet the Fuller's eight criteria of legality,[118] coupled with a continuing practice of legality[119] and built upon shared understandings,[120] can generate a 'distinctive legal legitimacy and a sense of commitment' that create a true sense of legal obligation among the participants in the system.[121] Constructivist work, stressing that identities and interests are constructed and supported by intersubjective practice based on and mediated by rules and norms, offers further insights to examine the role of actors, language, interactions and networks in 'constructing' social reality and therefore international law.[122]

Another wave of scholarship that feeds into the legal consciousness research is of understanding the law as a language of communication, discourse and deliberation. At its core is the idea that law provides actors with a shared framework to communicate with each other with a view of reaching understandings. This perspective, stemming from European theories of communicative action and ideal speech act[123] and combined with their American version of deliberative democracy,[124] has been increasingly employed in recent international law and international relations studies to highlight the power of 'better argument' in international legal interactions.[125]

118 Ibid, 6, 351.

119 Brunnée and Toope, *Legitimacy and legality* at 69, 270, 284.

120 Ibid, 64.

121 Ibid, 7.

122 For helpful classification on constructivism research see Antjie Wiener and Uwe Puetter, 'The quality of norms is what actors make of it: Critical constructivist research on norms' (2009) 5 Journal of International Law and International Relations 1–16 at 8. For behaviorist perspective see eg Jeffrey T. Checkel, 'Why comply? Social learning and European identity change' (2001) 55 International Organization 553–588. For societal perspective studying normative meaning see generally Kratochwil, *Rules, norms, and decisions* and Onuf, 'Do rules say what they do?'.

123 Jürgen Habermas, *The theory of communicative action. Vol. 1. Reason and the rationalization of society* (Cambridge, Polity Press 1986), John Langshaw Austin, *How to do things with words* (Oxford, Clarendon Press 1962) Jürgen Habermas, *The theory of communicative action. Vol. 2 Lifeworld and system: A critique of functionalist reason* (Cambridge, Polity Press 1987).

124 James Bohman, *Public deliberation: Pluralism, complexity, and democracy* (Cambridge, MA, MIT Press 2000), Joshua Cohen, 'Procedure and substance in deliberative democracy' in James Bohman and William Rehg (eds), *Deliberative democracy: essays on reason and politics* (MIT Press 2002) and Carlos Santiago Nino, *The constitution of deliberative democracy* (New Haven, Yale University Press 1998).

125 Thomas Risse, '"Let's argue!": Communicative action in world politics' (2000) 54 International Organization 1–39, Ian Johnstone, 'Security Council deliberations: The power of the better argument' (2003) 14 European Journal of International Law 437–480.

As the discussion above has shown, the themes of legal consciousness in international law closely echo Peczenik's conception of the legal consciousness as comprised of 'acts of understanding and the other feelings caused by those acts'. This blend of understanding, awareness and perception forms a psychological layer of international law and, as socio-legal scholars and constructivists teach us, can be built and reconstructed through mutual engagement in an on-going process of interaction.

2.1.4 *Legal Relationships within Normative Communities*

Normative, sociological and psychological facets of international law are complex and interrelated. It is through this internal complexity and interconnection of legal norms, legally relevant behaviour and legal consciousness that international law works and gains its authority and power. If international law is singularly conceived, its potential to constitute and influence actors' behaviour and guide relations in international arena is not to be fully realised. For example, continuous endeavours to design 'perfect' treaties and measure success of interstate cooperation based on qualitative and quantitative aspects of legal norms often remain blind to sociological and psychological aspects that should guide effective law making and implementation. If one admits that international law is a conglomerate of norms, behaviour relevant to law, and legal consciousness, then one should also acknowledge that assessing its performance based on only one of its elements – mainly normative – is hardly justifiable. Norms are important, but they have to be part of system that works. Enforceable legal norms emerge and can be realised only to the extent that available processes allow.

Therefore, the process elements of international law (legally relevant behaviour and legal consciousness) are so important. Only if international law is conceived as a system of norms and processes, its true purpose – which is to build and foster *legal relationships* among actors in the international arena – can be finally appreciated. Reframing analysis in this way gives a more dynamic picture of international law and its operation as well as helps to illuminate that international law is socially constructed, not objectively given. This is especially relevant, given that the crucial shift in international law is not within its normative facet, but in the processes through which international norms are negotiated and implemented.

Understanding that law is socially constructed and driven through changes in behaviour and consciousness brings forward the fundamental importance of the notion of 'community' for development and operation of international law. As ancient Romans profoundly noted *ubi societas, ibi jus* – wherever there is a society (community), there will be law. Elaborating on the notion of a community of states as defined in Article 53 of the 1969 Vienna Convention on the Law of Treaties, Lukashuk refers to a community as an independent social and political system with its own interests, 'which are not confined to the coinciding individual interests of states'.[126] Reference to 'the international community of states', an 'international society' or a 'community of states' can be found in treaties, case law and doctrine.[127] Suggesting similar communitarian ideas, Habermas coined the concept of 'a common life-world' that 'consists of a shared culture, a common system of norms and rules perceived as legitimate, and the social identity of actors being capable of communicating and acting';[128] while Rawls used the concept of an 'overlapping consensus' to support the view that there exist some common ground even among most contending worldviews.[129] In his analysis of deliberation in the UN Security Council, Johnstone – borrowing from Rawls and Habermas – describes the normative climate in which the Council operates as 'overlapping life-worlds' – if not a common life-world – among its members and argues that shared understandings make the discourse possible in this setting.[130]

---

126 Igor I. Lukashuk, 'The law of the international community' in *International law on the eve of the twenty-first century: Views from the International Law Commission* (United Nations 1997) at 53–54.

127 The term 'the international community of States as whole' is used in Article 53 of the Vienna Convention on the Law of Treaties. For discussion on the concept of the international community see *Case Concerning Barcelona Traction, Light and Power Co. Ltd (Belgium v. Spain)* [1970] ICJ Reports 3 at 32 para 33, Separate Opinion of the Judge Christopher Weeramantry, *Case Concerning the Gabčíkovo-Nagymaros Project (Hungary/Slovakia)* General List No 92 (1997) ICJ, 37 ILM 162 (1998) at 95. See eg James R. Crawford, 'Responsibility to the international community as a whole' (2001) 8 Indiana Journal of Global Legal Studies 303–322 at 314 and Dino Kritsiotis, 'Imagining the international community' (2002) 13 European Journal of International Law 961–992. For discussion on the concept of international society see eg Kai Alderson and Andrew Hurrell (eds), *Hedley Bull on international society* (Palgrave Macmillan 2000) at 3 and Barry Buzan, 'From international system to international society: Structural realism and regime theory meet the English school' (1993) 47 International Organization 327–352. See also Russell Buchan, 'A clash of normativities: International society and international community' (2008) 10 International Community Law Review 3–27. Most famously, Brunno Simma advocated for a more institutionalised international community and move 'from bilateralism to community interest' Bruno Simma, 'From bilateralism to community interest in international law' (1994) 250 Recueil des Cours 217.

128 Risse, '"Let's argue!"' at 10.

129 For Rawls, such common 'module' is a political conception of justice, which in an overlapping consensus is supported by citizens for reasons from within their opposing, but reasonable, outlooks. See John Rawls, 'The idea of an overlapping consensus' (1987) 7 Oxford Journal of Legal Studies 1–25 at 1.

130 Johnstone, 'Security Council deliberations' at 460.

He goes on to maintain that '[l]anguage is the glue that holds the "overlapping life-world" together; in international society, that language is the language of law'.[131] Additionally, Johnstone draws upon the work of Stanley Fish[132] to stress the significance of 'interpretive communities' in influencing actor's behaviour in international arena.[133] From a slightly differently angle, Peter Hass highlighted the role of epistemic communities or networks of knowledge-based experts in influencing behaviour.[134] Finally, disregarding universalist claims of community interests, a community of states or international community as misleading and unhelpful in the reality of deep cultural and social diversity across the globe,[135] Brunnée and Toope draws upon the insights from constructivism and cognitive anthropology to emphasise the importance of 'communities of practice' 'constituted by mutual engagement, not by shared values or goals'.[136] Such communities of practice are claimed to be essential in building up shared legal understandings and a practice of legality, which in turn leads to an international legal obligation to emerge and nourish.

All these concepts encompass a communitarian idea that emphasises interconnections and interrelations among actors; they differ, however, in identifying grounds that consolidate such communities or societies: shared values,

131 Ibid, 461. See also Aust, 'The normative environment for peace' at 27.

132 See Stanley Fish, *Is there a text in this class? The authority of interpretive communities* (Cambridge, MA/London, Harvard University Press 1980) and Stanley Fish, *Doing what comes naturally: Change, rhetoric, and the practice of theory in literary and legal studies* (Durham, NC, Duke University Press 1989).

133 Johnstone, 'Security Council deliberations' at 450.

134 Peter M. Haas,'Epistemic communities' in Daniel Bodansky, Jutta Brunnée and Ellen Hey (eds), *The Oxford Handbook of International Environmental Law* (Oxford University Press 2007), Peter M. Haas, 'Do regimes matter? Epistemic communities and Mediterranean pollution control' (1989) 43 International Organization 377. Cf Lawrence Susskind, Environmental diplomacy: Negotiating more effective global agreements (Oxford: Oxford University Press, 1994) at 64 arguing that in general, epistemic communities have rarely played a role in environmental governance.

135 Brunnée and Toope, *Legitimacy and legality* at 79.

136 Ibid, 353. The term 'communities of practice' was initially developed by cognitive anthropologists Jean Lave and Etienne Wenger who emphasised the situated nature of learning and remembering through activity as its core features. Wenger understands 'communities of practice' as 'groups of people who share a concern or a passion for something they do and learn how to do it better as they interact regularly' Wenger, Etienne 'Communities of practice: A brief introduction' (2006). Online: <http://www.ewenger.com/theory/≥ accessed 25 December 2013. See also Etienne Wenger, *Communities of practice: Learning, meaning and identity* (Cambridge University Press 1998).

culture, norms, interests, knowledge, beliefs and other feelings have been suggested by various authors as central to the idea of community.[137]

Merging key ideas to building communities with tripartite understanding of international law, three important aspects can be distilled. First, despite the diversity of doctrinal views on the formation and operation of communities, the underlying idea that 'connection to others matters' seems to be shared across theories and disciplines (sociological facet). Second, what these different perspectives have in common is that it is not a multitude of actors or collective reference that supplies 'community' with its meaning, but rather a sense of connections acquired through discursive interactions on the basis of shared references (psychological facet). Third, a common system of legal norms can serve as a basis on which such interactions centred and built upon (normative facet).

These three aspects lay a necessary foundation for framing the idea of 'normative community' as a specific social space where legal relationships between various actors develop and mature. The notion of normative community brings together normative, sociological and psychological facets of international law by requiring mutual engagement of actors in continuous interactions through the language of international law, by assigning a central role to legal norms, which provide the normative frame for any interactions, and by demanding changes in actors' behaviour, understanding, and perception in order to transform individual actions and understandings to collective ones. Within such normative communities, mutual learning, coordination of action and socialisation can be enhanced and power asymmetry among actors mitigated. Normative community formed in such a way then become the expression of a collective consciousness, which gives rise to sustained legal relationships.

In summary, this section argued that understanding of international law and its operation requires consideration of the tripartite of legal norms, legally relevant behaviour and legal consciousness. It was further suggested that understanding of the role and workings of international law could be further advanced if these three accounts are brought together and mutually constitutive relationships between them are examined more carefully. An important

137 Kritsiotis, 'Imagining the international community' at 990, Thomas Franck, 'Legitimacy in the international system' (1988) 82 American Journal of International Law 705–759 at 706, Franck, *Fairness* at 10–11, Chayes and Chayes, *The new sovereignty* at 6. Thomas Franck, 'Fairness in the international legal and institutional system. General course on public international law' in *Receuil des cours: Collected Courses of the Hague Academy of International Law 1993: III* (Martinus Nijhoff Publishers 1994) at 45.

means by which to do so is to study the properties of legal norms and processes that pay due regard to the three facets of international law and its task of building legal relationships within normative communities. Such a perspective on international law can open up new avenues for a better understanding of the operation of international water law in the Aral Sea basin, including its accomplishments, promises and failures.

2.2 Analytical Framework: Properties of Norms and Processes

International law operates through a system of legal norms and processes and, as the previous section demonstrated, the certain properties of these norms and processes are especially relevant to its development and operation. Given that international law is a social construct and therefore intersubjectively[138] constructed by a group of actors, predominantly nation-states, the properties of legal norms and processes that help to enhance (or diminish) intersubjective expectations and normatively shared meanings are of paramount importance to understanding how international law works. Indeed, an agreement is signed if the intersubjective – shared, collective – understanding of its terms has been found, even though the lack of thereof is often not realised until later; the issues of non-compliance are resolved if intersubjective expectations have been secured. As such, the intersubjective nature of international law as reflected in the properties of its norms and processes serves as a promising avenue for inquiries about the role and workings of international law in general and in the context of transboundary waters of the Aral Sea basin in particular. Hence, this section introduces a framework for analysing international law through two norm properties (stringency and determinacy) and four process properties (inclusiveness, transparency, discursiveness, and coherence) as the most indicative to the intersubjective nature of international law.

2.2.1 *Norm Properties: Determinacy and Stringency*

> [...] *the capacity of rule texts to describe, and conform, state behavior varies from rule to rule and time to time. Different rules of the international community appear to have different strength to exert compliance pull... That rules do, indeed, vary in their ability to predict and to induce conforming behavior is commonplace. This unexceptional proposition nevertheless*

138 See Rein Mullerson, *Ordering anarchy: International law in international society* (Martinus Nijhoff Publishers 2000) at 47.

> *tends to become the source of controversy when the discourse substitutes the world 'law' for 'rules'.*[139]
>
> *It is one thing to say that a rule exists. It is quite a different thing to figure out what that rule means or, more accurately perhaps, what it can be taken to mean.*[140]

Legal norms vary in the way they establish a required standard of conduct. They may set forth either a permission, a prohibition or a requirement; they may impose either an obligation of conduct or an obligation of result; they may convey either a precise or an indeterminate normative message; and they may be couched in either stringent or soft language. The last two characteristics, namely the determinacy and stringency of norms, are especially relevant to understanding the potential operation of international law because they disclose international law as a *collective* enterprise, where compromise is often reached at the expense of the deliberate ambiguity and softness of norm-text.

Norm determinacy or precision refers to the degree of specificity required in prescribing normative conduct that 'removes the opportunity to claim inadvertence or misinterpretation for those predisposed to violate'.[141] It distinguishes between norms signalling clear-cut obligations (often referred to as 'rule-like' prescriptions) and norms that set forth more open-ended requirements (often referred to as 'principle-like' prescriptions).[142] The difference in norm

139 Franck, *The power of legitimacy among nations* 28.

140 Jan Klabbers, 'The meaning of rules' (2006) 20 International Relations 295–301 at 299.

141 Ronald B. Mitchell, 'Compliance theory: Compliance, effectiveness, and behavior change in international environmental law' in Jutta Brunnée, Daniel Bodansky and Ellen Hey (eds), *Oxford Handbook of International Environmental Law* (Oxford University Press 2007) at 912. The same quality may also be termed as norm's precision (Bodansky, *The art and craft of international environmental law* and Miles Kahler, 'Conclusion: The causes and consequences of legalization' (2000) 54 International Organization 661–683), specificity (Andre Nollkaemper, *The legal regime for transboundary water pollution: Between discretion and constraint* (Dordrecht Martinus Nijhoff 1993)), transparency , elasticity or textual clarity (Franck, *The power of legitimacy among nations*), and flexibility (Philippe Sands, *Principles of international environmental law* (Cambridge, 2nd edn, Cambridge University Press 2003)).

142 See eg Ronald Dworkin, *Taking rights seriously* (Cambridge, Harvard University Press 1978) and Ulrich Beyerlin, 'Different types of norms in international environmental law: Policies, principles, and rules' in Daniel Bodansky, Jutta Brunnée and Ellen Hey (eds), *The Oxford Handbook of International Environmental Law* (Oxford University Press 2007). Max Weber, *Economy and society: An outline of interpretive sociology* vol 1 (Guenther Roth and Claus Wittich eds, Berkeley/London, University of California Press 1978).

precision can be seen, for example, in the articulation of a speed limit: determinate norm would clearly set up a specific maximum speed (e.g. 70 km per hour), whereas indeterminate norm would require people to drive at 'safe speed', leaving open the determination of what constitute a safe driving speed in a specific context.[143] Franck observes that norm determinacy, which is 'a necessary first step toward compliance', is most often achieved through textual clarity.[144] He also warns that rules are not always capable of simplistic formulation, and that complex problems may require complex solutions.[145] A norm's indeterminacy does not necessarily negate its substantive content, but rather indicates that its application is contingent on its context and interpretative framework.[146] Precise norms essentially define *ex ante* what conduct is permissible, while open-textured norms provide a normative standard, but leave more specific determination to *ex post* interpretation in a specific context which is essential to ensuring adaptability and flexibility in law. Two points need clarification with respect to the operation of open-textured norms.

First, to limit the discretion of states in an *ex post* determination, open-textured norms must be susceptible to being measured by factual and 'objective' standards. As it follows from the work of the International Law Commission (ILC) and the use of the term by authoritative legal scholars, an 'objective standard' does not necessarily imply the impartiality of assessment, it rather refers to certain criteria, such as due diligence or reasonableness, against which any individual state's conduct can be measured.[147] This further supports the point

---

Michael Barnett and Raymond Duvall, 'Power in international politics' (2005) 59 International Organization 39–75.

143 Daniel Bodansky, 'Rules vs standards in international environmental law' (2004) 98 American Society of International Law Proceedings 275–280 at 276.

144 Franck, *The power of legitimacy among nations* at 52. See also Chayes and Chayes, *The new sovereignty* at 118 and Kenneth O.W. Abbott and others, 'The concept of legalization' (2000) 54 International Organization 401–419 at 30.

145 Franck, 'Legitimacy in the international system' at 724.

146 See eg Franck, *The power of legitimacy among nations* at 81 and Chayes and Chayes, *The new sovereignty* at 118.

147 See Commentary to *the Draft articles on prevention of transboundary harm from hazardous activities* in Report of the International Law Commission on the work of its fifty-third session, UN Doc A/56/10 (2001), at 152, 165; Commentary to *the Draft articles on the law of the non-navigational uses of international watercourses* in Report of the International Law Commission on the Work of its Forty-sixth Session, UN Doc 2(2) (1994) Y B Int'lL Comm'n at 222, at 94, 102, 103, 108, and 128; Nollkaemper, *The legal regime for transboundary water pollution* at 368; F.V. Garcia Amador, 'Second report on international responsibility' (1957) 2 Yearbook of the International Law Commission 104 at 122; Owen McIntyre,

made above that a reference to objectivity in law implies rather intersubjectivity. The word 'objective' is therefore used in this book in such connotation. In this framing, 'objective' standards such as reasonableness or due diligence establish collectively shared contours of a required conduct which may change over time and which may be imbued with various meanings in different contexts.

Second, and closely related, is the significance of the context for the operation of international norms in general and open-textured norms in particular. As was noted in the discussion on the normative facet of international law, very few – if any – international norms can be applied neutrally without taking into account factual and legal contexts, or, in other words, an exercise of interpretation. For this purpose, the customary legal rules of interpretation codified in Articles 31 and 32 of the Vienna Convention on the Law of Treaties require attention to the text, context, and object and purpose of a treaty.[148] Besides, norm interpretation and subsequent application depends on other norms (other relevant rules or principles) and the wider legal environment in which they operate.[149] Therefore norm determinacy is influenced by the context, which reflects the changing character of contemporary society, new developments, realities and trends.[150] Both intersubjectivity and contextualisation connects norms with the relevant legal processes because shared meanings and understandings are inferred from legally relevant behaviour in a given context. For example, the open-textured norm to take 'appropriate' measures to control water pollution requires follow up activities the scope and intensity of which might change over time and depending on the context and the development level of the countries.

'The proceduralisation and growing maturity of international water law' (2010) 22 Journal of Environmental Law 475–497.

148 McLachlan, 'The principle of systemic integration and Article 31(3)(c) of the Vienna Convention' at 280.

149 ILC Report on fragmentation.

150 Contextualism as 'the manifestation of the spirit of the times' also brings into play the time dimension. For example, The European Court of Human Rights established that the European Convention is 'a living instrument which [...] must be interpreted in the light of present day conditions'. Tyrer v. UK, Series A, No 26, para 31 (1978). In the *Gabčíkovo-Nagymaros case*, the ICJ observed that 'what might have been correct application of law in 1989 or 1992 (less than ten year before), if the case had been before the Court then, could be a miscarriage of justice if prescribed in 1997' and that 'it would be an administration of law althogether out of touch with reality if the Court were to order the obligations (under the 1997 Treaty) to be fully reinstated'. *Gabčíkovo-Nagymaros case*, paras 134, 136.

It is also worth noting that often the form of instruments prescribing legal norms predetermines the language in which obligations are couched. Thus, in a preliminary report on the law of the non-navigational uses of international watercourses to the ILC, McCaffrey notes,

> It seemed to be generally recognized by the Commission that, in a framework text, it would be necessary or useful to use, to a reasonable extent, general legal formulations or standards such as 'good-neighbourly relations', 'good faith', participation in the benefits of a resource 'in a reasonable and equitable manner' and the duty not to cause 'appreciable harm' to the rights or interests of others.[151]

Similarly, Raustiala points out to 'systematic trade-offs between form and substance' that requires closer attention to the complex architecture of international agreements and treating agreement design holistically.[152]

In summary, norm determinacy assesses the specificity of behaviour required of states and in doing so calls attention to the form of instruments, legal and factual context, and requires on-going interaction in the search of intersubjective meanings of the norms.

The second property of norms considered in this book is their stringency. Norm stringency is the degree of normative force with which the norm is phrased.[153] It relates to the norm's mandatory quality.[154] Norms expressed through directive verbs such as 'shall, must, require, and may not' are stringent. Less stringent norms can be indicated through the use of verbs such as 'plan, may, and recommend' that convey a normative message in a more hortatory or programmatic way. Importantly, norm stringency should be understood as a spectrum, with different levels of 'control intention' shading into one another in the norm-text.[155] This recognises that an obligation may be couched in terms conveying a different degree of normative force and consequently

151 Stephen C. McCaffrey, 'Preliminary report on the law of the non-navigational uses of international watercourses' in *Yearbook of the International Law Commission, vol II(1), pp. 87–96, un Doc A/CN4/393* (1985) at 90, para 13.

152 Kal Raustiala, 'Form and substance in international agreements' (2005) 99 American Journal of International Law 581–614 at 582.

153 Jens Steffek, 'The legitimation of international governance: A discourse approach' (2003) 9 European Journal of International Relations 249–275, at 251.

154 Bodansky, *The art and craft of international environmental law* at 1034 (distinguishing between the terms 'mandatory' as refereed to the language and 'binding' as referred to the legal status of an norm).

155 Ibid. See also Wiersema, 'The new international law-makers?'.

different intentions and expectations about the required standard of conduct. Recent practice in the Permanent Court of Arbitration is illustrative in this regard. In the case regarding the Convention for the Protection of the Marine Environment of the North-East Atlantic[156] (the *OSPAR Convention* case), the arbitral tribunal cast some light on norm stringency by defining it as 'a cascading standard of expression providing for the particular obligations'.[157] To analyse the obligations imposed on Contracting Parties under the OSPAR Convention with respect to access to information, the Tribunal classified a hierarchy of obligations or different levels of engagement of treaty obligation. The Tribunal stated:

> For the achievement of [the Convention's] aims the framers of the OSPAR Convention have carefully applied differential language to provide for stipulated levels of engagement of treaty obligation to achieve the objectives. There is a cascading standard of expression providing for the particular obligations imposed on a Contracting Party. For example, there are mandatory provisions that provide for Contracting Parties:

- to take some act ('shall apply', 'shall include', 'shall undertake', 'shall cooperate' or 'shall keep');
- actively to work towards an objective ('take all possible steps', 'implement programs', 'carry out programs');
- to deal with issues of planning for the objective ('establish programs', 'adopt', 'define', 'draw up', 'develop', 'take account of'); and
- to take measures ('take', 'adopt', 'plan', 'apply', 'introduce', 'prescribe', 'take into account').

> At a lesser level of engagement, other provisions provide for information to be dealt with ('collect', 'access information') or that systems be set up ('provide for', 'establish').[158]

As can be seen from the above, norm stringency, displaying the degree of normative force with which the norm is couched, is useful to an understanding of

156 Convention for the Protection of the Marine Environment of the North-East Atlantic, 32 ILM 1069 (1992).

157 *Dispute Concerning Access to Information under Article 9 of the ospar Convention (Ireland v. United Kingdom)* Final Award of 2 July 2003, Permanent Court of Arbitration, OSPAR Arbitral Tribunal. [OSPAR Award] at 412 paras 129, 34.

158 Ibid, 412, paras 129, 34.

the existence of the different levels of 'control intention' embedded in the norm-text.

Norm determinacy and norm stringency are alike in the sense that they both help to capture the degree of consensus achieved by the concerned parties as to the form of expression and the content of any norm.[159] But there is also a clear analytical distinction between them. The latter shows the different degree of the 'control intention' expressed by the states as to the normative force of obligations; while the former mostly illustrates the degree of states' discretion with respect to the implementation of obligations in a particular context and requires the mutual engagement in the search of intersubjective meanings of the norms.

Thus, analysis of legal norms on the basis of their determinacy and stringency provides a deeper understanding of their nature and potential operation, sensitive to the time-context considerations. It serves as a reminder that different types of norms may require different forms of implementation and operationalisation. It is worth noting that if states decide to reserve more flexibility in their future conduct by phrasing norms in indeterminate or soft language, they should be aware of risks arising from diminished legal certainty and collective expectations that often must be restored through a sound procedural system. The latter point sheds light on the complex interrelations between norm and processes, which are the key to understanding its operation.

2.2.2 *Process Properties: Inclusiveness, Transparency, Discursiveness and Coherence*

> *To understand law is to understand the processes of interaction associated with the idea of 'law'.*[160]

The discussion in the first section of the chapter illuminated that legally relevant processes are built-in to the normative, sociological and psychological accounts of international law. As per the nature of these processes, sociological and psychological accounts were instrumental to point out the significance of on-going interactions among various actors by whom and through which international law operates. This section therefore examines properties of international legal interactions which serve to generate, elaborate and refine shared understandings and collective expectations about the meaning and

159 See eg Brown Weiss and Jacobson, *Engaging countries* at 1.

160 Roger B.M. Cotterrell, *The sociology of law: An introduction* (London, 2nd edn, Butterworths) at 148.

implementation of the norms with a view to addressing (or preventing) the lack of norm stringency and determinacy. Four characteristics of an international legal interaction that resonates with normative, sociological and physiological accounts and condition its effective operation are distilled from the theoretical deliberations of process-based scholars; all of the characteristics being closely interrelated to each other. Broadly defined, these encompass inclusiveness, transparency, discursiveness, and coherence. It is argued that these properties are helpful for understanding the workings of international law by addressing the questions of who, under what conditions, in what way and in which settings is involved in international legal interactions.

2.2.2.1 Inclusiveness

Inclusiveness or participation refers to a process of taking part and relating to others and therefore suggests both action and connection.[161] Inclusiveness of process helps to unfold what actors are involved in international legal interactions, in what capacity, and how they relate to and connect with each other.

As was discussed above, nation-states, individuals and non-state collectivities, such as governmental and non-governmental organisation, are currently playing diverse roles in various legally relevant processes, including norm evolution, development, interpretation, and implementation at the international level.[162] Acknowledging this diversity of actors, inclusive process does not require, however, all actors to be involved in all interactions, rather it stresses the need to be aware of different actors whose contribution may be useful or necessary to reach scientifically-informed, collective, participatory or other kinds of decision, which will be accepted by its addresses as legitimate. It is also necessary to be aware of the implications of the delimitation of actors on

---

161 Wenger, *Communities of practice* at 55.

162 See eg Jacobson and Brown Weiss, 'Assessing the record and designing strategies to engage countries', Oran R. Young, 'Political leadership and regime formation: On the development of institutions international society' (1991) 45 International Organization 281–308, Andrew Moravcsik, 'A new statecraft? Supranational entrepreneurs and international cooperation' (Spring 1999) 53 International Organization 267–306, Oran R. Young, 'Comment on Andrew Moravcsik, "A new statecraft? Supranational entrepreneurs and international cooperation"' (1999) 53 International Organization 805–809, and Laura A. Dickinson, 'Military lawyers on the battlefield: An empirical account of international law compliance' (2010) 104 American Journal of International Law 1–28, Ulrich Fastenrath, 'A political theory of law: Escaping the aporia of the debate on the validity of legal argument in public international law' in Ulrich Fastenrath and others (eds), *From bilateralism to community interest: Essays in honour of Bruno Simma* (Oxford University Press 2011) at 69.

the process and outcome of negotiation and deliberation. Adding or substracting parties changes the constellation of interests upon which compromise will be sought, and it may affect efficiency of decision-making, by imposing extra costs on participants, delaying outcomes or even stalling processes.[163] Finally, as constructivism and situated learning studies demonstrate, both participation *and* non-participation shape actors' identities.[164] The fact that actors define themselves through practices they engage in (or not) illuminates the importance of understanding how actors relate to and connect with each other.

Inclusiveness of process is also to be understood in terms of the membership in communities. Activities of certain communities take place in institutionalised forums, such as international organisations or the bodies of the conventions; others require only a sense of being part of it, identifying with it or belonging to it, such as 'epistemic' or 'interpretive' communities.[165] Institutions have been considered as 'a focused and intensified arena of public justification',[166] as the must platform to promote norms[167] and increase process determinacy.[168] For example, collective decision-making bodies such as Conferences of Parties serve today as the primary format through which member-States as well as non-state entities work at international settings. Similarly, specialised bodies, established to fulfil certain regulative or managerial functions within particular regimes, such as river commissions, have an important role to play in a regime development and performance.[169] These international institutions are increasingly conceived not just as structure or mechanisms through which states act, but also as autonomous and powerful agents on their own.[170]

---

163 See eg Gehring, 'Treaty-making and treaty evolution' at 471, Ian Johnstone, 'Legislation and adjudication in the UN Security Council: Bringing down the deliberative deficit' (2008) 102 American Journal of International Law 275–308 at 282. See also Lawrence Susskind, Sarah McKearnan and Jennifer Thomas-Larmer, *The consensus building handbook: A comprehensive guide to reaching agreement* (Thousand Oaks, CA, Sage 1999).

164 Wenger, *Communities of practice* at 164.

165 Ibid, 5. Adler, *Communitarian international relations*.

166 Chayes and Chayes, *The new sovereignty* at 119, 125. See also Thomas Franck, 'The power of legitimacy and the legitimacy of power: International law in an age of power disequilibrium' (2006) 100 American Journal of International Law 88–106 at 88.

167 Finnemore and Sikkink, 'International norm dynamics and political change' at 899.

168 Franck, 'Legitimacy in the international system' at 725.

169 *Case Concerning Pulp Mills on the River Uruguay* (*Argentina v. Uruguay*) ICJ General List No 135 (2010) 55 para 184.

170 See eg Robert O. Keohane and Joseph S. Nye, 'Transgovernmental relations and international organizations' (1974) 27 World Politics 39–62 and Michael Barnett and Martha

In summary, by uncovering what actors and in what capacity they are involved in international legal interactions, how they relate to and connect with each other, inclusiveness sets out the contours of the relevant actors and communities that make a difference in international law. To have a clearer understanding how these actors interact and what holds communities together, consideration of other properties of interaction is required.

2.2.2.2 Transparency

Transparency has been defined as 'a process by which information about existing conditions, decisions and actions is made accessible, visible and understandable'.[171] Transparency as 'a device signalling the trustworthiness'[172] of actors plays an important role in international settings by facilitating coordination, providing reassurance and exercising deterrence,[173] by creating a greater clarity about law's prescriptions,[174] by increasing the credibility of commitments and reputational concerns,[175] by enhancing the trust of the public to decision-making, and creating a greater degree of internal acceptance of commitments.[176]

Finnemore, 'The politics, power and patologis of international organisations' (Autumn 1999) 53 International Organization 699–732. Frank Biermann and Bernd Siebenhüner eds., Managers of global change: The influence of international environmental bureaucracies, (2009), Karen N. Scott, 'International environmental governance: Managing fragmentation through institutional connection' (2011) 12 Melbourne Journal of International Law 1–40 at 15 and Klabbers, 'Constitutionalism and the making of international law: Fuller's procedural natural law' at 92, Chayes and Chayes, *The new sovereignty* at 280, Johnstone, 'Security Council deliberations' at 442–443.

171 *Summary of reports on the international financial architecture by the G22 Working Group on transparency and accountability, Working Group on strengthening financial systems and Working Group on international financial crises* (International Monetary Fund, 1998) at 5.

172 Carolyn Ball, 'What is transparency?' (2009) 11 Public Integrity 293–308.

173 Chayes and Chayes, *The new sovereignty*, 135–136.

174 Franck, *The power of legitimacy among nations*.

175 Oran R. Young, 'Building regimes for socioecological systems: Institutional diagnostics' in Oran R. Young, Leslie A. King and Heike Schroeder (eds), *Institutions and environmental change: principal findings, applications, and research frontiers* (MIT Press 2008). Victor, Raustiala and Skolnikoff, *Implementation and effectiveness*.

176 See eg Aarhus Conventionand Stephen Stec and Susan Casey-Lefkowitz, *The Aarhus Convention: An implementation guide* (New York/Geneva, United Nations 2002). For a critique of the argument that transparency by itself will increase compliance see also George W. Downs, David M. Rocke and P.N. Barsoom, 'Is the good news about compliance good news about cooperation?' (1996) 50 International Organization 379–406.

Whether a process by which legally relevant information and decisions are made accessible, visible and understandable can be explored with the reference to textual and substantive transparency. Textual transparency refers to linguistic transparency of the text. The idea of textual transparency or transparency of commitments is well established in law with its requirements of promulgation and clarity that enable its addressees to know and understand what the law requires.[177] Textual transparency can be best analysed through the lens of stringency and determinacy introduced in this chapter as a property of legal norms. Addressing textual transparency within the process properties is justified by the fact that what is referred through the text is always subject to interpretation.

Substantive transparency takes place when a legal framework contains provisions related to information exchange, information disclosure to the public, reporting, compliance mechanisms and capacity building activities. The openness of law making, interpretation and implementation requires accessibility and clarity with regard to law making procedures as well as implementation of and compliance with commitments through visible monitoring or compliance (performance) review system as well as openness in the work of institutions and decision-making processes as a whole.[178]

Ultimately, textual and substantive transparency provide a picture of openness and accessibility to different actors of rules, procedures and settings of international legal interactions. With this knowledge, actors are better equipped to invoke the means of international law in their international relations.

Transparency essentially relates to other process features. Inclusiveness forms part of transparency as far as openness goes beyond simply informing the public and other actors and seeks to ensure that a process includes active participation of all actors. Greater involvement of various actors ensures that process and its outcomes are more open. In turn, transparency contributes to the process feature of inclusiveness, *inter alia*, by providing access to agenda setting and choice of forum that may prevent the exclusion or delegitimasation of certain actors. Similarly, transparency enables discursive interactions by ensuring openness of information and access to different settings. It is also important to address transparency across critical sectors, countries and

177 See eg Lon L. Fuller, *The morality of law* (New Haven, Conn., Yale University Press 1969), Franck, *The power of legitimacy among nations*, Brunnée and Toope, *Legitimacy and legality*.

178 Ronald B. Mitchell, 'Sources of transparency: Information systems in international regimes' (1998) 42 International Studies Quarterly 109–130 and Brown Weiss and Jacobson, *Engaging countries*.

institutions that highlights a close link with coherence. Finally, it should be borne in mind that transparent process – although being an asset in itself – shall yield positive outcomes in terms of decisions to be made. In other words, the caution is required to ensure 'workable' level of openness for decisions to be actually made not only discussed.

2.2.2.3 Discursiveness

The property of discursiveness builds upon and further develops the ideas of 'connections' and 'communities' introduced in the discussion of inclusiveness. To reiterate, it was argued that what supplies 'community' with its meaning is a sense of connections acquired through on-going interactions or 'the thriving network of discursive relationships occurring within' them.[179] Discursiveness complements the features of inclusiveness and transparency by setting up a *mode* of interaction in international legal processes. It refers to the quality of a process that allows participants to exchange reasons and search for intersubjective meaning (rather than for single right answers) in law making, interpretation, implementation and application through 'verbal interchange' such as communication, reasoning, argumentation and deliberation.[180]

Acts of shared understanding and reasoning – the key element of the physiological facet of law – are at the core of discursive interactions that employs the power of persuasion in international legal settings.[181] The idea of influencing behaviour toward reaching a shared understanding was pioneered by Max Weber in his study of legitimacy and developed further by Jürgen Habermas in the concept of communicative action.[182] Habermas argued that communicative action occurs,

---

179 Kritsiotis, 'Imagining the international community' at 990.

180 See eg Chayes and Chayes, *The new sovereignty* and John S. Dryzek, *Deliberative global politics: Discourse and democracy in a divided world* (Cambridge, Polity Press 2006). Bohman, *Public deliberation: Pluralism, complexity, and democracy* at 27, Johnstone, 'Security Council deliberations' at 282, 449.

181 Oxford Dictionaries, *'persuade'. Oxford Dictionaries. April 2010* (Oxford University Press) ('persuade', verb: (a) induce (someone) to do something through reasoning or argument; (b) cause (someone) to believe something, especially after a sustained effort; convince; and (c) provide a sound reason for (someone) to do something).

182 Weber, *Economy and society: An outline of interpretive sociology*, Habermas, *The theory of communicative action. Vol. 1. Reason and the rationalization of society*, Jürgen Habermas, *Between facts and norms: Contribution to a discourse theory of law and democracy* (Cambridge, MA, MIT Press 1996) and Habermas, *The theory of communicative action. Vol.2 Lifeworld and system: A critique of functionalist reason.*

> when the action orientations of the participating actors are not coordinated via egocentric calculations of success, but through acts of understanding. Participants are not primarily oriented toward their own success in communicative action; they pursue their individual goals under the condition that they can coordinate their action plans on the basis of shared definitions of the situation.[183]

The concepts of 'common life-world' and 'communities of practice' discussed in section 2.1.4 illustrate that the context of discursive interactions matters. Following Weber, Kratochwil asserts that action is meaningful if it can be placed in an intersubjectively shared context. For him, such context is based on and mediated by rules and norms.[184] This observation combined with the preceding discussion on the context-dependency of the norms illuminates the dual function of norms in an international legal discourse: (a) norms provide the context for interactions, but also (b) norms depend on the context for their interpretation and implementation. In other words, norms represent intersubjective frameworks of meanings, which evolve in the process of interactions about their interpretation and implementation.

Importantly, intersubjective meanings and understanding can only emerge as a result of *mutual* engagements in discursive process and social *learning*. Mutual learning and a reciprocity of understanding is possible through dialogue, in which 'our' expectations to be understood must be combined with genuine endeavours to grasp 'their' perspective.[185] Not only does such a process of reciprocal learning 'induce to believe' through increased understanding, as persuasion implies, but also adds to the construction of legality by strengthening legal consciousness.

From discursive perspective, interpretative process is also considered as a process of mutual involvement and collective enterprise rather than a unilateral act. Johnstone states that 'Interpretation of international law is the search for intersubjective understanding of the norm at issue: the interpretive task is to ascertain what law means to the parties to a treaty or subject of the law collectively rather than to any one of them individually. It is an interactive process, the parameters of which are set by an interpretive community'.[186]

183 Habermas, *The theory of communicative action. Vol. 1. Reason and the rationalization of society* cited in Risse, '"Let's argue!"' at 9.

184 Kratochwil, *Rules, norms, and decisions* at 24.

185 Jurgen Habermas, *Postmethaphisical thinking: Philosophical essays* (Polity Press 1992) at 138, Bodansky, *The art and craft of international environmental law* at 152.

186 Johnstone, 'Security Council deliberations' at 449–450. Cf. Dworkin, *Taking rights seriously*.

It should be noted, however, that intersubjectivity does not dismiss the need for 'subjectivity', understood as 'what the individual subject brings to the act of understanding; it is what allows her to construct the object of her interpretation so that she can understand it'.[187] Rather, 'individual cognition evolves together with intersubjective understandings'.[188]

In addition to interactions aimed at reaching shared understandings, justification (argumentation) or providing reasons for action and attitudes serve as another distinctive feature of discursive process. It is not enough that 'an argument' can be made; the argument must have the power to pursued and thereby generate adherence and belief[189] and be open to confirmation or disconfirmation in a justificatory discourse.[190] The power of persuasive argument lies in the justification made in terms acceptable to others.[191]

In sum, the process of dialogue, argumentation [legal justification], and reciprocal learning are at the core of understanding an international legal process in terms of discourse. The process is discursive, if it opens up possibilities for communicative interactions to reach shared understandings, such as mutual learning, in contrast to a mere strategic interaction provided by information sharing as an element of transparency;[192] and if it triggers a reasoning process grounded in *legal* arguments rather than political rhetoric.[193]

Discursive process builds upon the features of inclusiveness and transparency because an initial range of participants and openness is required for discourse to emerge. It also further develops these features: the more engagement in discursive settings, the stronger connections and a sense of community, as well as the better understanding and accessibility of information and reasons behind decisions taken. But sometimes more open and transparent debates can also jeopardize 'discursive bite' and the possibility to reach an agreement. In his analysis of deliberation in the UN Security Council, Johnstone warns,

> [Although the] Council expansion is clearly needed, [...] a larger Council could be less cohesive and reasoned discourse might become more difficult. As a thin normative consensus emerges, discourse based on shared

187 See Balkin, 'Understanding legal understanding' at 107.

188 Adler, *Communitarian international relations* at 5.

189 Johnstone, 'Security Council deliberations' at 448–450.

190 Steffek, 'The legitimation of international governance: A discourse approach' at 262

191 Cohen, 'Procedure and substance in deliberative democracy' at 414 and 416.

192 See eg Johnstone, 'Security Council deliberations' at 453.

193 Nicole Deitelhoff, 'The discursive construction of legal norms and institutions: Law and politics in negotiations on the International Criminal Court' (2007) SSRN and Brunnée and Toope, *Legitimacy and legality* at 304–305.

> understandings and intersubjective meanings, if not values, is possible. Conceivably a dramatic expansion of the Council would jeopardize that minimum consensus. Debates would be more open and inclusive but could lose their discursive bite.[194]

Finally, discursiveness is also closely linked to norm properties of determinacy and stringency that provide a normative frame within which discursive interactions about the meaning and interpretation of norms occurs. For instance, an indeterminate norm requires more active engagement of actors in discursive interactions to ascertain its actual meaning in a given time and context.

2.2.2.4 *Coherence*

Coherence or integration is about making connections within the law, between different legal regimes, between national and international domains, or between doctrine, knowledge and practice. In this rather broad framing, the property of coherence includes both horizontal and vertical connections within the international law, referred by Franck as 'coherence' and 'adherence' respectively,[195] but also goes beyond the international legal system to the national legal order. In addition to this *normative* coherence in law, the term 'coherence' as used in this study also includes *institutional* connections.

To operationalise these links, both normative and institutional integrative techniques are required. At the normative level, secondary rules of international law, such as rules of interpretation, rules of change and rules of responsibility, that 'define the normative context within which primary norms function and therefore affect the operation of such primary norms'[196] seems to serve as the main integrative feature of the international legal system.[197] For example, rules of interpretation helps to increase coherence within the international legal system by provide a framework for pulling together a wide range of sources operating at different levels of generality in order to ascertain the normative

194 Johnstone, 'Security Council deliberations' at 463, ft 103.

195 Franck, *The power of legitimacy among nations*. See also Dworkin, *Taking rights seriously* (using the term 'integrity') and Neil MacCormick, 'Coherence in legal justification' in Alexander Peczenik (ed), *Theory of legal science* (Reidel 1984).

196 André Nollkaemper, 'The power of secondary rules to connect the international and national legal orders' in Yuval Shany and Torner Broude (eds), *Multi-sourced equivalent norms in international law* (Hart Publishing 2011) at 47. See also Dirk Pulkowski, 'Universal international law's grammar' in Ulrich Fastenrath and others (eds), *From bilateralism to community interest: Essays in honour of Bruno Simma* (Oxford University Press 2011).

197 See eg ILC Report on fragmentation.

content of norms.[198] Scholars also make evident the power of secondary rules to connect the international and national legal orders. Nollkaemper, for instance, argues that because of an essential connection between primary and secondary norms of international law that can survive the migration of a primary norm into a different legal system, secondary rules of international law in certain cases might also be applicable to the interpretation, modification and termination of corresponding rules at national level.[199]

Institutional connections add to greater coherence in the international legal system. As some possible examples of institutional connections, transnational legal process and multilevel governance studies suggest that sound linkages between and within levels of regulative systems are crucial for desired changes to happen on the ground.

Horizontal linkages refer to interactions within levels, such as nations, issue areas, or agencies. It was argued that increased horizontal connections between nation states, treaty regimes and institutions offer the potential to facilitate better law making, implementation, and compliance.[200] Thus, the creation of cooperative arrangements and other institutional connections between treaties, especially in the fields of natural resources use and protection, can substantially improve the effectiveness of governance regimes by maximising the benefits that arise from a confluence between various treaties mandates.[201] Koyona convincingly illustrates benefits of horizontal dynamics between different regimes in her comprehensive analysis of the controversy between Ukraine and Romania concerning the Bystroe Canal Project in the Danube Delta. Particularly, she observes that 'complementary interaction' based on the practical cooperation between the institutions, including multiple processes under the MEAs concerned and the UNESCO Man and Biodiversity Programme have contributed to the effective management of the controversy.[202] In a wider context, Slaughter calls attention to transnational government networks that successfully operate to exchange information, coordinate regulatory efforts and resolve common problems; and characterises

198 McLachlan, 'The principle of systemic integration and Article 31(3)(c) of the Vienna Convention'.

199 Nollkaemper, 'The power of secondary rules to connect the international and national legal orders' at 49–50.

200 See eg Chayes and Chayes, *The new sovereignty*.

201 See eg Bradnee W. Chambers, *Interlinkages and the effectiveness of multilateral environmental agreements* (Tokyo, United Nations University Press 2008), *Compliance mechanism under selected multilateral environmental agreements* (UNEP Division of Environmental Law and Conventions, 2007) at 13, Scott, 'International environmental governance'.

202 Koyano, 'Effective implementation of IEAs' at 278.

resultant trans-governmental regulations, such as the memorandum of understandings between governmental institutions, as 'the fastest growing legal instrument'.[203]

Vertical connections put an emphasis on interactions between various levels, namely national, transboundary, regional and global. If horizontal discursive process mostly connotes with the effect of persuasion, vertical interactions seem to suggest more focus on the process of socialisation[204] and non-state actors' involvement. In this regard, insights from new 'organisational' legal scholarship can be informative with its focus on the mobilisation of social and cultural pressures to induce compliant behaviour at the national level.[205] It was argued, for example, that 'fostering greater compliance may sometimes be less a matter of writing new treaty provisions or increasing the activity of international courts and more a matter of subtly influencing organisational structures and cultural norms'.[206] Koh's transnational legal process theory promotes the mechanisms of 'vertical domestification',[207] while arguing that States obey international rules when they internalise the norms and incorporate them into their domestic legal structure 'through executive action, judicial interpretation, legislative action, or some combination of three'.[208] A similar approach in recognising the interplay between national and international arenas is adopted by Hathaway, when she claims that international and domestic 'collateral consequences' influence state behaviour.[209] Various theories and studies bring into play diverse arguments in favour of the importance of international and national factors,[210] but what is important for our discussion of

203 Slaughter, 'A liberal theory of international law' at 245.

204 Harold Koh, 'Internalization through socialization' (2005) 54 Duke law journal 975–982.

205 Ryan Goodman and Derek Jinks, 'Toward institutional theory of sovereignty' (2002–2003) 55 Stanford Law Review 1749–1788; Ryan Goodman and Derek Jinks, 'Incomplete internalization and compliance with human rights law' (2008) 19 European Journal of International Law 735–748.

206 Dickinson, 'Military lawyers on the battlefield: An empirical account of international law compliance' 3.

207 Koh, 'Bringing international law home' 636.

208 Harold Koh, 'The 1994 Roscoe Pound lecture: Transnational legal process' (1996) 75 Nebraska Law Review 181–207. The similar idea that more internalised norms attract compliance has been advanced by Henkin long before Koh. See Henkin, *How nations behave*.

209 Oona A. Hathaway, 'Between power and principle: An integrated theory of international law' (2005) 72 University of Chicago Law Review 469–536 at 473, 503.

210 Audie Klotz, 'Norms reconstituting interests: Global racial equality and U.S. sanctions against South Africa' (1995) 49 International Organization 451–478. Finnemore and Sikkink, 'International norm dynamics and political change' and Checkel, 'Why comply?', Anne-Marie Slaughter, 'International law in a world of liberal states' (1995) 6 European

vertical linkages is the fact that to understand international law and its operation it is not enough to look exclusively at international domain; its connections with domestic norms and processes must be examined more carefully.

Coherent process is ultimately linked to the process features of inclusiveness, transparency and discursiveness. Both vertical and horizontal linkages are reinforced through inclusive, transparent and discursive interactions. In turn, integrative feature adds to other process features, essentially by strengthening connections within and across levels of interaction. It contributes to inclusiveness by linking actors within levels, such as nations, issue areas or agencies as well as between levels, such as national, regional and international. It adds to transparency by improving information flow across sectors, countries and scales. It facilitates discursive interactions within and across levels. Finally, coherence contributes to greater norm determinacy and stringency by reinforcing normative and institutional connections.

2.2.2.5 *Conclusion on Process Properties*

Four features, namely inclusiveness, transparency, discursiveness and coherence, are considered in this section as being of particular relevance for understanding processes of international law. Although by no means exhaustive, these properties serve to capture a more realistic and dynamic image of international law through focus on various actors and certain features of the processes by whom and through which international law is generated, invoked, used and changed. These features are not disparate; rather they are closely interconnected, partially reinforcing and building on each other. For instance, connections to others and becoming part of communities are an important element of inclusiveness, but it is also an essential prerequisite for discursive interactions to occur. The inverse is also true: the more engagement in discursive settings, the stronger connections and sense of community. Similarly, broader participation in discursive processes is enriched by and feeds into transparency, *inter alia*, by making information and reasons behind decisions understandable and acceptable to others. Finally, both vertical and horizontal linkages are reinforced through inclusive, transparent and discursive interactions. Table 1 summarises the main characteristics of process properties and their interrelations with each other and norm properties of determinacy and stringency.

Journal of International Law 503–538, Joel P. Trachtman, 'International law and domestic political coalitions: The grand theory of compliance with international law' (2010) 11 Chinese Journal of International Law 127–158.

TABLE 1 *Process properties and their interrelations with each other*

Process properties	Relations with each other and norm properties
Inclusiveness	
A process of taking part and relating to others. Sets out a range of actors, collectivities and communities by addressing what actors are involved in process, in what capacity, and how they relate to and connect with each other.	· Positively interrelated with transparency: broader participation is enriched by and feeds into transparency. · Enables discourse by setting up its participants. The more engagement in discursive settings, the stronger connections and a sense of community. But the greater participation may also jeopardize the possibility of reaching reasoned consensus within discursive process. · Defines actors from different sectors, countries and scales. · Greater inclusiveness may both diminish (e.g. actors with sharply different interests) and increase (e.g. experts knowledge) norm determinacy and stringency.
Transparency	
A process by which information about existing conditions, decisions and actions is made accessible, visible and understandable. Provides for openness and accessibility to different actors of rules, procedures and settings of international legal interactions. Facilitates trust building and mitigates power asymmetry.	· Positively interrelated with inclusiveness: more open process is ensured by and feeds into inclusive interactions. · Enables discourse by ensuring openness of information and access to different settings. Requires caution in ensuring 'workable' level of openness for decisions to be made. · Positively correlates with coherence: transparency is required at all levels and scales. · Norm determinacy and stringency are constitutive to transparency. In turn, better information may enhance norm determinacy.

TABLE 1 *Process properties and their interrelations with each other* (Cont.)

Process properties	Relations with each other and norm properties
Discursiveness	
A dialogue process of exchange of reasons and reciprocal learning in which actors generate, elaborate and refine shared understandings and expectations about norms. Sets up a mode of interaction, such as dialogue, reasoning, argumentation and social learning (in contrast to strategic interaction).	· Built upon and further develops inclusive process, especially the ideas of 'connections' and 'communities'; the more engagement in discursive settings, the stronger connections and a sense of community. · Built upon and further develops transparent process, especially by making information and reasons understandable and acceptable to others. But sometimes more open and transparent debates can also jeopardize 'discursive bite' and the possibility to reach an agreement. · Norm determinacy and stringency shape the parameters of discursive interactions about their meaning and interpretation.
Coherence	
A process of making connections within the law, between different legal regimes, between national and international domains. Establishes normative and institutional connections at horizontal and vertical scales.	· Both vertical and horizontal linkages are reinforced through inclusive, transparent and discursive interactions. · Contributes to inclusiveness by linking actors within levels, such as nations, issue areas or agencies as well as between levels, such as national, regional and international. · Positively interrelated with transparency: ensures information flow across sectors, countries and scales. · Facilitate discursive interactions within and across levels. · Contributes to greater determinacy and stringency by providing normative and institutional connections.

Inclusiveness, transparency, discursiveness and coherence have been identified in this section as being most indicative to the intersubjective nature of international law and helpful to generate, elaborate and refine shared understandings and collective expectations about the meaning and implementation of the norms with a view of addressing (or preventing) the lack of norm stringency and determinacy. This is why process features and norm features are closely linked. Legal norms and their application are shaped by the degree of subjective and intersubjective understandings of the content of these norms, reached in the continuous process of transparent, discursive and integrative interactions between actors. It can be argued therefore that legally relevant behaviour and legal consciousness together – as captured by the four process features – form an adequate response to the indeterminacy and elasticity of law.

Conclusion

This chapter set up a theoretical and analytical foundation of the book by addressing two rather broad and generic questions (i) What is international law and how it operates? and (ii) How to analyse international law and its operation? This general discussion serves as an essential preliminary to a more specific inquiry on international law operation in the context of transboundary watercourses in the Aral Sea basin.

The first section has proposed to look at international law as a complex phenomenon comprised of legal norms (normative facet), legally relevant behaviour (sociological facet) and legal consciousness (psychological facet), which are so deeply interconnected and yet so often isolated. This conceptual understanding of law, initially introduced by Peczenik, was used as a departure point to examine in a more systematic manner what international law is and how it works. The literature review has shown that studies of international law would benefit from a closer attention to the complex interplay of its normative, sociological and psychological facets through which international law gains its authority and power.

Against this theoretical background, the second section has developed a framework for analysing international law through properties of its norms and processes, which takes normative, sociological and psychological accounts seriously. It maintained that two properties of norms (determinacy and stringency) and four properties of processes (inclusiveness, transparency, discursiveness and coherence) connect all three accounts and therefore can provide a sound framework for examining the mutually constitutive relationship between them, and ultimately, understanding the role and workings of international law.

As per norm properties, analysis of legal norms on the basis of their determinacy and stringency helps to illustrate that different types of norms may require different forms of implementation and operationalisation. It also sheds light on the complex interrelations between norm and processes, which are the key to understanding its operation. Often international legal norms may be couched in indeterminate or soft language because they are constructed within the very field that they regulate. A need for generality and flexibility in law as well as complexity of the physical and social realities as a subject of regulation adds to explanation. Hence, in the international domain the nature of legal norms stems from and is closely interrelated with the process of norm evolution and application.

Further, the chapter has demonstrated that norm indeterminacy and elasticity can be addressed by process elements embedded in legally relevant behaviour and legal consciousness. Strictly speaking, the distinction between legally relevant behaviour and legal consciousness is made exclusively for analytical purposes. In practice, this distinction is blurred because the conduct of actors in international arena is closely intertwined with the acts of understandings and perceptions/expectations of appropriate behaviour. The requirement of on-going actions and interactions about and through the law is what glues these two facets together. Their separate consideration in this chapter was, however, necessary to illuminate the lack of attention to the psychological facets of international law, despite its significance for the operation of the law. Ultimately, the chapter argued that legally relevant behaviour and legal consciousness together form an adequate response to the indeterminacy and elasticity of law because formal legal norms and their application are shaped by the degree of subjective and intersubjective understandings of the content of these norms, reached in the continuous process of interactions between actors. More specifically, the chapter stressed that the processes of international legal interactions should be inclusive, transparent, discursive and integrative for the effective operation of international law. In other words, it matters who is involved in international interactions, in what capacity, in what way and in which settings. Crucially, these properties are to be considered jointly as being closely interconnected, partially reinforcing and building on each other.

Against this theoretical and analytical background, the next part studies international water law as applied to the Aral Sea basin through these properties of norms and processes. This analytical framework allows a more specific assessment of the role of international norms and processes in building and maintaining peaceful relations between the countries sharing transboundary waters in the basin.

PART 2

International Water Law in the Aral Sea Basin

The following five chapters deal with international water law as applied to the Aral Sea basin. Chapter 3 provides an overview of the basin, its main transboundary water challenges and legal instruments at sub-regional, regional and global levels. Treaty provisions related to scope, substantive and procedural norms, compliance and dispute settlement are examined through the lenses of norm determinacy and stringency in Chapters 4 and 5. Then, Chapter 6 analyses state practice of the Aral Sea basin countries against the process properties of inclusiveness, transparency, discursiveness, and coherence. The main findings and recommendations of the study are summarised in Chapter 7.

CHAPTER 3

Setting the Scene

The Aral Sea Basin

Given the importance of factual and legal context for understanding international law and its operation stressed in Chapter 2, this chapter introduces the physical characteristics of the Aral Sea basin and provides the socio-economic and geopolitical context in which transboundary water interactions in the subregion take place. It also outlines the legal architecture of transboundary water cooperation in the Aral Sea basin comprised of a diverse patchwork of bilateral and multilateral treaties, inherited from the Soviet past and adopted in recent decades at sub-regional, regional and global levels. In doing so, this chapter sets the scene for an in-depth assessment of norms and processes of international water law in the basin.

3.1 Transboundary Waters of the Aral Sea Basin: Challenges and Opportunities

3.1.1 *Physical Characteristics of the Basin*

The Aral Sea basin, covering an area of 1,550,000 km^2, is the largest basin in Central Asia.[211] It embodies the entire territory of Tajikistan and Uzbekistan, the major part of Turkmenistan (excluding the Krasnovodsk region), southern part of Kazakhstan (the Kzyl-Orda and the South Kazakh regions), three regions of the Kyrgyz Republic (Osh, Djalalabad, and Naryn), part of northern Afghanistan, and north-eastern Iran.[212] The Amudarya and Syrdarya are the two major rivers belonging to the basin of the Aral Sea (see Figure 1).

The Amudarya is the biggest river in Central Asia in terms of annual water runoff (79.4 km^3/year) and its basin is shared by Afghanistan, the Kyrgyz Republic, Tajikistan, Turkmenistan and Uzbekistan. The Amudarya river originates in Tajikistan (where 74% of flow is formed), the Kyrgyz Republic (2%),

211 CAWATERinfo, 'Aral Sea Basin'. Online: <http://cawater-info.net/aral/geoe.htm> accessed 7 April 2013.

212 See Ibid and I. Severskiy and others, *Global International Waters Assessment Aral Sea, GIWA Regional assessment 24* (Kalmar, University of Kalmar on behalf of United Nations Environment Programme 2005). Given that the portion of Iran in the basin is insignificant, the present study will not address the involvement of Iran in regional water cooperation.

 | DOI 10.1163/9789004274266_004

FIGURE 1 *The Aral Sea basin and its water resources*

Afghanistan and Iran (13.9%),[213] then forms the border between Afghanistan and Uzbekistan (8.5%), crosses the territory of Turkmenistan (1.7%) and returns to Uzbekistan where it discharges into the Aral Sea. It is 2540 km long from the headwaters of the Pyandzh, its main tributary, to the Aral Sea, and has a catchment area of 309,000 km^2. The Pyandzh and Vakhsh are the biggest tributaries of the Amudarya. Other tributaries include Kafirnigan, Kunduz, Pamir, Surkhandarya and Zeravshan rivers.[214] The flow regulation in the

213 Estimates on Afghanistan's contribution to the Amudarya flow vary. Variations in the estimates primarily depend on which parts of Northern Afghanistan and its various sub-basins are considered as part of Amudarya basin. See Victor A. Dukhovny and Vadim Sokolov, *Assessment of water resources in the Northern Afghanistan, its use and impact on the region of the Amudarya River Basin* (Scientific Information Center of Interstate Commission for Water Coordination in Central Asia, 2002), Masood Ahmad and Wasig Mahwash, *Water resource development in Northern Afghanistan and its implication for Amu Darya Basin* (World Bank, Working Paper no 36, 2004) and David W. Rycroft and Kai Wegerich, 'The three blind spots of Afghanistan: Water flow, irrigation development, and the impact of climate change' (2009) 7 China and Eurasia Forum Quarterly 115–133.

214 Some assessment consider the Zeravshan as an independent river, since it lost connections with the Amudarya due to the development of irrigation in the lowland parts of the

Amudarya basin is provided by two main reservoirs, namely the Nurek on the Vakhsh (total capacity 10.5 km^3) and the Tuyamuyun on the Amudarya (total capacity 7.3 km^3), and a network of small reservoirs and their associated canals. Given that there are still possibilities for further, including long-term, flow regulation in the basin, a number of new dams and reservoirs are planned, the largest of which includes the Rogun on the Vakhsh and the Dashtidjumn on the Pyandzh.

The Syrdarya is the longest river in Central Asia and its basin crosses the territories of Kazakhstan, the Kyrgyz Republic, Tajikistan and Uzbekistan. The Syrdarya is formed by the confluence of the Naryn and Karadarya rivers. About 75.2% of the Syrdarya flow originates in the Kyrgyz Republic. The river then flows across Uzbekistan and Tajikistan and discharges into the Aral Sea in Kazakhstan. About 15.2% of the flow of the Syrdarya is formed in Uzbekistan, about 6.9% in Kazakhstan, and about 2.7% in Tajikistan. The Syrdarya is up to 3019 km long from its main tributary, the Naryn headwaters, to the Aral Sea, and has a catchment area of 219,000 km^2. The other tributaries of the Syrdarya include Karadarya, Chirchik, Angren and Keles. The flow of the rivers within the Syrdarya basin is almost completely regulated. Major reservoirs include the Toktogul on the Naryn (total capacity 19,500 km^3), the Kayrakkum (total capacity 4,160 km^3) and the Chardara (total capacity 5,700 km^3) on the Syrdarya, and the Andijan on the Karadarya (total capacity 1,900 km^3).

Extensive water diversions from the Amudarya and the Syrdarya for expanding irrigation have led to the drying up of the Aral Sea, once the world's fourth largest terminal lake. In 1960, the Aral Sea covered a surface area of 64,490 km^2 (with islands); its maximum length was 428 km, and maximum width 284 km.[215] Since the early 1960s, the water balance, morphology and ecology of the Aral Sea have changed drastically, with the maximum water level having declined by more than 26 m, the surface area having decreased by 88%, the water volume decreased by 92%,[216] and water salinity having risen to 90–150 g/l.[217] As a result, the Aral Sea has in fact divided into two water bodies in the Small Aral Sea in the north and the Large Aral Sea in the south.[218] After

catchment area. See eg *Our waters: Joining hands across borders. First assessment of transboundary rivers, lakes and groundwaters* (UN Economic Commission for Europe, 2007) at 72.

215 Joop de Schutter and Victor A. Dukhovny (eds), *South Prearalie – New Perspectives*. Project 'Science for Peace' (Ecotec Resource & SIC ICWC 2003).

216 Philip Micklin, 'The past, present, and future Aral Sea' (2010) 15 Lakes & Reservoirs: Research and Management 193–213 at 194.

217 Igor S. Zonn and others, *The Aral Sea Encyclopedia* (Springer, Verlag Berlin Heidelberg 2009).

218 The Syrdarya flows into the Small Aral Sea, and the Amudarya into the Large Aral Sea.

this separation, the regimes of the Small Aral Sea and the Large Aral Sea have developed differently. A dike and dam constructed in 2005 by the Government of Kazakhstan with the World Bank support to block water outflows from the Small Aral Sea has helped to stabilize its water level at 42 m, to lower its salinity and improve its ecological conditions and to revitalize its fisheries. The situation with the Large Aral Sea is less encouraging: its water level is low (23 m) and salinity very high (>200 g/l).[219] As a result, about 4.5 mln ha of the seabed have become exposed and have turned into a vast solonchak desert – Aralkum, which has changed the local climate and intensified desertification in the region.[220]

3.1.2 *Socio-Economic Uses and Environmental Concerns*

The social and economic development of the CARs and Afghanistan depends on the waters of the Amudarya and the Syrdarya, and there are many competing claims over the use of their waters for hydropower, irrigation, and the environment.

Water resources are an important source of electricity generation in the Aral Sea basin countries, constituting 27.3% of their total electricity consumption.[221] Upstream, Tajikistan and the Kyrgyz Republic cover up to 90% of their domestic energy needs and export electricity to other CARs and Russia – the latter country imports approximately 10% of the total exports by the two former CARs.[222] Tajikistan possesses vast amount of hydropower resources (40GW), of which about 10% (4,326 MW) has been developed.[223] The proposed Rogun hydropower plant (HPP) (3600 MW 13,000 GWh) on the Vakhsh and the Dashtidjumn HPP (4000 MW 15,600 kWh) on the Pyandzh would increase significantly the hydropower generation capacity of the country. Hydropower potential of Kyrgyzstan is estimated in 18,500 MW, and its

---

219 Micklin, 'The past, present, and future Aral Sea' at 195.

220 See Zonn and others, *The Aral Sea Encyclopedia* at 23 stating that the area of solonchaks has increased from 85 thou ha to 273 thou ha.

221 Sagit Ibatullin, Vladimir Yasinsky and Alexander Mironenkov, *Impact of climate change to water resources in Central Asia* (Eurasian Development Bank, Sector Report No 6, 2009) at 7.

222 *Central Asian Human Development Report. Bringing down barriers: regional cooperation for human development and human security* (UNDP Regional Bureau for Europe and the Commonwealth of Independent States, 2005) at 86.

223 ADB, Report and Recommendation of the President to the Board of Directors, Project Number: 42189 'Proposed Asian Development Fund Grant Republic of Tajikistan: Nurek 500 kV Switchyard Reconstruction Project' (October 2008). Online: <www.adb.org/Documents/RRPs/TAJ/42189-TAJ-RRP.pdf> accessed 10 April 2013.

installed capacity is about 2,950 MW.[224] Such dominant reliance on hydropower makes these countries vulnerable to climate change and variability. For instance, low water levels in hydropower stations in very cold and dry 2007–2008 has depressed electricity generation, leaving industries and households with no access to heating and water supply, which led to severe socio-economic consequences in Tajikistan and Kyrgyzstan. In 2009, electricity generation dropped by 18.5% in the Kyrgyz Republic during the first 11 months of 2008, and by 8% in Tajikistan for the year as a whole.[225] Although the hydropower situation in Afghanistan, another water tower of the sub-region, is difficult to assess as years of conflict have left the power grids severely damaged, Afghanistan Human Development Report 2011 states that the impact of 30 years of turmoil had reduced the power generation capacity from 454 MW to 250 MW and suggests that new dams will be necessary if the country is to process a sustainable source of energy.[226]

Irrigated agriculture accounts for more than 90% of the total water withdrawals in the basin, and plays a vital role in supporting the economy and livelihoods.[227] In 2012, agricultural output supported by irrigation accounted for 15% of the gross domestic product in Turkmenistan, 19% in Uzbekistan, 20% in the Kyrgyz Republic, 25% in Afghanistan, and 26% in Tajikistan.[228] Although

224 Almaz Stamalaev, 'Development of the Renewable Energy Sector in the Kyrgyz Republic (Ministry of Energy of the Kyrgyz Republic)' (International Energy Efficiency Forum and Workshop on Investments in Energy Efficiency and Renewable Energy Projects 28–30 September 2010 Astana, Kazakhstan). See also Ibatullin, Yasinsky and Mironenkov, Impact of climate change to water resources in Central Asia at 36 noting that when in the last century the hydropower potential of the two countries was assessed, it was done without taking climate change into account, and therefore now the assessment needs to be revised.

225 *Central Asia regional risk assessment: Responding to water, energy, and food insecurity* (UNDP Regional Bureau for Europe and CIS, 2009) at 6. See also Victor A. Dukhovny and Joop de Schutter, *Water in Central Asia: Past, present, future* (Taylor & Francis Group 2011) at 279.

226 *Afghanistan Human Development Report 2011. The forgotten front: Water security and the crisis in sanitation* (Centre for Policy and Human Development, Kabul University 2011) at 64 ('Afghanistan requires storage and infrastructural capacity and other support to alleviate the country's water scarcity problems and offset climate shocks. [...] The government is attempting to grapple with the crisis by investing in medium- to large-scale water storage infrastructure. It has identified at least 31 major infrastructural projects, including the construction of 15 storage dams at an estimated total of almost $10 billion').

227 Jakob Granit and others, *Regional Water Intelligence Report Central Asia* (Stockholm International Water Institute 2010) at 15.

228 World Bank (2013). Online: <http://data.worldbank.org/>accessed 11 January 2014.

the national economy of Kazakhstan is less dependent on irrigated agriculture (5%), farming has substantial importance in the lowlands of the Syrdarya. Similarly, Ahmad and Mahwash state that, although the Amudarya basin constitutes only 12% of the Afghan territory, it supports about 25% of the Afghan population.[229] An estimated 22 million people depend directly or indirectly on irrigated agriculture in CARs.[230] Currently, 60% of Central Asia's population lives in rural areas, and almost half of the rural population lives in poverty, directly or indirectly depending on natural resources to sustain their livelihoods.[231] Additionally, agricultural demand for water in the basin is most likely to increase as a result of the expansion of irrigated lands in Northern Afghanistan – in furtherance of Afghanistan's 2007 Water Strategy and as supported by a flow of international investment in the sector.[232]

Clearly, both hydropower production and irrigated agriculture are crucial for the sub-region. The difficulties arise, however, in accommodating the different seasonal requirements of these two dominant water uses. Since the highest demand for electricity occurs in the coldest time, the interests of hydropower production require the releases of water from upstream reservoirs in winter. Conversely, irrigated agriculture depends on water releases in the summer months. In the Soviet time, a system of reservoirs and hydropower stations along the Amudarya and Syrdarya rivers accumulated their flow during the non-irrigation season and provided reliable water supply for

---

229 Ahmad and Mahwash, Water resource development in Northern Afghanistan and its implication for Amu Darya Basin at 1.

230 *Central Asian Human Development Report. Bringing down barriers: regional cooperation for human development and human security* at 86.

231 World Bank, 'Data by country' (2014). Online: <http://data.worldbank.org> accessed 11 January 2014.

232 Klemm and Shobair, The Afghan part of Amu Darya Basin. Impact of irrigation in Northern Afghanistan on water use in the Amu Darya Basin at 10 (stating that 'By 2020, the three planned major irrigation projects would comprise an additionally irrigated area of some 200,000 ha resulting in a total irrigated area in the Afghan part of the Amu Darya Basin (without the Northern Basins whose rivers do not contribute water to the Amu Darya) of approximately 600,000 ha corresponding to an annual maximum of 6,000 million mi water withdrawn from Payndzh, Amu Darya itself and the major 'boundary' rivers Kokcha and Kunduz'.). See also, 'Speech by Mr Nabiel, Ministry of Foreign Affairs, Afghanistan'(stating 'We had designed ambitious projects for irrigation and hydropower before 1978–1979, but the war prevented us to implement them. Now is the time we start implementing some of them and we ask for the understanding and cooperation of our neighbours'.). Avoiding water wars at 1 and 13 (stating that in 2009 the United States provided approximately $46.8 million in assistance for water-related activities in Afghanistan and Pakistan).

agriculture. Power generation was secondary to agricultural needs, and fossil fuel from downstream states alleviated electricity deficits in the upstream countries. Upon independence, the economic basis of this regional arrangement was undermined. Fossil fuel prices went up, energy trade between the countries was put on a commercial footing, and upstream countries, poor in fossil fuel, declared their interests in the generation of electricity, and changed the use of reservoirs from irrigation to hydropower production.

This shift was especially noticeable in the Syrdarya basin where switching the operation of the Toktogul reservoir from irrigation to electricity production resulted in a substantial change in flow patterns, with the peak of water releases in winter rather than in summer. As a result, farmers reliant upon irrigation faced water shortages. What is more, south Kazakhstan and Uzbekistan had to deal with the threat of their lowlands inundation since the frozen waterways and canals were unable to handle excessive water releases in winter. Some of the water from winter releases was therefore diverted wastefully into the Arnasai depression.[233]

In the Amudarya basin, flow regulation issues are shaped by Tajikistan's plans for building new dams on the Vakhsh and Pyandzh tributaries. Presently, only seasonal flow regulation is carried out in the basin, namely by the Nurek and Tuyamuyun reservoirs. If done right and operated accordingly, the proposed Rogun hydropower project is said to introduce long-term flow regulation in the interests of irrigation, hydropower production and water supply.[234] However, the project raises concerns as to its ecological and seismic safety, as well as socio-economic and cultural impacts across the sub-region.[235] The World Bank currently is supporting the preparation of an assessment study for

233 As for now, the Arnasai is a part of the Aydar Arnasai Lakes System, the largest lake system in the Republic of Uzbekistan. These lakes were formed as a result of emergency dumping of water from the Chardara reservoir in the catastrophically high-water year of 1969 (20.1 km^3). See The Aydar Arnasai Lake System (Uzbekistan). Information Sheet on Ramsar Wetlands – 2008 Ramsar Uzbekistan 2UZ002. Online: <http://ramsar.wetlands.org> accessed 11 January 2014.

234 Victor A. Dukhovny and Anatoliy Sorokin, *Assessment of the impact of Rogun reservoir on Amudarya river water regime. In Russian* (SIC ICWC, 2007).

235 Address by President Islam Karimov at the meeting of heads of the IFAS founding states. Permanent Mission of the Republic of Uzbekistan to the United Nations (28 April 2009). Online: <www.un.int/wcm/content/site/uzbekistan/pid/9548> accessed 7 April 2011. Kazakhstan has recently supported Uzbekistan's position. J Lillis 'Uzbekistan: Nazarbayev Makes Diplomatic Trade-Off With Karimov' Eurasia Insight (18 March 2010). Online: <www.eurasianet.org/departments/insightb/articles/eav031810pr.shtml> accessed 7 April 2013.

the proposed Rogun HPP to examine its techno-economic, environmental, and social impacts.[236]

The changes in river flow following the construction of reservoirs and the excessive water withdrawals for irrigation have profoundly affected the quality of water and modified the deltas of the rivers and floodplain environment. One of the most telling examples of this is the devastating degradation of the Aral Sea, its ecosystem, and surrounding areas. The Aral Sea, once the world's fourth-largest lake, today consists only of a series of separate bodies of water surrounded by a vast saline desert. Increased water salinity, the degradation of deltas and the decrease of their areas led to a severe reduction in biodiversity in the sub-region.[237] The situation is accompanied by poor water quality as a result of agricultural discharges, which is especially critical in the lowlands of Kazakhstan, Turkmenistan, and Uzbekistan, resulting in increased illness (e.g., kidney disease, oncological and acute infectious diseases), and adult and child mortality rates.[238] Further to that, unsustainable irrigation practices over several decades led to soil salinization in the areas around the Aral Sea, which substantially complicates agricultural activities and requires pre-season salt leaching by application of significant amounts of water.[239]

The shrinkage of the Aral Sea has also affected the climate of the sub-region, with both summer and winter temperatures becoming more extreme. Global climate change exacerbates the situation further. UNEP's 2005 Global International Waters Assessment forecasts that, by 2050, the glaciers on the mountains of Central Asia may shrink by 1/3 in area and volume if the current rate of 0.8–1.0% decrease per year continues.[240] In the 20th century, the glaciers of Tajikistan decreased on average by 20–30%; and the glaciers of Afghanistan, on the left bank of Pyandzh, by 50–70%.[241] Glacial retreat causes

236 World Bank, 'Assessment Studies for Proposed Rogun Regional Water Reservoir and Hydropower Project in Tajikistan'. Online: <http://go.worldbank.org/ZQXIA8J0H0> accessed 7 April 2013.

237 Severskiy and others, *Global International Waters Assessment Aral Sea, GIWA Regional assessment 24* at 30.

238 *Environmental performance review of Uzbekistan: Second Review* (United Nations Economic Commission for Europe, 2010).

239 Victor A. Dukhovny and Vadim I. Sokolov. 2001. *Diagnostic Study. Rational and Effective Use of Water Resources in Central Asia* (UN Special Program for Economics of Central Asia. Tashkent–Bishkek, 2001).

240 Severskiy and others, *Global International Waters Assessment Aral Sea, GIWA Regional assessment 24* at 45.

241 Ibatullin, Yasinsky and Mironenkov, Impact of climate change to water resources in Central Asia at 16.

flood events in the short-term, and declines in long-term water availability, thus intensifying the aridity of the sub-region.[242] According to some projections, by 2050, the runoff of the Syrdarya and the Amudarya rivers may decrease by up to 6–10% and 10–15%, respectively.[243] Given that currently the volume of water resources used already exceeds available supplies,[244] further declines in water availability could threaten the region's water security profoundly. The intensity of droughts, floods and other extreme events, such as mudflows and avalanches, is also expected to increase in the sub-region.[245] Climate change seems to hit at stationarity, a foundational concept in hydrology that stands for the idea that natural systems fluctuate within an unchanging envelope of variability.[246] Assuming climatic stationarity, hydrologists could predict probability distributions arising from historic records. In a new non-stationary world, such projections are dubious. Consequently, changes in the climatic and hydrological systems will further affect ecosystems, human health, and economies; intensify the tense competition over water between agricultural and hydropower sectors; and challenge traditional water planning and management techniques.[247]

Dam safety is another issue occupying a special place in sub-regional water cooperation. While bringing multiple benefits in terms of seasonal and long-term flow regulation, large dams also bear a significant potential threat. In the case of natural events and anthropogenic accidents, disastrous effects may

242 Ibid, 30.

243 Ibid, 28.

244 Due to the use of return waters, the volume of water resources used in the Aral Sea Basin exceeds available supplies; in the Syrdarya Basin 130–150% of available water resources are used and in the Amudarya Basin, 100–110%. See Nariman Kipshakbaev and Vadim Sokolov, *Water resources of the Aral Sea Basin-formation, distribution, usage. Water resources of Central Asia. In Russian* (SIC ICWC, 2002).

245 Bates and others, *Climate Change and Water. Technical Paper of the Intergovernmental Panel on Climate Change* at 87 and Ibatullin, Yasinsky and Mironenkov, Impact of climate change to water resources in Central Asia at 22, 24 and 27.

246 P.C.D. Milly and others, 'Stationarity is dead: Whither water management?' (2008) 319 Science 573–574 (arguing that 'stationarity is dead because substantial anthropogenic change of Earth's climate is altering the means and extremes of precipitation, evapotranspiration, and rates of discharge of rivers').

247 Bates and others, *Climate Change and Water. Technical Paper of the Intergovernmental Panel on Climate Change* at 87 and 88 (stating that 'consequences of enhanced snow and glacier melt, as well as rising snow lines, would be unfavourable for downstream agriculture in several countries of south and central Asia' and 'changes in runoff could have a significant effect on the power output of hydropower-generating countries such as Tajikistan, which is the third largest hydro-electricity producer in the world').

occur across the sub-region. The natural ageing of dams in Central Asia, many of which were built 30 to 40 years ago, requires close supervision of their technical condition and the execution of proper repair and rehabilitation work.[248] The high seismic activity of the sub-region adds another layer of complication for dam operations and calls for extra-care in their construction.[249] Serious risk, with severe transboundary implications, comes from the high-mountain Lake Sarez (Tajikistan), with an unsafe natural 567-metre-high landslide dam, which was formed at the Mugrab River in 1911 as the result of a severe earthquake.[250] A breach of the dam at Lake Sarez could affect up to 6 million people and flood approximately 52,000 km^2 in the territories of Afghanistan, Tajikistan, Turkmenistan and Uzbekistan.[251]

To complicate the situation further, the Aral Sea basin is the world's top-10 polluted areas in terms of uranium radioactive waste.[252] About two million m^3 of uranium tailings are located in the upper reaches of the Syrdarya basin, in 92 toxic waste sites in the Kyrgyz Republic, inherited from the Soviet past. The fact that these sites are located close to rivers heightens the potential for transboundary impacts and requires active cooperation between the countries concerned.

The above overview highlights some of the major water-related challenges facing the countries of the Aral Sea basin. The countries' economies and the livelihoods of their populations depend profoundly on the availability and quality of the basin's waters, and are vulnerable to seasonal climate and weather conditions. Such dependency has compromised a delicate ecological balance in the basin and put under stress its environmental integrity. It has

248 *Dam Safety in Central Asia: Capacity-Building and Regional Cooperation* (UN Economic Commission for Europe Water Series No 5, 2007) at 1.

249 *Central Asian Human Development Report. Bringing down barriers: regional cooperation for human development and human security* at 116 (stating that 'The entire southern part of Central Asia lies in one of the world's most active seismic belts. Severe earthquakes, causing great damage to people and infrastructure, have been common in that region'). See also *Disaster risk reduction in Central Asia, building partnerships to secure development gains* (European Commission Humanitarian Aid (ECHO), United Nations International Strategy for Disaster Reduction Secretariat – Central Asia and Caucasus (UNISDR – CA) 2009).

250 *Sarez Lake: Latest achievements and unresolved problems* (United Nations International Strategy for Disaster Reduction Secretariat – Central Asia and Caucasus (UNISDR – CA) 2007); *Usoi landslide dam and lake Sarez: An assessment of hazard and risk in the Pamir mountains, Tajikistan* (United Nations International Strategy for Disaster Reduction Secretariat (UNISDR), 2000).

251 Dam Safety in Central Asia: Capacity-Building and Regional Cooperation at 6.

252 Granit and others, Regional Water Intelligence Report Central Asia at 7.

also aggravated the competition for resources between sectors, such as irrigated agriculture and hydropower production; and ultimately between upstream and downstream countries trying to reach energy and food self-sufficiency. A complex web of water, energy and environmental problems in the sub-region can be addressed in a holistic, mutually beneficial and peaceful manner only through collaborative actions whether that is cooperation to increase economic and social benefits or cooperation to mitigate negative effects.

3.2 Legal Instruments that Govern Transboundary Waters in the Aral Sea Basin

The CARs have recognised the need to address water-related problems in a coordinated way at the top political level, including by establishing the Aral Sea Basin Programme (ASBP) – a programme of concrete actions to improve the environmental and socio-economic condition in the Aral Sea basin and attract much-needed investment.[253] Additionally, in the past two decades, the countries adopted a number of sub-regional agreements, established new institutions, and joined regional and global environmental and water-related treaties. Some of these legal arrangements are to be traced back to the pre-independence period; others were adopted in recent decades. A brief overview of these treaties follows in order to sketch the legal architecture of transboundary water cooperation in the sub-region.

3.2.1 *Treaties at Sub-Regional Level*

In Soviet times, the use and management of the Amudarya and Syrdarya basins by five CARs was regulated according to the Schemes of Complex Water Resources Use and Protection, which have been endorsed by the central management of the Ministry of Reclamation and Water Management of the USSR.[254] In 1992, the countries reiterated the validity of those schemes in the

253 In 1994, the heads of CARs decided to adopt the Programme of concrete actions for environmental improvement in the Aral Sea basin over the next 3–5 years (ASBP-1) and to approve the main provisions of the strategy for addressing problems of the Priaralie and the Aral Sea basins in light of regional socio-economic development. In 2002 they approved the Programme of concrete actions on environmental and socio-economic improvement in the Aral Sea basin for 2003–2010 (ASBP-2). In 2009, they mandated relevant agencies to develop ASBP-3 that was approved in 2013.

254 See Resolution of the Expert Sub-Commission to the Gosplan (State Planning Committee) State Expert Commission of the USSR (12 March 1982); Protocol of the Scientific and

Almaty Agreement, which was adopted by all CARs as newly independent States to manage jointly shared waters.[255] In addition, the 1993 Kzyl-Orda Agreement, also adopted among all five CARs, includes a range of 'common objectives' to be pursued to mitigate the Aral Sea crisis.[256] The 1999 Agreement on the Status of the International Fund for Saving the Aral Sea and its organisations, along with the statutes of each particular organisation, further articulate the functions and duties of the interstate water institutions established in the 1992 Almaty Agreement and the 1993 Kzyl-Orda Agreement.[257]

There exist also other sub-regional agreements to address water-related issues, ranging from specific arrangements on water and energy trade to general environmental treaties. The 1996 Chardjev Agreement, between Uzbekistan and Turkmenistan, regulates water management issues, including water allocation in the Amudarya's lower reaches.[258] Also in 1996, Kazakhstan, the Kyrgyz Republic and Uzbekistan committed to foster economic cooperation on the use of fuel and water resources, construction and operation of gas

---

Technical Council of the Ministry of Water Resources Management of the USSR on Approval of the Principles of Inter-Republican Water Allocation of the Syrdarya River Basin Resources No 413 (29 February 1984); Protocol of the Scientific and Technical Council of the Ministry of Water Resources Management of the USSR on Approval of the Principles of Inter-Republican Water Allocation of the Amudarya River Basin Resources No 556 (10 September 1987); Decision of the Gosplan State Expert Commission of the USSR No 11 (5 March 1982).

255 1992 Almaty Agreement.

256 Agreement between the Republic of Kazakhstan, the Kyrgyz Republic, the Republic of Tajikistan, Turkmenistan, and the Republic of Uzbekistan on Joint Actions for Addressing the Problems of the Aral Sea and its Coastal Area, Improving the Environment, and Ensuring the Social and Economic Development of the Aral Sea Region, Kzyl-Orda (signed 26 March 1993). Online: <http://cawater-info.net/library/eng/l/kzyl-orda_agreement.pdf> (an unofficial English translation).

257 Statute of the International Fund for saving the Aral Sea (IFAS), Ashgabad (adopted 9 April 1999 by the Decision of the Heads of the CARs); the Statute of Executive Committee of IFAS of 1997, 1999, 2002 and 2009; the Statute of ICSD of 2000; Statute of the Interstate Commission for Water Coordination in Central Asia (ICWC), Tashkent (approved 5 December 1992 by ICWC members) and Statute of the Interstate Commission for Water Coordination in Central Asia (ICWC), Almaty (approved 18 September 2008 by ICWC members); the Statue of BWO Amudarya of 1992; the Statute of BWO Syrdarya of 1992; the Statute of the Secretariat of the ICWC of 1993; the Statute of the Secretariat of the ICSD of 2001, the Statute of the SIC ICWC of 1996, the Statute of SIC ICSD of 2001.

258 Agreement between Turkmenistan and the Republic of Uzbekistan on Cooperation over Water Management Issues, Chardjev (signed 16 January 1996). Online: <http://www.cawater-info.net/library/rus/uzb_tur_1.pdf> (an unofficial English translation).

pipelines, mostly touching the Syrdarya basin.[259] Two years later, those same countries concluded a watercourse-specific agreement on the use of the water and energy resources of the Syrdarya basin, with the aim of producing a cooperative framework.[260] Tajikistan joined the latter agreement in 1999. Given the close connection between energy and water resources in the sub-region, the 1999 Agreement on Parallel Operation of the Energy Systems of Central Asian States aims to foster more effective operation of the energy system towards establishing a sub-regional 'integral market for electricity'.[261] Kazakhstan, the Kyrgyz Republic and Uzbekistan also entered into an agreement that regulates wider environmental issues by stipulating the areas of cooperation in the use and protection of natural resources.[262] In 1999, those three countries, plus Tajikistan, adopted a treaty on cooperation in the sphere of hydrometeorology.[263] The 2006 Framework Sustainable Development Convention, signed by the Kyrgyz Republic, Tajikistan and Turkmenistan, with its entry into force pending, seeks to ensure effective environmental protection for the sustainable development of Central Asia.[264]

The above sub-regional agreements define rights and obligations only with respect to the five CARs. Afghanistan, a riparian country to the Amudarya, is not formally involved in sub-regional water management. However, the legal

259 Agreement between the Government of the Republic of Kazakhstan, the Government of the Kyrgyz Republic and the Government of the Republic of Uzbekistan on the Use of Fuel and Water Resources, Construction and Operation of Gas Pipelines in Central Asian Region, Tashkent (signed 5 April 1996).

260 1998 Syrdarya Agreement.

261 Agreement between the Government of the Republic of Kazakhstan, the Government of the Kyrgyz Republic, the Government of the Republic of Tajikistan and the Government of the Republic of Uzbekistan on the Parallel Operation of the Energy Systems of Central Asian States, Bishkek (signed 17 June 1999). Online: <http://www.cawater-info.net/library/eng/l/parallel-agreement.pdf> (an unofficial English translation).

262 Agreement between the Government of the Republic of Kazakhstan, the Government of the Kyrgyz Republic and the Government of the Republic of Uzbekistan on Cooperation in the Area of Environment and Rational Nature Use, Bishkek (signed 17 March 1998). Online: <http://www.cawater-info.net/library/eng/l/nature_use.pdf> (an unofficial English translation).

263 Agreement between the Government of the Republic of Kazakhstan, the Government of the Kyrgyz Republic, the Government of the Republic of Tajikistan and the Government the Republic of Uzbekistan on Cooperation in the Sphere of Hydromet, Bishkek (signed 17 June 1999). Online: <http://www.cawater-info.net/library/rus/gov4.pdf>.

264 Framework Convention on Environmental Protection for Sustainable Development in Central Asia, Ashgabad (signed 22 November 2006 by the Kyrgyz Republic, Tajikistan and Turkmenistan, not yet in force).

basis for such cooperation exists within applicable customary and treaty norms. Several agreements were concluded between Afghanistan and Russia (and, later, the USSR) on frontier matters that touch upon water use issues, including: the 1843 Agreement between Russia and the Great Britain; the 1887/1985 Protocol on Delimitation; the Exchange of Notes of 11 March 1985 between Great Britain and Russia; the 1921 Treaty of Friendship between Afghanistan and the Soviet Union; the 1931 Treaty concerning neutrality and non-aggression between the USSR and Afghanistan;[265] the 1946 Frontier Agreement between Afghanistan and the USSR;[266] the 1958 Treaty concerning the regime of the Soviet-Afghan state frontier;[267] the 1958 Protocol between the USSR and Afghanistan on the joint execution of works for the integrated utilization of the water resources in the frontier section of the Amudarya;[268] the 1968 Agreement on economic and technical cooperation during the period 1967–1972;[269] and the 1978 Treaty of friendship, good-neighbourliness and cooperation.[270] According to the rules of treaty succession, these agreements would still be in force to the extent that they create rights and obligations 'attaching to' the parts of the Amudarya basin to which they relate within the meaning of Article 12 of the Vienna Convention on Succession of States in respect of Treaties.[271]

265 Treaty between the Union of Soviet Socialist Republics and Afghanistan of neutrality and non-aggression (signed 24 June 1931) 157 UNTS 371.

266 Frontier Agreement between Afghanistan and the Union of Soviet Socialist Republics (including Exchange of Notes), Moscow (signed 13 June 1946, entered into force 17 January 1947) 31 UNTS 158.

267 Treaty between the Government of the Union of Soviet Socialist Republics and the Royal Government of Afghanistan concerning the regime of the Soviet-Afghan state frontier (with annexes and Protocols), Moscow (signed 18 January 1958) 321 UNTS 166 (1959).

268 Protocol between the Union of Soviet Socialist Republics and Afghanistan on the Joint Execution of Works for the Integrated Utilization of the Water Resources in the Frontier Section of the Amudarya, Kabul (signed 25 June 1958). Online: <www.cawater-info.net/library/eng/afghanistan_ussr_en.pdf>.

269 Agreement on economic and technical co-operation during the period 1967–1972 (with annexes) (signed 6 February 1968) 31 UNTS 124 (1970).

270 Treaty of friendship, good-neighbourliness and co operation Moscow (signed 5 December 1978) 1145 UNTS 133 (1979).

271 Succession of States does not affect [...] obligations [or...] rights established by a treaty [...] relating to the use of any territory [...] and considered as attached to that territory (article 11) [or] relating to the regime of a boundary (article 12). Vienna Convention on Succession of States in Respect of Treaties, (adopted 23 August 1978, entered into force 6 November 1996) 1946 UNTS 3 (1978). See also *Case Concerning the Gabčíkovo-Nagymaros*

Finally, a review of sub-regional instruments would be incomplete without mention of numerous declarations and statements adopted by the Heads of Central Asian States on water-related issues. Even though these 'soft law' documents are not legislative in form, some provisions of these instruments seek to regulate water-related issues by establishing guiding principles, modifying interstate institutional bodies, or recognising the agreements signed by the heads of water authorities. The legal significance of these instruments is also evident from their formal and stringent language ('shall', 'duties', 'decide').[272] These instruments include Nukus Declaration (1995), Ashgabat Declaration (1999), Tashkent Statement (2001), Dushanbe Declaration (2002), and Joint Statement of the Heads of States – Founders of IFAS (2009).[273]

3.2.2 *Treaties at Regional and Global Levels*

At the regional level, the five CARs cooperate under the umbrella of the Commonwealth of Independent States (CIS or Commonwealth) and the United Nations Economic Commission for Europe (UNECE).

The cooperation under the auspices of Commonwealth is based on its Charter, which, among other things, deals with environmental issues.[274] The

---

Project (Hungary/Slovakia) General List No 92 [1997] ICJ, 37 ILM 162 [1998] at 72, para 123 (where the Court considered that Article 12 reflects a rule of customary law).

272 See eg Nukus Declaration of the Central Asian States and International Organisations on the Problems of Sustainable Development in the Aral Sea Basin, Nukus (adopted 5 September 1995) and Ashgabad Declaration of the Heads of States of the Republic of Kazakhstan, the Kyrgyz Republic, the Republic of Tajikistan, Turkmenistan and the Republic of Uzbekistan, Ashgabad (adopted 9 April 1999).

273 1995 Nukus Declaration, Almaty Declaration of the Heads of States of the Republic of Kazakhstan, the Kyrgyz Republic, the Republic of Tajikistan, Turkmenistan and the Republic of Uzbekistan, Almaty (adopted 28 September 1997), Issik-Kul Declaration on Regional Cooperation between the Central Asian States, Issik-Kul (adopted 1995) ibid, 1999 Ashgabad Declaration, Joint Statement made by the Heads of States of the Republic of Kazakhstan, the Kyrgyz Republic, the Republic of Tajikistan, Turkmenistan and the Republic of Uzbekistan, Ashgabad (adopted 9 April 1999), Tashkent Statement made by the Heads of States of the Republic of Kazakhstan, the Kyrgyz Republic, the Republic of Tajikistan and the Republic of Uzbekistan, Tashkent (adopted 28 December 2001), Dushanbe Declaration of the Heads of States of the Republic of Kazakhstan, the Kyrgyz Republic, the Republic of Tajikistan, Turkmenistan and the Republic of Uzbekistan, Dushanbe (adopted 6 October 2002) and 2009 Almaty Joint Statement.

274 Charter of the Commonwealth of Independent States Moscow (adopted 22 June 1993) 34 ILM 1279 (1995).

1992 Agreement on Interaction in the Field of Ecology and Environmental Protection fleshes out the specifics of such cooperation.[275] In 1998, the countries adopted an agreement on informational cooperation in the field of ecology and environmental protection, which has been ratified by Kazakhstan, the Kyrgyz Republic and Tajikistan.[276] At the same date, Belarus, the Russian Federation, Kazakhstan and Tajikistan signed an agreement on the main principles of interactions in the field of rational use and protection of the transboundary watercourses of Commonwealth (1998 CIS Transboundary Waters Agreement).[277] This agreement refers to the 1966 Helsinki Rules and the 1992 UNECE Water Convention and is substantially grounded on the latter's provisions. Among the CARs, only Tajikistan is a party to the 1998 CIS Transboundary Waters Agreement. Kazakhstan has signed the treaty, although it has not ratified it yet, with a reservation that interactions in the field of rational use and protection of transboundary watercourses shall be a subject to separate agreements between parties concerned.

In the early 2000s, the CARs turned towards regional environmental frameworks under the auspices of the UNECE. In 1999, Turkmenistan was the first among the CARs to join the Aarhus Convention on access to information, public participation in decision-making and access to justice in environmental matters.[278] This step was followed by Kazakhstan, the Kyrgyz Republic and Tajikistan in 2001. In the same year, Kazakhstan and the Kyrgyz Republic acceded to the Espoo Convention, which obliges parties to notify and consult each other on all major projects likely to have a significant adverse environmental impact across borders .[279] In 2004, Tajikistan took formal steps with a view to becoming a contracting party to the Espoo Convention, but did not

275 Agreement on Interaction in the Field of Ecology and Environmental Protection, Moscow (signed 8 February 1992; all CARs are parties). Online: <http://www.cawater-info.net/library/rus/moscow3.pdf>.

276 Agreement on Informational Cooperation in the Field of Ecology and the Environmental Protection, Moscow (11 September 1998; among others ratified by Kazakhstan, the Kyrgyz Republic and Tajikistan). Online: <http://www.cawater-info.net/library/rus/moscow.pdf>.

277 Agreement between Government of the Republic of Belarus, the Government of the Russian Federation, the Government of the Republic of Kazakhstan and the Government of the Republic of Tajikistan on the Main Principles of Interaction in the Field of Rational Use and Protection of the Transboundary Water Bodies, Moscow (adopted 11 September 1998, in force for Belarus, Russian Federation and Tajikistan 6 June 2002). Online: <www.cawater-info.net/library/rus/moscow4.pdf>.

278 Aarhus Convention.

279 Espoo Convention.

complete ratification process so far.[280] Also in 2001, Kazakhstan was the first CARs to accede to the Convention on the transboundary effects of industrial accidents[281] and to the 1992 UNECE Water Convention, which aims to prevent, control and reduce transboundary impact.[282] Uzbekistan and Turkmenistan joined the 1992 UNECE Water Convention in 2007 and 2012, respectively. Although Afghanistan is not a member of the UNECE, now it can accede to the 1992 UNECE Water Convention, given its recent opening to the countries outside the region. The 1992 UNECE Water Convention has been initially negotiated as a regional instrument, but in 2003 the Parties adopted an amendment to allow accession by countries outside the UNECE region, which came into force on 6 February 2013 and turned the convention into a global legal instrument.[283]

Out of the Aral Sea basin countries, only Uzbekistan is a party to another global framework agreement – the 1997 UN Watercourses Convention,[284] having acceded to it in 2007. In a complementary way to the sub-regional and regional treaties, the 1997 UN Watercourses Convention seeks to regulate 'uses of international watercourses and of their waters for purpose other than navigation and to measures of protection, preservation and management related to the uses of those watercourses and their waters.'[285]

In addition, all CARs, plus Afghanistan, are parties to global multilateral environmental treaties relevant to transboundary waters. These include the Convention on Biological Diversity that promotes the conservation of biological diversity, the sustainable use of its components, and the fair and equitable sharing of the benefits arising out of the utilisation of genetic resources;[286] Convention on Desertification, which aims to combat desertification and mitigate the effects of drought through effective actions at all levels;[287] and

---

280 Tajikistan promulgated the Decree of 1287 on Accession to UNECE Convention on environmental impact assessment in a transboundary context on 17 February 2004, but the Depositary of the Convention has not yet received the ratification documents.

281 UNECE Convention on the Transboundary Effects of Industrial Accidents, Helsinki (adopted 17 March 1992, entered into force 19 April 2000) 31 ILM 1330 (1992).

282 1992 UNECE Water Convention.

283 Amendment to Articles 25 and 26 of the Convention on the Protection and Use of Transboundary Watercourses and International Lakes, (adopted by decision III/1 of the Meeting of the Parties to the Convention of 28 November 2003, entered into force 6 February 2013) 1992 UNECE Water Convention, amendment to arts 25 and 26.

284 1997 UN Watercourses Convention.

285 Ibid, art 1.

286 Convention on Biodiversity.

287 Convention on Desertification.

Convention on Climate Change, which sets an overall framework for intergovernmental efforts to tackle climate change.[288] The five CARs also work together under the Ramsar Convention, which provides a cooperative framework for the conservation of wetland habitats.[289]

In summary, there is a range of treaties applicable to the transboundary waters of the Aral Sea basin. Nevertheless, there is still no watercourse-specific agreement on the Amudarya basin that would cover the whole basin and involve all riparian countries, including Afghanistan. The 1998 Syrdarya Agreement includes all riparians, but its functional scope is limited to water and energy exchange. The 1992 Almaty Agreement, the only overarching instrument for the Aral Sea basin, fails to include Afghanistan and its catchment area into a joint management framework. The Commonwealth and UNECE agreements have not been ratified by all basin states.

288 Convention on Climate Change.

289 Ramsar Convention.

CHAPTER 4

Scope and Substantive Norms in the Aral Sea Basin

*Norm Properties**

The preceding chapter has provided an overview of transboundary water problems in the Aral Sea basin and located the legal instruments governing countries' relationships over their shared waters. The purpose of this chapter is to outline the scope of the legal regime and ascertain the nature of substantive norms of international water law in the Aral Sea basin through the lenses of norm determinacy and stringency. Norm determinacy and stringency has been identified in Chapter 2 as properties essential to understanding the role and workings of international law. The main question to be explored in this chapter is therefore whether provisions related to scope and substantive norms establish a required standard of conduct for the Aral Sea basin states in determinate and stringent terms. To evaluate norm determinacy, the chapter examines whether a norm is couched in determinate (precise) or indeterminate (open-textured) terms.[290] To explore norm stringency, the chapter studies whether a norm is expressed in mandatory or hortatory/programmatic language – 'shall, must, require, and may not' or 'should, may, and recommend'.

4.1 Scope

The matter of scope deals with the geographical or hydrological extent of water and other related resources covered by a legal regime, defines the types of uses or activities governed by its provisions, and determines the range of legal actors eligible to participate in the watercourse utilisation.[291]

In terms of the geographical or hydrological extent of the waters covered by each legal regime, the 1992 Almaty Agreement recognises 'water resources of interstate sources' as 'common and integral' for the basin. The current scope of

---

* This chapter has drawn upon material from within Dinara Ziganshina, 'International Water Law in Central Asia: The Nature of Substantive Norms and what Flows from It', (2012) Volume 2(1) Asian Journal of International Law 169–192 © Asian Journal of International Law, published by Cambridge University Press, reproduced with permission.

290 See eg Bodansky, *The art and craft of international environmental law* at 102.

291 Sergei Vinogradov, Patricia Wouters and Patricia Jones, *Transforming potential conflict into cooperation potential: The role of international water law* (Paris, UNESCO 2003) 46.

© KONINKLIJKE BRILL NV, LEIDEN, 2014 | DOI 10.1163/9789004274266_005

water allocation and regulation under this agreement, as revalidation of the Soviet rules, covers the main stem of the Pyandzh, Vakhsh, Kafirnigan and Amudarya rivers in the Amudarya basin, and the main stem of the Syrdarya and Chirchik rivers in the Syrdarya basin. The 2006 Framework Sustainable Development Convention, if it enters into force, will apply the scope of a legal regulation to 'all territories under national jurisdictions of the Contracting Parties with special regard to the Aral Sea basin area' and 'all kind of activities exercised by the Contracting Parties within its jurisdiction'.[292] Existing instruments do not extend the scope of regulation to transboundary groundwater and only partly include freshwater ecosystems, which will be discussed in more detail in section 4.2.3.

In this context, countries can benefit from the 1997 UN Watercourses Convention and the 1992 UNECE Water Convention, which reflect contemporary approaches to water use and protection by defining a hydrological scope based on the concepts of a 'watercourse' (or a river system) and an 'ecosystem'.[293] The 1997 UN Watercourses Convention determines the rights and obligations of 'watercourse states'[294] with respect to a 'watercourse', defined as 'a system of surface waters and groundwaters constituting by virtue of their physical relationship a unitary whole and normally flowing into a common terminus'.[295] Given that the Convention seeks to regulate 'uses of international watercourses and of their waters for purpose other than navigation and to measures of protection, preservation and management related to the uses of those watercourses and their waters',[296] its scope appears to include land-based activities which might affect the protection, preservation and management related to an international watercourse. Some scholars interpret this provision as implicitly adopting a drainage basin approach, which finds further support in the Convention's substantive rules and principles – especially

292 2006 Framework Convention on Sustainable Development in CA, art 2.

293 ILC Commentary to 1994 Draft Articles at 90–91; 'UNECE Guide to Implementing the Convention' (2009) Meeting of the Parties to the Convention on the Protection and Use of Transboundary Watercourses and International Lakes, 5th Session Geneva 10–12 November 2009 UN Doc ECE/MPWAT/2009/L2at 23 art 1(2).

294 1997 UN Watercourses Convention, art 2(c): 'Watercourse State' means a State Party to the present Convention in whose territory part of an international watercourse is situated, or a Party that is a regional economic integration organization, in the territory of one or more of whose Member States part of an international watercourse is situated.

295 Ibid, arts 2(a) and 2(b): 'International watercourse' means a watercourse, parts of which are situated in different States.

296 Ibid, art 1.

Article 20 – discussed below.[297] On its part, the 1992 UNECE Water Convention distinguishes two categories of states – 'Parties' and 'Riparian Parties'[298] – and deals with 'transboundary waters' defined as 'any surface or ground waters which mark, cross or are located on boundaries between two or more States; wherever transboundary waters flow directly into the sea, these transboundary waters end at a straight line across their respective mouths between points on the low-water line of their banks'.[299]

In addition to the explicit reference to groundwater and the idea of 'hydrologic system composed of [...] rivers, lakes, aquifers, glaciers, reservoirs and canals',[300] the 1997 UN Watercourses Convention and the 1992 UNECE Water Convention have a broadened scope that includes provisions related to freshwater ecosystems. The ILC commentary to 1994 Draft Articles refers to 'ecosystem' as 'an ecological unit consisting of living and non-living components that are interdependent and function as a community'.[301] UNECE Recommendations include in the definition of 'water-related ecosystems', 'ecosystems such as forests, wetlands, grasslands, and agricultural land that play vital roles in the hydrological cycle through the services they provide'.[302]

Concerning legal actors eligible to participate in the utilisation of the resource, the existing sub-regional agreements define rights and obligations only with respect to the five CARs. Afghanistan, a riparian country to the Amudarya basin, is not formally involved in sub-regional water management,

297 Attila Tanzi, *The Relationship between the 1992 UNECE Convention on the Protection and Use of Transboundary Watercourses and International Lakes and the 1997 UN Convention on the Law of the Non Navigational Uses of International Watercourses* (UN ECE, Report of the UN ECE Task Force on Legal and Administrative Aspects, 2000) at 7 and Alistair Rieu-Clarke, Patricia Wouters and Flavia Loures, 'The role and relevance of the UN Convention of the Law and of the Non-Navigational Uses of International Watercourses to the EU and its member states' (2008) Thematic and Regional Assessments of the Relevance and Applicability of the 1997 UN Convention on the Law of the Non-navigational Uses of International Watercourses at 11.

298 1992 UNECE Water Convention: 'Party' means, unless the text otherwise indicates, a Contracting Party to this Convention and 'Riparian Parties' means the Parties bordering the same transboundary waters.

299 Ibid, art 1(1).

300 See eg ILC Commentary to 1994 Draft Articles at 90.

301 Ibid, 118–119 refers to 'ecosystem' as 'an ecological unit consisting of living and non-living components that are interdependent and function as a community'.

302 'UNECE Recommendations on Payments for Ecosystem Services in Integrated Water Resources Management' (2006) Meeting of the Parties to the Convention on the Protection and Use of Transboundary Watercourses and International Lakes, 4th Session Bonn 10–12 November 2006 UN Doc ECE/MPWAT/22.

although any significant water resources development on the territory of Afghanistan can potentially affect downstream use. The 1987 Protocol of the Scientific and Technical Council of the Ministry of Melioration and Water Management of the USSR, which established still valid water distribution limits for the Amudarya basin, deducted Afghanistan's estimated water withdrawal (2.1 billion cubic meters) from the river's flow to estimate water availability for allocation purposes among the five CARs. Clearly, the absence of a new treaty between all riparian countries does not preclude them from using the waters of an international watercourse[303] as long as this use in conformity with the norms of customary law and other international legal commitments. Nevertheless, the 1997 UN Watercourses Convention is useful in promoting a basin-wide approach to the management of international watercourses. Article 4(1) of the 1997 UN Watercourses Convention entitles each watercourse state 'to participate in the negotiation of and to become a party to any watercourse agreement that applies to the entire international watercourse, as well as to participate in any relevant consultations'. It also provides that 'a watercourse State whose use of an international watercourse may be affected to a significant extent by the implementation of a proposed watercourse agreement that applies only to a part of the watercourse or to a particular project, programme or use is entitled to participate in consultations on such an agreement and, where appropriate, in the negotiation thereof in good faith with a view to becoming a party thereto, to the extent that its use is thereby affected'.[304]

States other than riparians seem to be eligible to participate in certain water-related activities in the Aral Sea basin. Thus, due to historical ties and geopolitical considerations, Russia has been an active observer in the subregion. Formally, Article 3 of the 1993 Kzyl-Orda Agreement grants the Russian Federation an observer status in the work of the Interstate Council in addressing the Aral Sea crisis and the rehabilitation of the disaster zone.[305] It stipulates further that Russia shall provide the required financial and technical assistance for a range of related activities. Given that the Russian Federation is

303 See ILC Commentary to 1994 Draft Articles at 94 para 17 ('[...]watercourse States are not under an obligation to conclude an agreement before using the waters of international watercourse. To require conclusion of an agreement as a pre-condition of use would be to afford watercourse States the power to veto a use by other watercourse States of the waters of international waters by simply refusing to reach agreement [...] Nor does it find support in State practice or international judicial decisions (indeed, the *Lake Lanoux* arbitral award negates it)').

304 1997 UN Watercourses Convention, art 4(2).

305 1993 Kzyl-Orda Agreement, art 3.

not a signatory to the agreement, the legal consequences of such provisions are rather limited. The Vienna Convention on the Law of Treaties provides that, as a general rule, '[a] treaty does not create either obligations or rights for a third states without its consent'.[306] According to Articles 35 and 36, an obligation must be intended by parties and *expressly* accepted by the third States, whereas a right might be *tacitly* accepted.[307] As such, the provisions of the 1993 Kzyl-Orda Agreement might be viewed as creating rights in favour of Russia, but not imposing obligations. Interestingly enough, the structure of the 1992 UNECE Water Convention – that envisages two major categories of obligations relating to *all* Parties (Part I) and relating to Riparian Parties (Part II)[308] – also allows some space for speculation on the scope of other states' obligations with respect to transboundary waters; the issue discussed in more details further in this chapter.

Summing up, the global and regional instruments clearly require countries to apply 'watercourse system' and an ecosystem approach in defining the scope of legal regulation. The sub-regional agreements – although specified the scope of transboundary water management – still need more clear provisions related to groundwater and freshwater ecosystems.

4.2 Substantive Norms

The principle of equitable and reasonable use and the no-harm rule are considered to be two basic norms of international water law. Emerging as specific applications of those norms are procedures and obligations related to the sustainable and optimal management, use and protection of international watercourses and their ecosystems.

4.2.1 *The Principle of Equitable and Reasonable Use*

The principle of equitable and reasonable use is broadly recognised as 'a general rule of law for the determination of the rights and obligations of states' with respect to international watercourses.[309] Article 5 of the 1997 UN

306 Vienna Convention on the Law of Treaties, Vienna (adopted 23 May 1969, entered into force 27 January 1980) 8 ILM 679, art 34.

307 Ibid, art 35–37.

308 1992 UNECE Water Convention, arts 1(3) and 1(4): 'Party' means, unless the text otherwise indicates, a Contracting Party to this Convention and 'Riparian Parties' means the Parties bordering the same transboundary waters.

309 ILC Commentary to 1994 Draft Articles at 98.

Watercourses Convention codifies this fundamental customary norm of international water law, providing that watercourse States 'shall in their respective territories utilize an international watercourse in an equitable and reasonable manner'[310] and 'shall participate in the use, development and protection of an international watercourse in an equitable and reasonable manner'.[311] Article 6(1) provides a non-exhaustive list of factors and circumstances that should be taken into account in a determination of 'equitable and reasonable utilisation'. These include:

(a) Geographic, hydrographic, hydrological, climatic, ecological and other factors of a natural character;
(b) The social and economic needs of the watercourse States concerned;
(c) The population dependent on the watercourse in each watercourse State;
(d) The effects of the use or uses of the watercourses in one watercourse State on other watercourse States;
(e) Existing and potential uses of the watercourse;
(f) Conservation, protection, development and economy of use of the water resources of the watercourse and the costs of measures taken to that effect;
(g) The availability of alternatives, of comparable value, to a particular planned or existing use.[312]

The high degree of this norm's indeterminacy can be already detected from this broad range of factors and circumstances to be considered and from the fact that the list itself is not exhaustive. Article 6(3) further provides that '[t]he weight to be given to each factor is to be determined by its importance in comparison with that of other relevant factors'.[313] Although Articles 5 and 6(1) do not require anything more than a unilateral appraisal of what equitable and reasonable use is, in the first instance, Article 6(2) does require the states concerned to enter into consultations in the application of Article 5 or Article 6(1) 'when the need arises'. As such, the determination of equitable and reasonable use, in some instances, may invite watercourse countries to engage into

310 1997 UN Watercourses Convention, art 5(1).

311 Ibid, art 5(2).

312 Ibid, art 6.

313 Further, 1997 UN Watercourses Convention, art 6(3) states, 'The weight to be given to each factor is to be determined by its importance in comparison with that of other relevant factors. In determining what is a reasonable and equitable use, all relevant factors are to be considered together and a conclusion reached on the basis of the whole'.

discursive interactions to ascertain what *relevant* and *important*[314] factors and circumstances in a particular context, time or settings are. Consequently, the questions of 'equity' and 'reasonableness' have to be tackled, contingent to an intersubjectively shared context. Given the open-textured nature of the norm, such collective appraisals seem to be highly desirable to reach mutually agreeable outcomes.

The ILC commentary to the 1994 Draft Articles explains that only 'reasonable and beneficial' uses will be relevant to a determination of what is equitable.[315] Hence, prior to establishing what constitutes an 'equitable use' by weighing and balancing the competing interests of states, states should ascertain what constitutes a 'reasonable use' by consulting contemporary conceptions of rationality.[316] For its part, the principle of equity requires, *inter alia*, that 'not only the absolute injury caused to the neighbouring state' be considered, but also 'the relation of the advantage gained by one to the injury caused to the other'.[317] Although no factor or use is accorded inherent priority when balancing the interests of states, nonetheless when there is a conflict between different uses 'special regard' should be given to 'the requirements of vital human needs'.[318] The terms 'vital human needs' and 'special regard' also raise questions over their determinacy and stringency.

'Vital human needs' is defined in the Statement of Understanding attached to the 1997 UN Watercourse Convention as 'sufficient water to sustain human life'.[319] The Statement clarifies that water necessary to sustain human life includes 'both drinking water and water required for the production of food in order to prevent starvation', where the latter is only relevant in the rural context where the population depends on agriculture.[320] Specific inclusion of

314 van Dijk, 'Relevance in text and context: Discussion of Joseph E. Grimes' preprint "Context structure patterns"' (maintaining that discourse 'has the important property that it may show what information is 'important', 'prominent' or 'relevant' in a particular context, time or settings').

315 ILC Commentary to 1994 Draft Articles at 98, para 9. See also Alistair Rieu-Clarke, *A fresh approach to international law in the field of sustainable development: Lessons from the law of international watercourses* (London, IWA Publishing 2005) 104.

316 Rieu-Clarke at 106.

317 *Württemberg and Prussia* v. *Baden* (the *Donauversinkung* case), German Staatsgerichshof 1927, [1927] Annual Digest of Public International Law Cases 128 at 131, cited in ILC Commentary to 1994 Draft Articles at 105, para 16.

318 1997 UN Watercourses Convention, art 10.

319 Statement of Understanding accompanying the UN Convention on the Law of the Non-Navigational Uses of International Watercourses, New York (11 April 1997) UN Doc A/51/869.

320 Ibid.

these uses does not preclude a situation where, depending on the context, other uses may be found 'vital'. Further guidelines can be found in other hard-law and soft-law instruments in the field of water resources and human rights. Thus, the 2004 Berlin Rules on Water Resources describes water needed for immediate human consumption to include 'drinking, cooking, and washing', and for other uses necessary for the immediate sustenance of a household to include 'watering livestock for household use and keeping a kitchen garden'.[321] The 2002 General Comment 15 on the Right to Water under the 1966 UN International Covenant on Economic, Social and Cultural Rights refers to a broader term of 'personal and domestic uses' defined to encompass drinking use (water consumption through beverages and foodstuffs), personal use (disposal of human excreta), washing of clothes, food preparation (including food hygiene), and personal and household hygiene (including personal cleanliness and hygiene of the household environment).[322] In the latter classification, water required for the production of food in order to prevent starvation is not explicitly covered.

The qualifying term 'special regard' refers to the weight to be given to vital human needs, without affording them an absolute priority.[323] Such weight should be determined on a case-by-case basis, which may also require taking into account related provisions of other treaties and non-binding instruments. The most relevant of those are instruments that deal with the concept of a human right to water.[324]

Most recently, the UN General Assembly has recognised the right to safe and clean drinking water and sanitation as a human right that is essential for the full enjoyment of life and all human rights.[325] The key concepts, guidelines and objectives related to the human right to water are established in General Comment 15 on the Right to Water, which provides that 'the human right to water entitles everyone to sufficient, safe, acceptable, physically accessible

321 International Law Association, *Berlin Rules on Water Resources* in [2004] Report of the Seventhy-First International Law Association Conference, Berlin, arts 3(20), 14(1) and 17.

322 UN Economic and Social Council, Committee on Economic, Social and Cultural Rights *General Comment 15 (2002) The right to water (arts 11 and 12 of the International Covenant on Economic, Social and Cultural Rights)* 20 January 2003 UN Doc E/C.12/2002/11.

323 Cf. ILA's 2004 Berlin Rules, art 14(1) (stating that 'In determining an equitable and reasonable use, States shall first allocate waters to satisfy vital human needs').

324 Although a human right to water as such has not been recognised in 1997, when UN Watercourses Convention was adopted; arguably subsequent developments can be relevant in the context of the intertemporal doctrine in international law.

325 UN General Assembly Resolution *The human right to water and sanitation* 28 July 2010 UN Doc A/RES/64/292.

and affordable water for personal and domestic uses'.[326] With regard to international watercourses, the General Comment provides that 'international cooperation requires State parties to refrain from actions that interfere, directly or indirectly, with the enjoyment of the right to water in other countries'.[327] The General Comment goes on to provide that 'any activities undertaken within the State party's jurisdiction should not deprive another country of the ability to realise the right to water for persons in its jurisdiction'.[328] Thus, the General Comment may serve as normative guidelines that provide for standards and benchmarks to consider in determination of the human right to water.

The sub-regional agreements in the Aral Sea basin also contain some – rather broad – provisions that may be useful in determining 'special regard' to be given to 'vital human needs' in the basin. Thus, in the 1993 Kzyl-Orda Agreement, the Central Asian states recognize as common objectives a need to improve sanitary and hygiene requirements and medico-biological living conditions, especially for the sea zone residents, and to address the urgent problem of a clean drinking water supply for the sub-region.[329] Further, in the 2006 Framework Convention on Sustainable Development, the countries have agreed to cooperate on the development of norms and procedures that would ensure that joint measures to provide safe drinking water to their population are undertaken.[330]

By way of summary, these considerations may be relevant in the determination of 'special regard' and 'vital human needs' to guarantee that transboundary water management is equitable and reasonable for all, including the most vulnerable.

Although historically the principle of equitable and reasonable use has been developed as a basis for water allocation, the norm also embraces the issues of water quality and ecosystem considerations. Article 5(1) of the 1997 UN Watercourses Convention clearly requires that 'an international watercourse shall be used and developed...with a view to attaining optimal and sustainable utilization thereof'.[331] The 1992 UNECE Water Convention adds to this development. Article 2(2)(c) provides that '[t]he Parties shall [...] take all appropriate measures [...] to ensure that transboundary waters are used in a

326 General Comment 15 on the Right to Water, para 2.

327 Ibid, para 31.

328 Ibid, para 31.

329 1993 Kzyl-Orda Agreement, art 1.

330 2006 Framework Convention on Sustainable Development in CA, art 9(3)(d).

331 1997 UN Watercourses Convention, art 5(1).

reasonable and equitable way, taking into particular account their transboundary character, in the case of activities which cause or are likely to cause transboundary impact'.[332] The Guide to Implementing the Convention points out that:

> Article 2(2)(c) should be read in conjunction with article 2(5)(c), according to which 'water resources shall be managed so that the needs of the present generation are met without compromising the ability of future generations to meet their own needs'. This is fully in line with the contemporary developments of international customary water law according to which the principle of equitable use incorporates that of sustainable development. That is to say that a use of an international water body may not be considered as equitable, therefore legal, if it is not sustainable.[333]

Thus, although the principle of equitable and reasonable use is couched in strong terms ('shall utilize', 'shall participate', 'shall take all appropriate measures') and thus imposes an obligation of action, the actual determination of conduct is complicated by the norm's complex and open-textured nature. The determination of equitable and reasonable use is in all cases dictated by the objective application of its two-fold standard of 'equity' and 'reasonableness', necessarily including consideration of vital human needs and the protection of watercourses. The principle of equitable and reasonable use pays due regard to changing needs by requiring that balancing of the relevant factors must be responsive to the circumstances of individual cases. This is not to negate, however, the inherent flexibility of this norm that is considered by many analysts to be its strength,[334] but also entailing a considerable level of uncertainty in its application.

To meet this challenge, the concept of equitable participation forms an essential part of the equitable and reasonable use principle. As the ILC's commentary explains, '[t]he core of this principle is cooperation between watercourse States through participation, on an equitable and reasonable basis, in measures, works, activities aimed at attaining optimal utilization of

332 1992 UNECE Water Convention, art 2(2)(c).

333 'UNECE *Guide to Implementing the Convention*' at 33, para 102. See also *Gabčíkovo-Nagymaros case* and *Pulp Mills case*. Owen McIntyre, 'The proceduralisation and growing maturity of international water law. Case Concerning Pulp Mills on the River Uruguay (Argentina v Uruguay), International Court of Justice, 20 April 2010' (2010) 22 Journal of Environmental Law 475–497.

334 See Rieu-Clarke at 158.

international watercourse, consistent with adequate protection thereof'.[335] The character of the principle of cooperation attempts to direct conduct towards a particular goal. It gives some guidance, although abstract, for assessing the performance of interstate cooperation both in substantive and procedural terms. As for the substance of cooperation, it determines that 'attaining optimal utilization' and 'adequate protection of the watercourse' is the objective of interstate cooperation. By making reference to the principle of 'good faith', it sets a general and indeterminate, but an essential procedural prerequisite for cooperation. To provide more precision, the Guide to Implementing the 1992 UNECE Water Convention points out that '[a]ddressing such problems through collective action requires a number of initially unilateral decisions towards cooperation'.[336] The principle of equitable and reasonable use therefore imposes constraints on the exercise of national sovereignty and requires states, *inter alia*, to develop national laws and policies to implement its objectives. Accordingly, the effective application of this regulatory norm requires 'affirmative conduct' from riparian states both at the basin and the national levels.[337] The subsequent chapter considers in more detail the procedural requirements of cooperation in international water law.

Finally, as was mentioned above, the principle of equitable and reasonable use does not set forth a legal entitlement to the use of shared waters by States other than the riparians; nevertheless, the structure of the 1992 UNECE Water Convention that envisages two major categories of obligations, one relating to Parties (Part I) and the other to Riparian Parties (Part II)[338] allows some room for speculation on the scope of other States' obligations to ensure an equitable and reasonable use under this Convention. Article 2(2)(c) of the 1992 UNECE Water Convention requires the Parties – not only the Riparian Parties – to 'take all appropriate measures [...] to ensure that transboundary waters are used in a reasonable and equitable way'.[339] Read in tandem with the preambular provision that 'the effective accomplishment of [the Convention's tasks] can only be ensured by enhanced cooperation',[340] this article 2(2)(c) seems to

335 ILC Commentary to 1994 Draft Articles at 97.

336 'UNECE *Guide to Implementing the Convention*' at 9, para 25.

337 Stephen C. McCaffrey, 'Convention on the Law of the Non-Navigational Uses of International Watercourses' (2008) United Nations Audiovisual Library of International Law. Online: <http://untreaty.un.org/cod/avl/pdf/ha/clnuiw/clnuiw_e.pdf> accessed 22 July 2013.

338 1992 UNECE Water Convention, arts 1(3)–(4): 'Party' means, unless the text otherwise indicates, a Contracting Party to this Convention and 'Riparian Parties' means the Parties bordering the same transboundary waters.

339 Ibid, art 2(2)(c).

340 Ibid, preamble.

emphasise a need for cooperation to ensure that the use of transboundary waters is equitable and reasonable not only by Riparian Parties, but also other Parties to the Convention. As the Guide to Implementing the Convention puts it, 'each Riparian State is not left alone in its dealing with other riparians, while expectations become the concern of all other Parties sitting in the Meeting of the Parties' through the collective institutional regime.[341]

Since what constitutes 'equitable and reasonable' is not capable of a precise definition within the global and regional framework instruments, the norm necessitates the adoption of more specific arrangements (e.g. agreements, joint bodies) that can develop an increasingly complex pattern of detailed rules and standards for a particular watercourse. The Aral Sea basin countries do not contest or negate the status of the equitable and reasonable use principle as the governing norm of international water law and widely voice their adherence to this norm in formal and semi-formal settings. Nonetheless, the sub-regional agreements in the basin contain no explicit provisions on the principle of equitable and reasonable use. Some preambular recitals in such treaties and soft law instruments vaguely refer to 'adherence to the principle of international water law',[342] 'established international practice',[343] 'equitable solution in utilization of water and energy resources [...] in accordance with norms of international law',[344] and 'solving the issues of joint management of water resources on the basis of common regional principles and equitable regulation of their consumption'.[345] The case can be made that the main

341 'UNECE *Guide to Implementing the Convention*' at 10, para 26. 'Cooperative conduct from other than riparian states to ensure equitable and reasonable use of transboundary waters gains relevance and importance in the context of the globalised world that struggles to achieve water security and ensure water for all'. See Victor Dukhovny, 'Water and globalization: case study of Central Asia' (2007) 56 Irrigation and Drainage 489–507. Arjen Y. Hoekstra and Ashok K. Chapagain, *Globalization of water: Sharing the planet's freshwater resources* (Oxford, Blackwell Publishing 2007), and Patricia Wouters, Sergei Vinogradov and Bjørn-Oliver Magsig, 'Water security, hydrosolidarity and international law: A river runs through it...' (2009) 19 Yearbook of International Environmental Law 97–134 Ibid. See also *United Nations Millennium Declaration*, 8 September 2000, GA Res. 55/2, UN Doc A/RES/55/2 at 2, para 5.

342 1993 Kzyl-Orda Agreement.

343 1998 CIS Agreement on Transboundary Waters.

344 1998 Syrdarya Agreement.

345 1992 Almaty Agreement. See also soft law instruments: 1997 Almaty Declaration and 1999 Ashgabad Joint Statement (stating that transboundary water management must be based on ecosystem approach, equitable and reasonable use and no-harm rules), 2001 Tashkent Statement (reaffirming that concerned actions in water and energy resources management should be based on recognised principles and norms of international law).

provisions should be interpreted and applied in line with the preamble as indicated in Article 31(2) of the Vienna Convention, which sets forth that the treaty text includes its preamble and annexes,[346] and normally the treaty's object and purpose is found in its preamble. The significance of preambular provisions in the legal regulation of the transboundary water management in the Aral Sea basin can be demonstrated by the fact that the principal provision of the 1992 Almaty Agreement – that the Parties will 'respect…the vested pattern and principles of water allocation and [will rely upon] current regulations for water allocation from interstate sources' – is stipulated in its preamble.[347]

The 1992 Almaty Agreement validates the Soviet Schemes for Complex [Integrated] Water Resources Use and Protections,[348] which provide for detailed regulations on water allocation and use between the Central Asian countries. However, the 'equity' of these norms has been questioned. For instance, representatives of some riparian states raised concerns that the agreement favours a *status quo* that does not take into account current political, economic, and social circumstances and the new national interests of the states.[349] Indeed, existing legal arrangements were not designed to accommodate changing circumstances, nor can they be easily amended. As a result, many treaties became stagnant and lost their effectiveness. The negotiations of new agreements have not succeeded so far. In contrast the principle of

346 1969 Vienna Convention, art 31(2). See also Gerald Fitzmaurice, 'The law and procedure of the International Court of Justice 1951–4: Treaty interpretation and other treaty points' (1957) British Yearbook of International Law 203–293 at 209.

347 1992 Almaty Agreement, preamble.

348 Separate schemes for two principal river basins—the Scheme of Complex Water Resources Use and Protection for the Amudarya River and the Scheme of Complex Water Resources Use and Protection for the Syrdarya River—provide detailed provisions for water allocation, use, management, and protection. See *Resolution of the Expert Sub-Commission to the Gosplan (State Planning Committee) State Expert Commission of the USSR* (12 March 1982); *Protocol of the Scientific and Technical Council of the Ministry of Water Resources Management of the USSR on Approval of the Principles of Inter-Republican Water Allocation of the Syrdarya River Basin Resources No 413* (29 February 1984); *Protocol of the Scientific and Technical Council of the Ministry of Water Resources Management of the USSR on Approval of the Principles of Inter-Republican Water Allocation of the Amudarya River Basin Resources No 556* (10 September 1987); *Decision of the Gosplan State Expert Commission of the USSR No 11* (5 March 1982) (on file with author).

349 See ADB TA 6163-REG: Improved Management of Shared Water Resources in Central Asia. Online: <http://cawater-info.net/reta/documents/index_e.htm> accessed 22 December 2013; Dinara Kemelova and Gennady Zhalkubaev, 'Water, conflict, and regional security in Central Asia revisited' (2003) 11 New York University Environmental Law Journal 479–502.

equitable and reasonable use, being responsive to the necessities of time and place, adopts a flexible all-encompassing approach to reconciling a broad range of existing and new economic, social, and environmental issues and ultimately provides for a legal framework for such discussions and, if necessary, adjustments.[350] It also allows for the engagement of other riparian states such as Afghanistan in transboundary water management in the region. Hence, it seems inaccurate to assume that the 1997 UN Watercourses Convention, centred around the principle of equitable and reasonable use, 'protects the first developer [in the basin] from the start' or 'freeze[s] power relations that prevailed at a particular time period'.[351]

It has further been argued that the principle of equitable and reasonable use is better able to reconcile competing interests in the sub-region than the concept of 'benefit sharing'[352] embedded in the sub-regional agreements on water and energy trade-off between the riparian states to the Syrdarya.[353] Thus, Tarlock and Wouters argue that the application of the concept of benefit sharing among riparian States can prejudice the application of the equitable and reasonable use principle through introducing 'unequal bargaining among states; the premature "sale" of future use opportunities; and the increased risk of aquatic ecosystem degradation'.[354] To avoid these failures, Article 4 of a draft agreement on the Syrdarya river basin, prepared as a result of collaborative efforts by regional and national working groups, seeks to codify the equitable and reasonable use of water resources of the basin by which the parties agreed to 'be guided'.[355]

There exists no provision on equitable and reasonable use in the treaties with Afghanistan. The 1946 Afghan-Soviet Frontier Agreement only goes as far as to govern the utilisation of the waters of the river Kushka and the

---

350 Rieu-Clarke at 158.

351 Wegerich and Olsson, 'Late developers and the inequity of "equitable utilization" and the harm of "do no harm"'at 709 and 714.

352 The benefit sharing, defined as 'any action designed to change the allocation of costs and benefits associated with cooperation', has gained its advocates and skeptics in application to shared waters. Claudia W. Sadoff and David Grey, 'Beyond the river: The benefits of cooperation on international rivers' (2002) 4 Water policy 389–403.

353 See 1998 Syrdarya Agreement.

354 Dan Tarlock and Patricia Wouters, 'Are shared benefits of international waters an equitable apportionment?' (2007) 18 Colorado Journal of International Environmental Law and Policy 523–536. See also Dukhovny, 'Water and globalization: case study of Central Asia'.

355 Draft Agreement on the Syrdarya River Basin (Version 2007) (on file with author), art 4.

construction of a dam on the river Murghab.[356] The 1958 Treaty states in stringent terms that '[q]uestions concerning the use of waters that are connected with frontier waters shall be governed by special agreements between the Contracting Parties'[357]- agreements that have yet to be negotiated and adopted.

In summary, the stringency of the equitable and reasonable use principle varies from the mandatory scale of engagement in the 1997 UN Watercourses Convention and 1992 UNECE Water Convention to the lesser level of framing in the sub-regional treaties' preambular provisions. As far as determinacy is concerned, the qualifying adjectives 'equitable and reasonable' are not without ambiguity and are contingent to the extent that their determination applies to a specific factual context of norm application. Nonetheless, the discretion of states is constrained by the requirement of considering objective factors embedded in the norm itself.[358] The standard can be further contextualised through procedural obligations such as the duty to cooperate, to exchange information, to notify on planned measures, to conduct assessments and the like, and through the more detailed requirements of watercourse-specific agreements.[359]

4.2.2 *The No-Harm Rule*

Another fundamental substantive norm applicable to international watercourses is the no-harm rule. It derives its normative foundation from *sic utere tuo ut alienum non laedas*, or the good neighbourliness principle, and it is now part of the corpus of international customary and treaty law relating to transboundary watercourses.[360] Article 7(1) of the 1997 UN Watercourses

356 1946 Soviet-Afghan Frontier Agreement, Note III released Afghanistan from prohibition to use water from the river Kushka north of Chihil Dukter, but provided that it 'shall not increase the quality of water taken from the river Kushka in this area and shall observe the *status quo* in this respect'. The Agreement is also endorsed the Soviet Government's waiver to construct a dam on the river Murghab and to utilize the Afghan bank of the river for this purpose, on condition that the Afghans, too, would forego construction of such a dam on their territory 'as would diminish the flow of water from this river on to Soviet territory'.

357 1958 Soviet-Afghan Frontier Treaty, art 16.

358 The criteria specified in article 6 of 1997 UN Watercourses Convention.

359 Patricia Birnie, Alan Boyle and Catherine Redgwell, *International law and the environment* (Oxford, 3rd edn, Oxford University Press 2009) at 553.

360 The customary status of the obligation not to cause transboundary harm has been sufficiently established after the *Trail Smelter case Trail Smelter Case* (*United States v Canada*) III Reports of International Arbitral Awards 1905 (1941). See eg Stockholm Declaration, principle 21; Rio Declaration, principle 2; Treaty between Great Britain and the United States Relating to Boundary Waters, and Questions arising between the United States and

Convention envisages the no-harm rule in stringent, but indeterminate language, providing that '[w]atercourse States shall, in utilizing an international watercourse in their territories, take all appropriate measures to prevent the causing of significant harm to other watercourse States'.[361] The ILC's commentary to Article 7 explains that '[t]he obligation of due diligence contained in article 7 [...] is an obligation of conduct, not an obligation of result'.[362]

In a similar fashion, Article 2(1) of the 1992 UNECE Water Convention provides that '[t]he Parties shall take all appropriate measures to prevent, control and reduce any transboundary impact'.[363] The Guide to implementing the 1992 UNECE Convention, in recognising 'a reasonable amount of flexibility' of this due diligence obligation, defines a non-exhaustive list of minimum requirements to comply with Article 2(1) based on the provisions of other articles and annexes of the Convention on 'best environmental practice' and 'water-quality objectives and criteria'.[364] The Guide states, in particular, that in case of a problem about compliance by a Party with this obligation of prevention, that Party is to show, *inter alia*, that:

(a) It has taken 'measures for the prevention, control and reduction of water pollution [...] at source' (art. 2 (3));
(b) Such measures do not 'result in a transfer of pollution to other parts of the environment' (art. 2 (4));

Canada (adopted 11 January 1909, entered into force 5 May 1910) 36 Stat 2448, Washington [1909 US-Canada Boundary Waters Treaty]; UN Convention on the Law of the Sea (adopted 10 December 1982, entered into force 16 November 1994) 21 ILM 1261 (1982). See also Stephen C. McCaffrey, *The law of international watercourses – non-navigational uses* (Oxford, Oxford University Press 2001) at 415; Attila Tanzi and Maurizio Arcari, *The United Nations Convention on the Law of International Watercourses: A framework for sharing* (Patricia Wouters and Sergei Vinogradov eds, The Hague, Kluwer Law International 2001) at 142.

361 1997 UN Watercourses Convention, art 7(1).

362 ILC Commentary to 2001 Draft articles at 103, para 4.

363 1992 UNECE Water Convention, art 2(1). See also art 1(2) according to which

> 'Transboundary impact' means any significant adverse effect on the environment resulting from a change in the conditions of transboundary waters caused by a human activity, the physical origin of which is situated wholly or in part within an area under the jurisdiction of a Party, within an area under the jurisdiction of another Party. Such effects on the environment include effects on human health and safety, flora, fauna, soil, air, water, climate, landscape and historical monuments or other physical structures or the interaction among these factors; they also include effects on the cultural heritage or socio-economic conditions resulting from alterations to those factors.

364 'UNECE *Guide to Implementing the Convention*' at 29, para 95.

(c) It has taken legal, administrative, economic, financial and technical measures to apply low and non-waste technology in order to prevent emission of pollutants at source (art. 3 (1 (a)));
(d) It has introduced a licensing regime of wastewater discharges also providing for monitoring and control of the authorized discharges based on the best available relevant technology (ibidem, (b, c));
(e) It applies biological treatment (or equivalent processes) to municipal wastewater, or, at least, concrete steps to that effect have been undertaken (ibidem, (e));
(f) It applies measures for the reduction of nutrient inputs from industrial and municipal sources (ibidem, (f));
(g) It applies appropriate measures and best environmental practices (in conformity with annex II) for the reduction of inputs of nutrients and hazardous substances from diffuse sources, especially agriculture (ibidem, (g));
(h) It has developed contingency planning (ibidem, (j));
(i) It has taken measures to prevent the pollution of groundwaters (ibidem, (k)).[365]

The terms of both the 1997 UN Watercourses Convention and the 1992 UNECE Water Convention clearly suggest that States are not under an absolute obligation to guarantee that no significant harm will occur to other watercourse States. McCaffrey further points out that 'it is not factual harm *per se*, but injury to a legally protected interest that the law prohibits'.[366] Article 7(2) introduces even more flexibility and ambiguity into the norm and its relationship with the equitable and reasonable principle by stating,

> Where significant harm nevertheless is caused to another watercourse State, the States whose use causes such harm shall, in the absence of agreement to such use, take all appropriate measures, having due regard for the provisions of articles 5 and 6, in consultation with the affected State, to eliminate or mitigate such harm and, where appropriate, to discuss the question of compensation.

The ILC's commentary to the 1994 Draft Articles explains that this provision is 'setting forth a process aimed at avoiding significant harm as far as possible

365 Ibid, 29–30.

366 Stephen C. McCaffrey, *The law of international watercourses – Non-navigational uses* (Oxford, 2nd edn, Oxford University Press 2007) at 347.

while reaching an equitable result in each concrete case'.[367] In doing so, this article seeks to clarify a delicate balance between the equitable and reasonable use principle and the no significant harm rule, the issue that was one of the most contested and debated at the UN negotiations, with upper riparians being in favor of the equitable and reasonable principle and lower riparians being in favor of the no-harm rule.[368] The resultant formula seems to suggest that the no-harm rule does not supersede the equitable and reasonable use principle by which 'a legally protected interest' is to be established, adjusted, and protected, but rather these norms work in a tandem. As Tanzi observes, the wording of Articles 5–7 'seems perfectly crafted in order to provide absolutely the same weight to both' and 'the combined operation' of these two norms is envisaged to provide 'a balanced normative setting' to be used on a case by case basis by the States concerned.[369] This means, *inter alia*, that these norms shall constrain the conduct and protect the legitimate interest of all States, irrespective of their geographical location on a watercourse, on an equal footing.

Also it should be noted that, as the ILC's commentary to 1994 Draft Articles explains, a 'use which causes significant harm to human health and safety is understood to be inherently inequitable and unreasonable'.[370] In turn, the ILC's commentary to the 2001 Draft Articles on the prevention of transboundary harm from hazardous activities provides a useful clarification on the meaning of the word 'significant':

> [T]he Commission is aware that it is not without ambiguity and that a determination has to be made in each specific case. It involves more factual considerations than legal determination. It is to be understood that 'significant' is something more than 'detectable,' but need not be at the level of 'serious' or 'substantial'. The harm must lead to a real detrimental

367 ILC Commentary to 1994 Draft Articles.

368 Stephen C. McCaffrey, 'The contribution of the UN Convention on the law of the non-navigational uses of international watercourses' (2001) 1 International Journal of Global Environmental Issues at 253–254. See also McCaffrey, *The law of international watercourses – Non-navigational uses* at 370–371, Tanzi and Arcari, *The UN Convention on the Law of International Watercourses* at 176–179, Salman M.A. Salman, 'The Helsinki Rules, the UN Watercourses Convention and the Berlin Rules: Perspectives on international water law' (2007) 23 International Journal of Water Resources Development 625–640. See ILA's 2004 Berlin Rules.

369 Tanzi and Arcari, *The UN Convention on the Law of International Watercourses* at 178–179.

370 ILC Commentary to 1994 Draft Articles at 104.

> effect on matters such as, for example, human health, industry, property, environment or agriculture in other States.[371]

The no-harm rule, requiring from the Parties a significant level of engagement, can be found in the treaty law relating to the environment under the auspices of the Commonwealth. Article 2 of the 1998 CIS Agreement on Transboundary Waters requires Parties 'to refrain from water management activities that may cause negative impact on environment, including water bodies', 'to take measures in order to prevent and eliminate surface and ground water pollution and depletion', and 'estimate damages caused to water bodies by use in a neighbouring state according to a unified methodology'.[372] As per the preambular recitals of the 1992 CIS Agreement on Environmental Interaction, 'economical and other activities within the territory of a state *shall* not cause harm to the environment, the quality of life and economic activities in other states'.[373]

In the Aral Sea basin, Article 3 of the 1992 Almaty Agreement requires its Parties 'to refrain from actions on their respective territories that might affect interests of other contracting Parties and cause them harm, lead to deviation from agreed volumes of water discharges and pollution of water sources'.[374] According to this provision's clear-cut formulation, its addressees must take all measures needed to ensure that no transboundary harm originates from their respective territories. It illustrates the application of a very strong level of expression. The article does not discuss nor provide guidance to establishing the threshold of harm incumbent upon states[375] such as whether significant,[376] appreciable,[377] substantial,[378] or serious[379] transboundary damage is

371 ILC Commentary to 2001 Draft articles at 165.

372 1998 CIS Agreement on Transboundary Waters, art 2.

373 1992 CIS Agreement on the Environmental Interaction.

374 1992 Almaty Agreement, art 3.

375 McCaffrey, *The law of international watercourses – Non-navigational uses* at 433, 435.

376 1997 UN Watercourses Convention, art 7.

377 Article 7 of the draft articles was adopted on first reading by the ILC in 1991. *Draft Articles on the Law of Non-navigational Uses of International Watercourses*, Report of the ILC on the Work of its Forty-third Session, UN. GAOR, 46th Sess, Supp (No 10), UN Doc A/46/10 (1991), reprinted in [1991] 2(2) YB. Int'l L Comm'n 1, at 66.

378 International Law Association, '*Helsinki Rules on the Uses of the Water of International Rivers*' (International Law Association, Helsinki 1966), reprinted in S Bogdanovic, *International law of water resources: Contribution of the International Law Association (1954–2000)* (Kluwer Law International, The Hague 2001) [1966 Helsinki Rules], art X.

379 Philippe Sands, 'Water and international law: Science and evidence in international litigation' (2010) 22 Environmental Law and Management 151–161; *Declaration of the UN*

prohibited. The prohibition of harm is not restricted to damage to the environment, but extends to 'the interests of other states', including an obligation to secure the agreed volumes of water flow and avoid water pollution. Arguably, it may imply that even when there are no physical spillovers, unilateral actions are illegal if they, for example, affect other states' economic interests.[380] The question may arise whether this provision indeed prohibits any transboundary harm, whether it in fact asks for the impossible.[381] The more plausible and internally consistent reading of this article in terms of the objective and purpose of the agreement suggests that this provision imposes significant limits on the *unilateral* actions of states within their jurisdictions and requires that any possibly harmful activity must be co-ordinated and concerted among the parties. This conclusion is supported by the way in which the title and preambular provisions of the agreement are formulated to reflect its spirit of 'joint management' and 'consolidation and coordination of actions'.[382]

Apart from the Almaty Agreement, the 1998 Environmental Cooperation Agreement requires Kazakhstan, the Kyrgyz Republic, and Uzbekistan to cooperate and 'coordinate their actions in building new facilities in frontier areas or in any areas that might have adverse transboundary impact'[383] 'with a view to attaining practical results'.[384] Finally, Article 9(3)(e) of the 2006 Sustainable Development Convention encourages States to set up rules and procedures concerning measures to be taken to prevent and reduce water pollution to a level that does not harm the territories of downstream countries.[385]

Treaties with Afghanistan also require the avoidance of harm arising from the use of frontier rivers. The 1958 Soviet-Afghan Frontier Treaty states in stringent terms: '[t]he location and direction of frontier watercourses shall as far as possible be preserved unchanged'; '[n]either Contracting Party shall cause an artificial displacement of river beds'; '[m]ineral deposits in the immediate vicinity of the frontier line shall be so prospected or worked and agricultural

Conference on Environment and Development (Rio de Janeiro, 13 June 1992) *in Report of the United Nations Conference on Environment and Development*, Annex I, UN Doc A/Conf.151/26 (Vol. I) reprinted in 31 ILM 876 (1992).

380 Daniel Bodansky, 'What's so bad about unilateral action to protect the environment?' (2000) 11 European Journal of International Law 339–347, at 342.

381 See Brunnée and Toope, at 26–27.

382 Jacobson and Brown Weiss, 'A Framework for analysis' at 4. See also *Case Concerning Military and Paramilitary Activities in and Against Nicaragua* (*Nicaragua v. United States of America*) Merits, Judgment of 27 June 1986, [1986] ICJ Rep 14, at para 275.

383 1998 Environmental Cooperation Agreement, art 2.

384 Ibid, preamble.

385 2006 Framework Convention on Sustainable Development in CA, art 9(3)(e).

operations so conducted as not to harm the territory of the other Party'.[386] More to the point, Article 19 states that the Parties shall reach an agreement before introducing any changes that may influence the flow of water or cause other damages. Specifically,

1. Existing bridges, dams, dikes and other similar structures on frontier watercourses shall be preserved and may be used.
2. Bridges, dams and other similar structures likely to hinder navigation or influence the flow of water shall not be erected on frontier watercourses except by agreement between the two Parties.
3. New dikes which might affect the flow of water and the state of the banks, and also cause damage thereto, may not be erected on frontier watercourses except by agreement between the two Parties.
4. Should the need arise for reconstruction or demolition of any installations on frontier rivers that might change the water level of those rivers, the necessary work may not be undertaken without the consent of the other Party.[387]

In summary, all relevant instruments seem to cast the no-harm rule in forceful language ('shall, 'under an obligation', and 'requires') whereas the level of the norm's determinacy, specifying these actions, varies. It requires the countries of the Aral Sea basin to meet a due diligence standard of conduct in the use of international watercourses under customary law as reflected in the 1997 UN Watercourses and the 1992 UNECE Water Conventions. The content of 'due diligence' cannot be distilled in abstraction and 'cannot be reduced to a clear and accurate definition which might serve as an objective standard for deciding, *regardless of the circumstances*, whether a State was "diligent" [emphasis added].[388] This is 'an eminently flexible concept that is designed to take into account the facts and circumstances of each particular case'.[389] It thus refers to a number of elements such as the relevant state's capacity, the risk that harm is caused or the degree of care, and the nature of the interest to which the harm is caused considered in the context of all the circumstances of the case.[390] The

386 1958 Soviet-Afghan Frontier Treaty, arts 9(1), 9(3) and 24(2).

387 Ibid, art 19.

388 Garcia Amador, at 122.

389 McCaffrey, *The law of international watercourses – Non-navigational uses* at 373.

390 The *Alabama* tribunal defines 'due diligence' as 'a diligence proportioned to the magnitude of the subject and to dignity and strength of the power which is exercising it' and thus relates it to the nature of the activity and the relevant state's capacity (a developed country would often be held to a higher standard of care than a developing one). See

ILC's commentary provides, for instance, that '[t]he State may be responsible [...] for not enacting necessary legislation, for not enforcing its laws [...] or for not preventing or terminating all illegal activity, or for not punishing the person responsible for it'.[391]

Further, the existing treaty law in the Aral Sea basin incorporates the no-harm rule in a way imposing significant restrictions on the activities within the territories of states *unless* these actions coordinated with the affected parties. The latter point indicates that by committing to the 1997 UN Watercourses Convention and the 1992 UNECE Convention, the Aral Sea basin countries will not be under any stricter requirements than arise for them from the existing treaties. At the same time, the 1997 UN Watercourses Convention can introduce more clarity in the legal relationship between the no-harm rule and the equitable and reasonable use principle, which is lacking in the existing applicable legal framework, and help to decipher the requirement of 'consolidation and coordination of action' essentially through its procedural system discussed below.

4.2.3 *Obligations Related to Environmental Protection*

The obligations related to the protection of international watercourses and their ecosystems are to be found in a range of customary and treaty obligations of the Aral Sea basin states.

With respect to the 1997 UN Watercourses Convention, Tanzi and Arcari observe that 'the environmental protection factor runs through virtually all the provisions of the convention',[392] starting with the notion of 'system of waters' used in Article 2. Given the unquestionable customary status of equitable and reasonable use principle, the Convention's provisions that embody the objective of protection of the watercourse and the principle of sustainability[393] within the framework of equitable and reasonable use clearly reflect a general

Alabama Claims Arbitration, reported in (1872) 1 Moore, International Arbitrations 495 at 572–573. The ILC Commentary to Article 3 of the 2001 Draft, at 155, para. 17, states: 'The main elements of the obligation of due diligence involved in the duty of prevention could be thus stated: the degree of care in question is that expected of a good Government'. Article 10 to the ILC Draft, at 374, also sets out factors to be taken into account, including the degree of risk of significant harm, the importance of activity, the degree of preparedness to contribute to the costs of prevention, the economic viability of the activity in relation to the costs of prevention, and the standards of prevention. See also Nollkaemper, *The legal regime for transboundary water pollution* at 44.

391 ILC Commentary to 1994 Draft Articles at 103.

392 Tanzi and Arcari, *The UN Convention on the Law of International Watercourses* at 225.

393 ILC Commentary to 1994 Draft Articles at 97.

duty of states and therefore are binding for the Aral Sea basin states.[394] Further, Tanzi considers that the concept of sustainability has played an essential role in reconciling 'the long-standing conflict between the "equitable and reasonable utilization" and the "no-harm" doctrines with respect to which [it] appears to be the lowest common denominator'.[395] Article 21(2) as a special application of the general principles contained in Article 5 [equitable utilization] and 7 [no harm][396] requires the Parties to exercise due diligence and to cooperate to

> prevent, reduce and control the pollution of an international watercourse that may cause significant harm to other watercourse States or to their environment, including harm to human health or safety, to the use of the waters for any beneficial purpose or to the living resources of the watercourse.

To clarify the relationship between these norms, McCaffrey explains that 'a use becomes inequitable and unreasonable to the extent that it causes pollution harm to other watercourse states'.[397]

Further, Articles 22 and 23 forcefully impose other due diligence requirements on watercourse states to take all of the necessary measures of which they are capable, financially and technologically concerning the introduction of alien species and protection and preservation of marine environment, respectively. Article 22 establishes rather ambiguous threshold of the permissible introduction of alien or new species into an international watercourse by referring to 'effects detrimental to the ecosystem of the watercourse resulting in significant harm to other watercourse States'.[398]

---

394 1997 UN Watercourses Convention.

395 Attila Tanzi, 'Reducing the gap between international water law and human rights law: The UNECE Protocol on Water and Health' (2010) 12 International Community Law Review 267–285, at 270.

396 ILC Commentary to 1994 Draft Articles at 122, para. 3.

397 McCaffrey, *The law of international watercourses – Non-navigational uses* at 385–386.

398 1997 UN Watercourses Convention, art 22 states that 'Watercourse States shall take all measures necessary to prevent the introduction of species, alien or new, into an international watercourse which may have effects detrimental to the ecosystem of the watercourse resulting in significant harm to other watercourse States'. 1997 UN Watercourses Convention, art 23 states that 'Watercourse States shall, individually and, where appropriate, in cooperation with other States, take all measures with respect to an international watercourse that are necessary to protect and preserve the marine environment, including estuaries, taking into account generally accepted international rules and standards'.

Finally, inspired by strong support in state practice, the 1997 UN Watercourses Convention introduced in mandatory terms a general obligation to protect and preserve the ecosystems of international watercourse that seeks to 'enhance a comprehensive and "holistic" approach to the issues of the protection of international watercourse'.[399] The ILC's commentary treats 'protection' as a specific application of the optimal and sustainable use of an international watercourse 'consistent with the adequate protection thereof' in Article 5 on equitable and reasonable use, and it refers to 'preservation' as to be applied to 'freshwater ecosystems that are in pristine or unspoiled condition' which are to 'be protected in such a way as to maintain them as much as possible in their natural state'.[400] Despite increasing support for the ecosystem approach in modern treaty practice and the work of international organisations, legal scholars are careful in attributing customary status to the obligation to protect and preserve the ecosystems of international watercourses, while treating it as a 'new', 'emerging', or 'developing' obligation.[401] Still, it is apparent that the 1997 UN Watercourses Convention provides an essential basis for the protection of international watercourses and their ecosystems in stringent terms, while assuming that more specific standards and rules will be developed for individual international watercourses at a basin level.

The 1992 UNECE Water Convention takes one step further in the protection of international watercourses and their ecosystems, establishing sound rules for the Parties to 'take all appropriate measures' in order 'to ensure that transboundary waters are used with the aim of ecologically sound and rational water management, conservation of water resources and environmental

399 Tanzi and Arcari, *The UN Convention on the Law of International Watercourses* at 238.

400 ILC Commentary to 1994 Draft Articles at 119.

401 See McCaffrey, *The law of international watercourses – Non-navigational uses* at 257 and 462 ('there is now at least an emerging obligation to protect international watercourses systems and their ecosystems against degradation', [w]hile this obligation may be described as 'new' or 'emerging', its basic elements are already part of general international law. The obligation, as formulated in Article 20 of the UN Convention, simply reflects advances in scientific knowledge about the interrelationships of natural systems); Birnie, Boyle and Redgwell, *International law and the environment* at 559–560. For the opposite view, see ILA's 2004 Berlin Rules at 28. The Berlin Rules were adopted by the International Law Association in 2004 as a result of revision of the Helsinki and other International Law Association Rules on International Water Resources. Four members of the ILA Water Resources Committee, namely Slavko Bogdanovic, Charles Bourne, Stefano Burchi, Patricia Wouters, submitted a dissenting opinion, stating that the Rules 'mark a radical and unwarranted departure from existing customary law'. See also Salman Salman, 'The Helsinki Rules, the UN Watercourses Convention and the Berlin Rules' on the status and role of the Berlin Rules.

protection', and 'to ensure conservation and, where necessary, restoration of ecosystems',[402] and providing a definition of 'transboundary impact' that encompasses environmental considerations.[403] The Convention stipulates that principles such as the precautionary principle, the polluter-pays principle, and intergenerational equity[404] shall guide the Parties in their implementation of the above measures, and it calls for measures to promote sustainable water resources management, including the application of the ecosystem approach.[405] Article 3 requires the development of limits on pollution discharges based on 'best available technology' or 'best environmental practices'. The Riparian Parties shall cooperate 'in order to develop harmonized policies, programmes and strategies...aimed at the protection of the environment of transboundary waters'.[406] The Convention's annexes further help to specify the content of due diligence requirement to protect the environment by defining the term 'best available technology' (Annex I), and providing guidelines for developing best environmental practices (Annex II), and water-quality objectives and criteria (Annex III). Further clarification on the ecosystem approach to water management can be found in the UNECE guidelines and recommendations. Thus, the 1993 Guidelines on the Ecosystem Approach in Water Management promotes the idea that the river basin should be considered as an entire ecosystem and water should not be managed in isolation from other ecosystem components, such as land, air, living resources and humans, present in a river basin.[407] Another relevant policy instrument is the 2006 Recommendations on Payments for Ecosystem Services in Integrated Water Resources Management (IWRM) seeks to provide guidance on the establishment and use of payment for ecosystem services to implement IWRM through

---

402 1992 UNECE Water Convention, art 2(2).

403 Ibid, art 1(2) reads,

> 'Transboundary impact' means any significant adverse effect on the environment resulting from a change in the conditions of transboundary waters caused by a human activity, the physical origin of which is situated wholly or in part within an area under the jurisdiction of a Party, within an area under the jurisdiction of another Party. Such effects on the environment include effects on human health and safety, flora, fauna, soil, air, water, climate, landscape and historical monuments or other physical structures or the interaction among these factors; they also include effects on the cultural heritage or socio-economic conditions resulting from alterations to those factors.

404 Ibid, art 2(5).

405 Ibid, art 3(1)(i).

406 Ibid, art 2(6).

407 'UNECE Guidelines on the ecosystem approach in water management' (1993) UN Doc ECE/ENVWA/31.

the promotion of the protection, restoration and sustainable use of water-related ecosystems – such as forests and wetlands – at all levels.[408]

The practice of international courts and arbitrations also illustrate increased attention to environmental considerations. Thus, in the *Gabčíkovo-Nagymaros case*, the ICJ ruled that, whenever necessary for the application of a treaty, 'new norms have to be taken into consideration, and [...] new standards given proper weight, not only when States contemplate new activities but also when continuing with activities begun in the past'.[409] In the *Iron Rhine Railway*, the Arbitral Tribunal found that 'international environmental law has relevance to the relations between the Parties' and applied contemporary concepts of customary international environmental law to treaties dating back to the nineteenth century.[410] Finally, in the recent *Indus Waters Kishenganga Arbitration*, the Court of Arbitration also interpreted and applied the 1960 Indus Waters Treaty 'in light of the customary international principles for the protection of the environment in force today' to decided that India is under an obligation to construct and operate the Kishenganga Hydro-Electric Project (KHEP) in such a way as to maintain a minimum flow of water into the Kishenganga/Neelum River below the KHEP at all times.[411] Indeed, an obligation to maintain a minimum flow of water of sufficient quality and quantity within an international watercourse in order to safeguard the ecological, chemical and physical integrity of a freshwater ecosystem finds considerable support in state practice.[412]

In addition to customary norms, the treaties relevant to the Aral Sea basin also stipulate obligations related to environmental protection. Under the Commonwealth umbrella, the 1992 CIS Agreement on Environmental Interaction, 'based on understanding of the integrity and indivisibility of the environment', stipulates in stringent terms that 'the Contracting Parties within their territories shall establish science-based norms for the inclusion of natural resources in economic and other activities and shall limit their irretrievable

408 'UNECE Recommendations on PES'.

409 *Gabčíkovo-Nagymaros case,* 7 at 78, para 140.

410 *Arbitration regarding the Iron Rhine Railway* (*Belgium v Netherlands*) Award, 24 May 2005, PCA Award Series (2007) at 59.

411 *Indus Water Kishenganga Arbitration* (*Pakistan v India*), Permanent Court of Arbitration, Partial Award of 18 February 2013, para 452 and Final Award of 20 December 2013, at 43.

412 See eg 1909 US-Canada Boundary Waters Treaty; Agreement on the Cooperation for the Sustainable Development of the Mekong River Basin (signed 5 April 1995) 34 ILM 864 (1995); Agreement for the Protection of the Rhine Against Chemical Pollution (signed 3 December 1976) 1979 UNTS 406. See also Albert E. Utton and John Utton, 'The international law of minimum stream flows', (1999) 10 Colorado Journal of International Environmental Law and Policy 7.

[consumptive] withdrawals, taking into account the need to ensure a universal ecological security and wellbeing'.[413] The terms of the 1998 CIS Agreement on Transboundary Waters require more engagement to achieve the environmental protection objectives. Using mandatory language, the instrument prescribes a set of general substantive and procedural measures for cooperation over 'protection of water bodies' referred to as 'an activity or a set of measures aimed at conservation and restoration of water bodies, including remedial measures for water pollution, clogging and depletion, negative economic intervention into water regime of rivers, water body and groundwater source'.[414] Among those, 'the Parties are obliged to refrain from water management activities that may cause negative impact on the environment, including water bodies' and 'to take measures in order to prevent and eliminate surface and ground water pollution and depletion'.[415]

The sub-regional agreements explicitly recognise the Aral Sea itself and its deltas as a legitimate water user. Article 1 of the 1993 Kzyl-Orda Agreement states that a 'common objective' of its Parties is to ensure that water flows to the Aral Sea in order to 'sustain[...] its lowered, but stable, ecologically acceptable, levels and by this means preserve[...] the Sea as an object of nature[...]'.[416] Moreover, a 1988 Decree of the Council of Ministers of the USSR established the requirements of minimum flows to the deltas of the Amudarya and Syrdarya basins and to the Aral Sea.[417]

In terms of additional ecosystem-related obligations, Article 3 of the 1993 Kzyl-Orda Agreement provides – at a lesser level of engagement – that 'common objectives' relating to the protection of the environment include the maintenance of appropriate water quality, restoration of degraded ecosystems in the Aral Sea region, and the development and implementation of a coordinated strategy for social and economic development that meets environmental security objectives for peoples of the basin.[418] This provision even appears to go beyond the provisions on protection and preservation envisaged in the

413 1992 CIS Agreement on the Environmental Interaction, preamble and art 2.

414 1998 CIS Agreement on Transboundary Waters, art 1.

415 Ibid, art 2.

416 1993 Kzyl-Orda Agreement, art 1.

417 A 1988 Decree of the Council of Ministers of the USSR on Measures for Radical Improvement of Ecological and Sanitary Situation in the Region of the Aral Sea, Enhancing the Efficiency and Use to Strengthen the Protection of the Water and Land Resources in its Basin. According to the Decree minimum inflows to the deltas of the Amudarya and Syrdarya and to the Aral Sea (including drainage waters) are as follows: 8.7 km^3 in 1990; 11 km^3 in 1995; 15 km^3 in 2000; and 20 km^3 by 2005.

418 1993 Kzyl-Orda Agreement, art 3.

1997 UN Watercourses Convention by encouraging the restoration of degraded ecosystems. But despite its positive intentions, the 1993 Kzyl-Orda Agreement's provisions seem to be expressed in rather declaratory terms or as overall goals rather than as precisely defined obligations. Nonetheless, they can be viewed as programmatic when read together with the title of the agreement ('On Joint Actions to Resolve the Problems…').[419]

According to the 1998 Environmental Cooperation Agreement, the parties shall cooperate in a wide range of environmental protection areas, including transboundary water resources conservation, rational use, and pollution prevention.[420] The 2006 Framework Convention on Sustainable Development, when it enters into force, will require parties 'to ensure effective environmental protection for sustainable development in Central Asia, including […] reduction and prevention of transboundary harm to the environment'.[421] The emphasis on effectiveness seems to suggest a stronger level of expression.

As per relations with Afghanistan, the 1958 Treaty between the USSR and Afghanistan requires the competent authorities of both Contracting Parties to 'take the necessary measures to protect the frontier waters from pollution by acids and waste products and from fouling by any other means'.[422] It further prohibits the nationals of the Counteracting Parties to fish in frontier waters using 'explosive, poisonous or narcotic substances that result in the destruction or mutilation of fish'.[423]

In addition to watercourse-specific treaties, a wide range of multilateral environmental agreements stipulate more general – but still binding on the Aral Sea basin states – provisions for environmental protection and preservation that contribute substantially to the protection of the ecosystems of international watercourses in Central Asia. The Ramsar Convention,[424] which arguably includes rivers in its broad definition of wetlands,[425] provides a

---

419 See C.G. Weeramantry, *Universalising international law* (Leiden/Boston, Martinus Nijhoff Publishers 2004) at 21 (observing that 'The Treaty brought into existence a certain regime which results from all of its provisions in conjunction. It forms a complete whole, the different provisions of which cannot be dissociated from others and considered apart by themselves').

420 1998 Environmental Cooperation Agreement, art 2.

421 2006 Framework Convention on Sustainable Development in CA, art 3.

422 1958 Soviet-Afghan Frontier Treaty, art 13.

423 Ibid, art 22(1)(a).

424 Ramsar Convention.

425 Ibid, art 1 defines 'wetlands' as 'areas of marsh, fen, peatland or water, whether natural or artificial, permanent or temporary, with water that is static or flowing, fresh, brackish or salt, including areas of marine water the depth of which at low tide does not exceed six metres'.

cooperative framework for the wise use of wetlands[426] and recognises in its preambular provisions the 'fundamental ecological functions of wetlands as regulators of water regimes and as habitats supporting a characteristic flora and fauna, especially waterfowl'.[427] With respect to transboundary aspects, it stipulates that '[t]he Contracting Parties shall consult with each other about implementing obligations [...] where a water system is shared by Contracting Parties'.[428] The Guidelines adopted by the 2002 Resolution of the Eighth Conference of the Contracting Parties encourage those parties with wetlands lying in shared river basins to apply the guidelines for the allocation and management of water to maintaining the ecological function of wetlands within the context of the management of water allocation in transboundary basins.[429] It should be noted that during the negotiation of the Syrdarya draft agreement the delegation of Uzbekistan has raised concerns about the status and water requirements of the Aydar Arnasai Lakes System that was formed in its territory due to anthropogenic activities on the sub-region's transboundary rivers.[430] Since the Aydar Arnasai Lakes System was registered as a Ramsar

426 The wise use of wetlands, the cornerstone of the Convention, has been defined first by the Conference of the Parties in 1987 as the 'sustainable use of wetlands for the benefit of mankind in a way that is compatible with maintaining the natural properties of the ecosystem'. This definition was revised in Resolution IX.1 Annex A (2005) as follows: 'Wise use of wetlands is the maintenance of their ecological character, achieved through the implementation of ecosystem approaches, within the context of sustainable development'. See Recommendation 3.3. Wise Use of Wetlands, 3rd meeting of the Conference of the Contracting Parties to the Convention on Wetlands, Regina, Canada, 27 May – 05 June 1987; Resolution IX.1 Annex A, 9th Meeting of the Contracting Parties to the Convention on Wetlands, Kampala, 2005; Ramsar FAQs: What is the 'wise use' of wetlands? Online: <http://www.ramsar.org/cda/en/ramsar-about-faqs-what-is-wise-use/main/ramsar/1-36-37%5E7724_4000_0__> accessed 15 January 2014.

427 Ramsar Convention, preamble.

428 Ibid, art 5.

429 *Guidelines for the Allocation and Management of Water for Maintaining the Ecological Functions of Wetlands*, Resolution VIII.1, 8th Meeting of the Conference of the Contracting Parties to the Convention on Wetlands (Ramsar, Iran, 1971) Valencia, Spain, 18–26 November 2002. Online: <http://www.ramsar.org/pdf/res/keyresviii01e.pdf> accessed 22 December 2013. See also *Guidelines for International Cooperation Under the Ramsar Convention*, Resolution VII.19, 7th Meeting of the Conference of the Contracting Parties to the Convention on Wetlands, San José, Costa Rica, 10–18 May 1999. Online: <http://www.ramsar.org/pdf/res/keyresvii.19e.pdf> accessed 22 December 2013.

430 The Aydar Arnasai Lakes System (the AALS) is the largest reservoir of Uzbekistan, consisting of freshwater lakes situated in the middle stream of the Syrdarya river and on the irrigated massif of the Golodnaya steppe and the Kyzylkum desert. It was formed as a

site in 2008,[431] the provisions of the Convention are directly applicable to the situation.

Another multilateral environmental agreement that envisages binding obligations related to international watercourses is the Convention on Biodiversity.[432] It states that the Parties shall 'as far as possible and as appropriate' 'integrate…the conservation and sustainable use of biological diversity into relevant sectoral or cross-sectoral plans, programmes and policies';[433] 'promote the protection of ecosystems, natural habitats and the maintenance of viable populations of species in natural surroundings';[434] 'rehabilitate and restore degraded ecosystems and promote the recovery of threatened species, *inter alia*, through the development and implementation of plans or other management strategies';[435] 'prevent the introduction of, control or eradicate those alien species which threaten ecosystems, habitats or species';[436] 'cooperate with other Contracting Parties, directly or, where appropriate, through competent international organisations, in respect of areas beyond national jurisdiction and on other matters of mutual interest, for the conservation and sustainable use of biological diversity'.[437] Similar to the Ramsar Convention, the Conference of the Parties to the Convention on Biodiversity undertakes significant efforts to specify the deliberately qualifying language of the treaty provisions.[438]

---

result of emergency dump of water from the Chardara reservoir in 1969 (20.1 km^3). In recent decades, Kazakhstan and Uzbekistan were forced to divert water into the AALS regularly, due to change in the operating regime of the Toktogul reservoir resulted in a substantial shift in flow patterns, with the peak of water releases in winter rather than in summer. A low carrying capacity of the riverbed downstream of the Chardara reservoir (400 to 600 m^3/sec in winter) did not allow to direct flow to the Aral Sea. Today, the AALS's size is about 42 km^3. See The Aydar Arnasai Lake System (Uzbekistan), Information Sheet on Ramsar Wetlands – 2008 Ramsar Uzbekistan 2UZ002. Online: <http://ramsar.wetlands.org>. G. Glysin, 'From Aral to Arnasay', in Ecological Almanac Simply Writing on Environment (in Russian 2005). Online: <http://kungrad.com/aral/book/arnasai/≥accessed 22 December 2013.

431 'The Aydar Arnasai Lakes System' (July 2008), Ramsar site No 1841. Online: <http://ramsar.wetlands.org> accessed 22 December 2013.

432 Convention on Biodiversity pursues the conservation of biological diversity, the sustainable use of its components and the fair and equitable sharing of the benefits arising out of the utilisation of genetic resources.

433 Ibid, art 6(b).

434 Ibid, art 8(d).

435 Convention on Biodiversity, art 8(f).

436 Ibid, art 8(h).

437 Ibid, art 5.

438 See 'Conference of the Parties Decisions'. Online: <http://www.cbd.int/decisions/cop/>accessed 22 December 2013.

In summary, the obligations to protect international watercourses and their ecosystems are reflected in a range of multilateral, regional, and sub-regional agreements establishing due diligence requirements for the Aral Sea basin states. The 1997 UN Watercourses Convention casts the relevant requirements in stringent terms, while assuming that more specific standards and rules will be developed for individual international watercourses at a basin level. The 1992 UNECE Water Convention introduces the widest spectrum of obligations on the matter in terms of their stringency and determinacy. Relevant provisions of multilateral environmental agreements that established in mandatory language, albeit 'softened' by such phrases as 'where appropriate', 'should be guided', 'promote', and 'as far as possible and as appropriate', are made more specific through decisions of the conference of the parties and the work of the respective scientific and technical bodies. In this respect, close linkages across treaties seem to be essential for effective implementation of the obligations related to environmental protection. The language of the sub-regional agreements is relatively precise in laying down guiding principles, but needs further specification of the practical measures to be taken, including developing national laws and policies to implement the stated environmental objectives. In addition to individual endeavours, procedural cooperation between States and through international river commissions is an important means of giving concrete content to the stated obligations and ensuring that these are consistently implemented and complied with.

4.3 Substantive Norms within a System of International Water Law

This chapter began the task of evaluating the norms of international law as applied to the transboundary waters in the Aral Sea basin through focusing on their determinacy and stringency. It explored the provisions related to the scope of regulation and the main substantive norms operating in the field, namely the principle of equitable and reasonable use, the no-harm rule, and obligations related to environmental protection of international watercourses.

By exploring the determinacy of substantive norms, the chapter has demonstrated that open-textured and elastic substantive norms prevail in international water law. For the most part, these substantive norms operate within a due diligence framework. The due diligence nature of obligations—along with the corresponding concept of 'appropriateness' of the measures—implies that a significant degree of flexibility and relativity must be applied to both contents and time-frame of the conduct of the parties.[439] Accordingly, textually

439 'UNECE *Guide to Implementing the Convention*'.

indeterminate standards such as equity, reasonableness, and appropriateness that dominate international water law as well as other areas of international law generally make it more difficult to define certain obligations and verify their fulfilment. However, the fact that substantive norms are generally couched in abstract terms does not affect the core of the rights and duties that arise therefrom. Instead, the determination of a required standard of conduct that flows from the principle of equitable and reasonable use, the no-harm rule, and the obligations to protect international watercourses is tied up with the specific context of the norm application and contingent upon the existence of an adequate procedural and institutional system in place. Consistency and objectivity in interpretation and application of contextual norms can be achieved through further specification (contextualisation) of norms, institutionalised decision-making process, or adjudication.[440] As the analysis suggests, however, the adequate level of specification of norms and their coherent interpretation with reference to each other have not been achieved in the context of the Aral Sea basin yet.

Addressing the stringency of norms was useful to an understanding of the existence of the different levels of 'control intention'[441] embedded in the norm-text. As evidenced in this chapter, the equitable and reasonable use principle and the no-harm rule, which represent well-established and highly contextual customary norms of international water law, are expressed in terms situated at the mandatory end of scale. At the same time, the obligations to protect ecosystems are mostly construed as requirements which 'more actively work towards' environmental objectives in the UNECE and the Commonwealth agreements and as programmatic obligations in the subregional agreements.[442]

By focusing on these properties of norms, and what flows from them, the chapter draws attention to the danger of assessing norms with no reference to their legal and factual context, the practice wide-spread in the Aral Sea basin as well as among social and political science scholarship globally. As McLachlan

440 As Patterson explained,

> Meaning—the basis of objectivity—is made possible by the harmony in action and judgment of participants in legal practice over time. Most importantly, it is in virtue of what participants in legal practice have in common that normativity and objectivity are possible.

Dennis Patterson, 'Interpretation in law' (2005) 42 San Diego Law Review 685–710 at 626. See also Franck, Chayes and Chayes, and Abbott et al.

441 Bodansky at 104, and Miles Kahler, 'Legalization as strategy: The Asia-Pacific case' (2000) 54 International Organization 549–571.

442 See The Arbitral Tribunal's hierarchy of obligations in *OSPAR Award.*

rightly commented, '[l]egal texts only make sense within the context of the system that gives them authority and meaning'.[443] This sentiment has been partly demonstrated in the foregoing analysis through focus on the interrelationship between norms.

Firstly, although the principle of equitable and reasonable use, the no-harm rule, and an emerging obligation to protect ecosystems qualify as independent norms in the field of international watercourses; these complement each other and work in tandem. Hence, understanding how these substantive norms relate to each other is a prerequisite for comprehending the nature of international water law and subsequently evaluating its performance and effectiveness. Thus, the practice in the Aral Sea basin suggests that riparian countries fail to comprehend international water law in this way and consequently substantiate their positions and claims based on the solid interpretation of customary and treaty provisions related to their case. Rather, they refer to the principle of equitable and reasonable use or the no-harm rule, without engaging into detailed inquiry of the normative content of these norms.

Secondly, the mutual support and complementarities of norms at the global, regional, and sub-regional levels are additional features of an international legal system that should be taken into account. For instance, whereas the sub-regional agreements typically stand as a *lex specialis* between the parties, the 1997 UN Watercourses and 1992 UNECE Water Conventions, which in part reflect customary international law, can also provide a framework for their interpretation, if the former do not comprehensively define the rights and obligations of the parties and serve as the sole ground for action in cases not covered by precise norms.[444] Again this opportunity has not been fully used in the context of the Aral Sea basin.

Finally, due to their complex and indeterminate nature, the substantive norms of international water law necessitate that a sound procedural and institutional system is in place to interpret, implement, and develop these norms. Clearly, the highly procedural and contextual character of substantive norms makes their operation in isolation impossible, and accordingly the assessment of their 'individual' effectiveness hardly justifiable. Still, the role of substantive norms in laying down normative benchmarks to follow is unquestionable.

The next chapter considers a set of provisions related to procedural cooperation, compliance and dispute settlement applicable to transboundary waters of the Aral Sea basin through the lenses of norm determinacy and stringency.

---

443 McLachlan, 'The principle of systemic integration and Article 31(3)(c) of the Vienna Convention' at 286.

444 Rieu-Clarke and Loures.

CHAPTER 5

Procedural System of Transboundary Water Cooperation in the Aral Sea Basin

*Norm Properties**

This chapter continues the examination of norms that govern transboundary water relations in the Aral Sea basin through the lenses of norm determinacy and stringency. The foregoing analysis of the substantive norms has shown that cooperation is constitutive to the equitable and reasonable use principle, no-significant harm, and environmental protection and imperative for giving them effect. The ILC designated a separate article to the general duty to cooperate in the 1997 UN Watercourses Convention couched in stringent terms and establishing an objective of interstate cooperation that of 'attaining optimal utilization and adequate protection of an international watercourse' and the basis of such cooperation that is 'sovereign equality, territorial integrity, mutual benefit and good faith'.[445] Various agreements relating to transboundary watercourses in the Aral Sea basin call for cooperation between the Parties, including the 1992 Almaty Agreement, the 1998 Syrdarya Agreement and many

* This chapter has drawn upon material from within Dinara Ziganshina, 'Procedural system of transboundary water cooperation in the Aral Sea Basin' in A. Kibariglu et all (eds.) *Water Law and Cooperation in the Euphrates-Tigrus Region: A Comparative and Interdisciplinary Approach* (Martinus Nijhoff Publishers, 2013) © reproduced with permission.

445 1997 UN Watercourses Convention, art 8 (General obligation to cooperate) reads,

> 1. Watercourse States shall cooperate on the basis of sovereign equality, territorial integrity, mutual benefit and good faith in order to attain optimal utilization and adequate protection of an international watercourse.
> 2. In determining the manner of such cooperation, watercourse States may consider the establishment of joint mechanisms or commissions, as deemed necessary by them, to facilitate cooperation on relevant measures and procedures in the light of experience gained through cooperation in existing joint mechanisms and commissions in various regions.

See also 1992 UNECE Water Convention , art 6(2) that states,

> The Riparian Parties shall cooperate on the basis of equality and reciprocity, in particular through bilateral and multilateral agreements, in order to develop harmonized policies, programmes and strategies covering the relevant catchment areas, or parts thereof, aimed at the prevention, control and reduction of transboundary impact and aimed at the protection of the environment of transboundary waters or the environment influenced by such waters, including the marine environment.

 | DOI 10.1163/9789004274266_006

others.[446] The 1994 ILC Commentary stresses that, within the law of international watercourses, the duty to cooperate provides 'an important basis for the attainment and maintenance of an equitable allocation of the uses and benefits of the watercourse and for the smooth functioning of the procedural rules'.[447] Being an autonomous legal obligation itself, the general duty to cooperate regarding transboundary waters also translates into specific procedural obligations to establish joint bodies, to exchange information with riparian states, to consult with each other, to notify regarding proposed activities, to conduct transboundary impact assessments, and to work together in emergency situations.[448]

The purpose of this chapter is to explore whether these procedural obligations are couched in stringent and precise terms as to establish a required standard of conduct for the Aral Sea basin countries. Besides, the chapter studies the determinacy and stringency of the provisions related to compliance and dispute settlement to get a whole picture of the legal regime in the basin. As was argued in Chapter 2, the norms expressed in stringent and precise language influence the ability of law to generate behavioural expectations as the very sense of the legal function.

5.1 Cooperation through Joint Bodies

It is widely recognised that transboundary water management is most effectively accomplished through joint bodies established by the states concerned.[449] Nonetheless, customary law does not oblige the riparian countries

---

446 See eg 1992 Almaty Agreement; 1996 Chardjev Agreement; 1998 Syrdarya Agreement; 2006 Framework Convention on Sustainable Development in CA, art 5(1) states that the Parties 'shall cooperate in the spirit of global and regional partnership'.

447 ILC Commentary to 1994 Draft Articles at 105 para 2.

448 See generally McCaffrey, *The law of international watercourses – Non-navigational uses*; Charles Bourne, 'Procedure in the development of international drainage basins' (1972) 22 University of Toronto Law Journal 172–206; Charles Bourne, 'Procedure in the development of international drainage basins: The duty to consult and to negotiate' (1972) 10 Canadian Yearbook of International Law 212–234; McIntyre, 'The proceduralisation and growing maturity of international water law'; Vinogradov, Wouters and Jones, *Transforming potential conflict into cooperation potential*; Tanzi and Arcari, *The UN Convention on the Law of International Watercourses*.

449 McCaffrey writes that the 'management of international watercourse systems through joint institutions is not only an increasingly common phenomenon, but also a form of cooperation between watercourse states that is almost indispensable if anything

to set up a joint commission, which is reflected in the hortatory language of the 1997 UN Watercourses Convention on the *possibility* of establishing a joint management mechanism.[450] In contrast, according to the 1992 UNECE Water Convention, the riparian parties are under a strict obligation to establish joint bodies to foster bilateral and multilateral cooperation.[451] The 1992 UNECE Water Convention further spells out the basic tasks of these bodies.[452]

---

approaching optimum utilisation and protection of the system of waters is to attained'. S McCaffrey, *Sixth Report on the Law of the Non-navigational Uses of International Watercourses*, [1990] 2(2) Y B Int'l L Comm'n, pt.2, at 41 UN Doc A/C.N.4/427 and Corr 1, and Add1, at para 7. See also *Pulp Mills case* (where the Court very clearly linked the functioning of cooperative institutions to the effective fulfilment of substantive obligations. It stated that the overall objective of optimum and rational utilisation 'must also be ensured through CARU, which constitutes "the joint machinery" necessary for its achievement' and, further, that '[i]n addition to its [procedural] role in that context, the functions of CARU relate to almost all aspects of the implementation of the substantive provisions of the 1975 Statute'.) In many river basins, the establishment of boundary or river basin commissions with different scope and functions is a widespread state practice, and an indispensable element in transboundary cooperation. See eg International Joint Commission established under 1909 US-Canada Boundary Waters Treaty; International Boundary Waters Commission is established under Treaty between the United States of America and Mexico relating to the Utilization of the Waters of the Colorado and Tijuana Rivers, and of the Rio Grande (Rio Bravo) from Fort Quitman, Texas, to the Gulf of Mexico [1944 US-Mexico Treaty] (adopted 3 February 1944, entered into force 8 November 1945) 3 UNTS 314, Washington; Niger Basin Authority is established by the Convention Creating the Niger Basin Authority, Faranah (signed 21 November 1980); Permanent Indus Commission is created under the Treaty between India and Pakistan Regarding the Use of the Waters of the Indus (adopted 19 September 1960, entered into force 1 April 1960) 419 UNTS 125 (1960).

450 1997 UN Watercourses Convention, art 24(1) states,

> Watercourse States shall, at the request of any of them, enter into consultations concerning the management of an international watercourse, which *may* include the establishment of a joint management mechanism. [emphasis added].

451 1992 UNECE Water Convention, art 9 provides, *inter alia*, that 'The Riparian Parties *shall* on the basis of equality and reciprocity enter into bilateral or multilateral agreements or other arrangements [...] and these agreements or arrangements *shall* provide for the establishment of joint bodies' [emphasis added].

452 Ibid, art 9(2) states,

> The tasks of these joint bodies shall be, *inter alia*, and without prejudice to relevant existing agreements or arrangements, the following: (a) To collect, compile and evaluate data in order to identify pollution sources likely to cause transboundary impact; (b) To elaborate joint monitoring programmes concerning water quality and

Treaties specific to the Aral Sea basin also envisage the need for joint bodies in forceful language. The 1992 Almaty Agreement established the Interstate Commission for Water Coordination (ICWC) in Central Asia as a body responsible for water management policy in the sub-region and subordinated to it two basin water organisations at the Amudarya and the Syrdarya rivers.[453] The ICWC is formed of the heads of water management authorities from the five Central Asian countries who meet on a quarterly basis to decide on water allocation and other issues. Also, the institutional framework of the ICWC and its executive bodies offers a forum for information exchange, capacity building, and conducting and coordinating research and pilot projects. As a matter of institutional improvement, the 1993 Kzyl-Orda treaty placed the ICWC under the newly established Interstate Council on the Aral Sea (ICAS).[454] In 1997, the ICAS was merged with the International Fund for Saving the Aral Sea (IFAS)[455]

---

quantity; (c) To draw up inventories and exchange information on the pollution sources mentioned in paragraph 2 (a) of this article; (d) To elaborate emission limits for waste water and evaluate the effectiveness of control programmes; (e) To elaborate joint water-quality objectives and criteria having regard to the provisions of article 3, paragraph 3 of this Convention, and to propose relevant measures for maintaining and, where necessary, improving the existing water quality; (f) To develop concerted action programmes for the reduction of pollution loads from both point sources (e.g. municipal and industrial sources) and diffuse sources (particularly from agriculture); (g) To establish warning and alarm procedures; (h) To serve as a forum for the exchange of information on existing and planned uses of water and related installations that are likely to cause transboundary impact; (i) To promote cooperation and exchange of information on the best available technology in accordance with the provisions of article 13 of this Convention, as well as to encourage cooperation in scientific research programmes; (j) To participate in the implementation of environmental impact assessments relating to transboundary waters, in accordance with appropriate international regulations.

453 1992 Almaty Agreement, arts 7 and 9.

454 1993 Kzyl-Orda Agreement, art 2.

455 The International Fund for saving the Aral Sea (IFAS) is an interstate organization founded to develop and finance environmental and scientific-practical projects and programs aimed at environmental improvement in areas under the impact of Aral disaster as well as at solving common socio-economic problems in the region. The IFAS has two intergovernmental bodies Interstate Commission for Water Coordination (ICWC) and Interstate Commission for Sustainable Development (ICSD). See 1999 IFAS Statute. In 2008, the IFAS was granted the observer status in the United Nations General Assembly. United Nations General Assembly *Resolution on Observer status for the International Fund for Saving the Aral Sea in the General Assembly* UN GAOR, 63d Sess, Agenda item 156, UN Doc A/C.6/63/L.13, 14 November 2008.

and its status was stipulated in a separate agreement.[456] In addition to the ICWC, the organisational structure of the IFAS includes the Interstate Commission for Sustainable Development (ICSD) that seeks to coordinate and manage sub-regional cooperation in the field of environment and sustainable development in Central Asia.[457] Both the ICWC and the ICSD have their own system of executive bodies to fulfill their respective functions.[458]

The instruments mandating the legal status and functions of the IFAS bodies and stipulating the coordination within its structure lack consistency and coherence that engender their determinacy. For example, the 1999 Agreement on the Status of IFAS and its Organisations lists the organisations of the IFAS, but does not clarify their functions and relationships with each other. As a result, contradictory provisions can be traced, for instance, in the Statute of the Executive Committee of the IFAS, which is to be approved by the president of the IFAS each time when a new president takes the office.[459] The 1997 and 2002 EC IFAS Statutes state that the EC IFAS is established, *inter alia*, 'to assist the ICWC and ICSD in their activities',[460] whereas the 2009 EC IFAS Statute

456 Agreement between the Republic of Kazakhstan, the Kyrgyz Republic, the Republic of Tajikistan, Turkmenistan, and the Republic of Uzbekistan on the Status of IFAS and its Organizations, Ashgabad (signed 9 April 1999). Online: <http://www.cawater-info.net/library/eng/ifas_e_1.pdf> (an unofficial English translation).

457 Statute of the Interstate Commission for Sustainable Development (ICSD), Ashgabad (aproved 18 October 2000 by the Decision of ICSD). The ICSD is comprised of 15 members, including three representatives from each of the CARs (Ministers of the Environmental Protection, deputy Ministers of Economic Affairs, representatives from science and other areas) appointed by respective governments.

458 2008 ICWC Statute, para 5.1. (ICWC executive bodies include Secretariat, Basin Water Organisation (BWO) 'Amudarya', BWO 'Syrdarya', Scientific Information Centre on water management problems (SIC) with its branches, Coordination-Metrological Centre (CMC) with national organisations, and Training Centre (TC) with its branches) and 2000 ICSD Statute, para 3.2. (ICSD working bodies include Secretariat, Scientific Information Centre (SIC) with its branches, and Advisory Council comprised of experts and representatives of NGOs and donors).

459 According to its Statute, the IFAS is governed by its President who is elected from the Heads of the CARs for a term defined by the Decision of the Council of the CARs' Heads. The EC IFAS is located in the country whose president is elected as the President of the IFAS. See 1999 IFAS Statute.

460 Statute of the Executive Committee of the International Fund for saving the Aral Sea (EC IFAS), Tashkent (approved 20 March 1997 by the Decision of the IFAS President № 2P-ИК, The President of the Republic of Uzbekistan I. Karimov) and Statute of the Executive Committee of the International Fund for saving the Aral Sea (EC IFAS), Dushanbe

provides that EC IFAS is established, *inter alia*, 'to coordinate the activities of the EC IFAS, the ICWC and the ICSD'.[461]

The attempts to advance the legal basis for institutional cooperation were undertaken within two Aral Sea Basin Programs with the support of the World Bank, European Union, and the Asian Development Bank (ADB). The commitments to improve the organizational structure and legal framework of the IFAS were expressed by the Presidents of five Central Asian countries at the IFAS summit in Almaty on 28 April 2009. As a follow-up to this meeting, the UNECE Programme on Regional Dialogue and Cooperation on Water Resources Management in Central Asia provided assistance to the IFAS Executive Committee in Kazakhstan and other regional institutions to analyse the needs for reforms in the institutional setting for transboundary water management in the sub-region.[462] Based on the 2009 Joint Statement of the Heads of State, inputs from sub-regional and national experts and proposals voiced during meetings, international consultants put forward two options of improving the institutional framework for cooperation in the sub-region. The first (softer) option suggests strengthening the existing mechanism for sub-regional cooperation through better coordination between interstate organisations, clarification of their responsibilities, and introduction of integrated water resources management principles and a fairer geographical distribution of seats of regional bodies.[463] The second (more radical) alternative advises countries to establish a new sub-regional organisation, transforming IFAS into a consolidated sub-regional organisation dealing with sustainable development, environmental protection and integrated water resources management and setting up international river basin commissions for the Amudarya and Syrdarya,

(approved June 2002 by the Decision of the IFAS President, The President of the Republic of Tajikistan E. Rahmonov).

461 Statute of the Executive Committee of the International Fund for saving the Aral Sea (EC IFAS), Almaty (approved 21 March 2009 by the Decision of the IFAS President, The President of the Republic of Kazakhstan N. Nazarbaev).

462 The project was financed by the Government of Germany through GIZ (German Technical Cooperation), in the framework of the Berlin Water Process. Online: <http://unece.org/env/water/cadialogue/cadwelcome.htm≥ accessed 22 December 2013.

463 'Strengthening the institutional and legal frameworks of the International Fund for Saving the Aral Sea: Review and proposals. Discussion paper' (2010) Prepared under the project 'Regional Dialogue and Cooperation on Water Resources Management', implemented by the IFAS Executive Committee and the United Nations Economic Commission for Europe (UNECE), supported by Deutsche Gesellschaft für Technische Zusammenarbeit (GTZ) GmbH at 23.

instead of the current BWOs.[464] These recommendations met a mixed response in the countries and remain a subject of further discussion.

5.2 Regular Information Exchange and Consultations

Regular information exchange and consultations have become key elements of the international legal body of procedural norms governing transboundary waters. They serve as tools for states to reach and maintain an equitable balance of uses and benefits, and prevent transboundary harm.[465]

As a matter of a general legal duty, the Aral Sea basin countries shall on a regular basis exchange readily available data and information concerning an international watercourse. This customary obligation[466] has been codified in stringent terms in the 1997 UN Watercourses Convention[467] and the 1992

---

464 Ibid, 29.

465 McCaffrey, *The law of international watercourses – Non-navigational uses* at 477 (stating that '[c]onsultations are a key element of the processes that maintain a fair balance of uses and prevent unreasonable harm'.), ILC Commentary to 1994 Draft Articles at 107–108. Higgins, *Problems and process* at 136 discussing the procedural law of cooperation in relation to transboundary watercourses, Rosalyn Higgins observed that '[i]t has [...] been regarded as insufficient to resolve conflict to have provided a list of criteria for the unilateral application by claimant states. Conflict can better be avoided by talking and by information sharing'.

466 The duty to exchange information finds support in numerous international agreements relating to international watercourses and is now part of customary international law. See eg Agreement between Bangladesh and India on Sharing of the Ganges Waters at Farakka (signed 5 November 1977) 17 ILM 103 (1978); 1960 Indus Waters Treaty; 1944 US-Mexico Treaty; Agreement between Niger and Nigeria concerning the Equitable Sharing in the Development, Conservation, and Use of their Common Water Resources (signed 18 July 1990) <http://www.fao.org>.

467 1997 UN Watercourses Convention, art 9 (Regular exchange of data and information) reads,

1. Pursuant to article 8, watercourse States shall on a regular basis exchange readily available data and information on the condition of the watercourse, in particular that of a hydrological, meteorological, hydrogeological and ecological nature and related to the water quality as well as related forecasts.
2. If a watercourse State is requested by another watercourse State to provide data or information that is not readily available, it shall employ its best efforts to comply with the request but may condition its compliance upon payment by the requesting State of the reasonable costs of collecting and, where appropriate, processing such data or information.

UNECE Water Convention.[468] Although 'shall' is also the main operative verb in the most of Commonwealth and sub-regional agreements, the language of these treaties is rather hortatory when requiring the countries to promote rather than ensure the exchange of information related to international watercourses. Thus, the 1998 CIS Agreement on Transboundary Waters requires countries 'to establish principles of cooperation',[469] and the 1992 Almaty Agreement provides that the Parties 'shall facilitate a wide information exchange'.[470]

---

3. Watercourse States shall employ their best efforts to collect and, where appropriate, to process data and information in a manner which facilitates its utilization by the other watercourse States to which it is communicated.

468 1992 UNECE Water Convention, art 13 (Exchange of information between riparian parties) states,

1. The Riparian Parties shall, within the framework of relevant agreements or other arrangements according to article 9 of this Convention, exchange reasonably available data, *inter alia*, on: (a) Environmental conditions of transboundary waters; (b) Experience gained in the application and operation of best available technology and results of research and development; (c) Emission and monitoring data; (d) Measures taken and planned to be take to prevent, control and reduce transboundary impact; (e) Permits or regulations for waste-water discharges issued by the competent authority or appropriate body.
2. In order to harmonize emission limits, the Riparian Parties shall undertake the exchange of information on their national regulations.
3. If a Riparian Party is requested by another Riparian Party to provide data or information that is not available, the former shall endeavour to comply with the request but may condition its compliance upon the payment, by the requesting Party, of reasonable charges for collecting and, where appropriate, processing such data or information.
4. For the purposes of the implementation of this Convention, the Riparian Parties shall facilitate the exchange of best available technology, particularly through the promotion of: the commercial exchange of available technology; direct industrial contacts and cooperation, including joint ventures; the exchange of information and experience; and the provision of technical assistance. The Riparian Parties shall also undertake joint training programmes and the organization of relevant seminars and meetings.

469 1998 CIS Agreement on Transboundary Waters, art 2 reads,

The Parties are obliged [...] to establish principles of cooperation governing the regular exchange of information and forecasts on radioecological monitoring, water chemistry and hydrometeorology of water bodies [...].

470 1992 Almaty Agreement, art 5 provides,

The Parties shall facilitate a wide information exchange on scientific and technical progress in the field of water management, complex use and protection of water resources, conducting joint studies to ensure scientific and technical support [for resolving the problems] and expert appraisals of project plans of water management facilities and economic assets.

In contrast, in the 1991 Statement the heads of the Central Asian countries' water authorities has expressed the need for information exchange in a more strong and demanding language that required the countries 'to ensure' exchange of information.[471] Finally, the obligation on information exchange in the Convention on Biodiversity is considerably less stringent than under general international law.[472]

To answer the question about the determinacy of the obligation to exchange information, the analysis of the applicable law will proceed with an inquiry as to how precise and clear the normative requirements on data and information to be exchanged are, and when and how these data and information should be exchanged.

As a general minimum requirement of customary international law, reflected in the 1997 UN Watercourses Convention, countries have to exchange 'readily available data and information' concerning an international watercourse. Although none of the instruments that impose the obligation to exchange of information and data defines the terms 'data' or 'information', it is clear from their ordinary meaning that those include both raw data and information in the form of analyses, forecasts and reports.[473] With respect to the qualifier of 'readily availability',[474] the 1994 ILC commentary explains that data

471 Statement made by the Heads of Water Management Authorities of the Central Asian Republics and Kazakhstan, Tashkent (adopted 12 October 1991), para 6 states that it is necessary 'to ensure exchange of full information on water resources use, water use infrastructure, legal and other documents that define status of water as a resource, and water use procedure in the republics'.

472 Convention of Biodiversity, art 17 (Exchange of information) reads,

1. The Contracting Parties shall facilitate the exchange of information, from all publicly available sources, relevant to the conservation and sustainable use of biological diversity, taking into account the special needs of developing countries.
2. Such exchange of information shall include exchange of results of technical, scientific and socio-economic research, as well as information on training and surveying programmes, specialized knowledge, indigenous and traditional knowledge as such and in combination with the technologies referred to in Article 16, paragraph 1. It shall also, where feasible, include repatriation of information.

473 See eg Stec and Casey-Lefkowitz, *The Aarhus Convention: An implementation guide* at 100 (explaining that 'the environmental information might include such items as analyses, summaries, sampling or monitoring data, background documentation, expert opinions, feasibility studies, draft impact statements, forecasts and agency reports').

474 1992 UNECE Water Convention, art 13(1) requires the Riparian Parties to exchange '*reasonably* available data' which, as Implementation Guide explains, 'does not substantially differ from the term "readily available"'. See 'UNECE *Guide to Implementing the Convention*' at 103, para 284.

and information is so if a watercourse state has those 'readily at its disposal, for example, that which it has already collected for its own use or easily accessible'.[475]

A watercourse state can also request 'not readily available' data or information from another watercourse state; and the latter 'shall employ its best efforts to comply with the request'.[476] The 1997 UN Watercourses Convention further provides that data and information subject to exchange relates to 'the condition of the watercourse, in particular that of a hydrological, meteorological, hydrogeological and ecological nature and related to the water quality as well as related forecasts'.[477] The ILC commentary spells out that this requirement 'is designed to ensure that watercourse States will have the facts necessary to enable them to comply with their obligations under article 5, 6 and 7'.[478] Nonetheless, this set of data and information, although non-exhaustive, seems to be restricted only to 'the condition of the international watercourse' rather than a wider range of factors relevant to equitable and reasonable utilisation stipulated in Article 6 of the Convention. Article 13 (1) of the 1992 UNECE Water Convention also establishes a non-exhaustive list of the data to be shared mainly related to watercourse protection and preservation,[479] while

475 ILC Commentary to 1994 Draft Articles at 108 para 4. See also the Commentary to Article XXIX of the *Helsinki Rules on the Uses of the Water of International Rivers* reprinted in S Bogdanovic, International law of water resources: Contribution of the International Law Association (1954–2000) (Kluwer Law International, The Hague 2001) at 133 (stating, in relation to 'readily available' information, that '...the basin State in question cannot be called upon to furnish information which is not pertinent and cannot be put to the expense and trouble of securing statistics and other data which are not already at hand or readily obtainable'.).

476 1997 UN Watercourses Convention, art 9(2) reads,

> If a watercourse State is requested by another watercourse State to provide data or information that is not readily available, it shall employ its best efforts to comply with the request but may condition its compliance upon payment by the requesting State of the reasonable costs of collecting and, where appropriate, processing such data or information.

477 Ibid, art 9(1).

478 ILC Commentary to 1994 Draft Articles at 107 para 2.

479 1992 UNECE Water Convention, art 13(1) states,

> The Riparian Parties shall, within the framework of relevant agreements or other arrangements according to article 9 of this Convention, exchange reasonably available data, *inter alia*, on: (a) Environmental conditions of transboundary waters; (b) Experience gained in the application and operation of best available technology and results of research and development; (c) Emission and monitoring data; (d) Measures taken and planned to be taken to prevent, control and reduce transboundary impact;

encouraging 'the widest exchange of information, as early as possible, on issues covered by the provisions of this Convention'.[480]

Both instruments contain provisions to protect certain categories of information. Article 31 of the 1997 UN Watercourses Convention exempts from the exchange information vital to national defence or security,[481] whereas Article 8 of the 1992 UNECE Water Convention protects information 'related to industrial and commercial secrecy, including intellectual property, or national security'.[482]

The scope of information subject to exchange in the Commonwealth treaties and treaties specific to states in the Aral Sea basin is rather wide, but the content is less specific. As for the type of information to be shared, these agreements refer to:

(a) 'Radioecological monitoring, water chemistry and hydrometeorology of water bodies'[483] and 'matters related to the Convention' (1998 CIS Agreement on Transboundary Waters)[484];
(b) 'Scientific and technical progress in the field of water management, complex use and protection of water resources', and the results of 'joint studies' and 'expert appraisals of project plans of water management facilities and economic assets' (1992 Almaty Agreement)[485];
(c) 'The level and volume of water in frontier rivers and [...] precipitation in the interior of the territory of the two Parties as might avert danger

---

(e) Permits or regulations for waste-water discharges issued by the competent authority or appropriate body.

480 Ibid, art 6 (Exchange of information) reads,

The Parties shall provide for the widest exchange of information, as early as possible, on issues covered by the provisions of this Convention.

481 Ibid, art 31 (Data and information vital to national defence or security) states,

Nothing in the present Convention obliges a watercourse State to provide data or information vital to its national defence or security. Nevertheless, that State shall cooperate in good faith with the other watercourse States with a view to providing as much information as possible under the circumstances.

482 1997 UN Watercourses Convention, art 8 (Protection of information) provides,

The provisions of this Convention shall not affect the rights or the obligations of Parties in accordance with their national legal systems and applicable supranational regulations to protect information related to industrial and commercial secrecy, including intellectual property, or national security.

483 1998 CIS Agreement on Transboundary Waters, art 2.

484 Ibid, art 3.

485 1992 Almaty Agreement, art 5.

or damage from flooding' (1958 Soviet-Afghan Frontier Agreement)[486];
(d) Ecology and environmental protection, including information about transboundary transport of pollutants and possible transboundary impact of planned measures (1998 CIS Informational Cooperation Agreement)[487]; and
(e) 'full information on water resources use, water use infrastructure, legal and other documents that define status of water as a resource, and water use procedure in the republics' (1991 Statement of the Heads of the CARs' water authorities).[488]

If taken together, these provisions are useful in defining the content of the information to be exchanged in the Aral Sea basin. However, as regional and basin-specific treaties, these instruments could have been even more specific in exemplifying the relevant data to be shared, according to the characteristics and needs of the basin. This would have been better provided the riparian countries with the material necessary to comply with their substantive obligations.

The language of existing instruments is sufficiently precise with respect to the time when data and information should be provided and less so on the ways of exchange. In requiring the 'regular' exchange of data and information, as distinct from *ad hoc* provision of information concerning planned measures (discussed below), this customary norm calls for establishing 'an ongoing and systematic process' of information flow between countries sharing an international watercourse.[489] Riparian countries are generally free to choose how to transmit relevant data and information – directly or indirectly, while the 1992 UNECE Water Convention indicates joint bodies as a preferential platform for information exchange.[490] States practice around the world, including Central

486 1958 Soviet-Afghan Frontier Treaty, art 17 states,

> The competent authorities of the Contracting Parties shall exchange as regularly as possible such information concerning the level and volume of water in frontier rivers and also concerning precipitation in the interior of the territory of the two Parties as might avert danger or damage from flooding. The competent authorities shall as necessary also agree on a mutual system of signals during periods of high water.

487 1998 CIS Informational Cooperation Agreement, arts 1 and 3.

488 1991 Statement of the Heads of the CARs' water authorities, para 6.

489 ILC Commentary to 1994 Draft Articles at 108 para 4.

490 See eg 1992 UNECE Water Convention, art 9(2) that includes the tasks of joint bodies (c) To draw up inventories and exchange information on the pollution sources mentioned in paragraph 2 (a) of this article; (h) To serve as a forum for the exchange

Asia, also demonstrates that the most effective way to establish a regular information exchange is through an institutional mechanism or a specific information system established for river basins concerned.

In Central Asia, the heads of the countries have identified the development of a sub-regional information exchange system as a priority area in the ASBPs.[491] The establishment of a unified information system on water resources use, monitoring of irrigation lands and hydrometeorological support is included in the main tasks of ICWC.[492] The Central Asia Regional Water Information Base (CAREWIB) project was developed in response to this, with the aims of ensuring transparency and public awareness and supporting decision making in the water sector.[493] The CAREWIB Information System and the CAWater-Info portal (www.cawater-info.net) are acknowledged as 'an official system for keeping records, collection, use and analysis of data, and modelling of water and land resources in the Aral Sea basin'.[494] Although Afghanistan neither is a member of the ICWC nor participates in the information exchange in the sub-region, the CAREWIB project collects and systematises the

of information on existing and planned uses of water and related installations that are likely to cause transboundary impact; (i) To promote cooperation and exchange of information on the best available technology in accordance with the provisions of article 13 of this Convention, as well as to encourage cooperation in scientific research programmes. See also Andrea K. Gerlak, Jonathan Lautze and Mark Giordano, 'Water resources data and information exchange in transboundary water treaties' (2011) 11 International Environmental Agreements 179–199 at 188 (observing that that indirect mechanisms of information exchange – in the form of prior notification and formalised communication – is far more common in international river basin that direct exchange mechanism).

491 'Database and Management Information System for Water and Environment' project was listed as a priority project in the ASBP-1. The ASBP-2 included as one of the activities 'Strengthening Material/Technical and Legal Basis for Interstate Organisations, Development of Regional Information System Designed to Manage Water Resources of the Aral Sea Basin'.

492 1992 ICWC Statute, para 2.6.

493 The project is funded by the Swiss Agency for Development Cooperation and implemented by the Scientific Information Centre of the ICWC with the assistance of UNECE and the UNEP/GRID-Arendal Office in Geneva, in close cooperation with five national water management organisations. For more information see online: <http://www.cawater-info.net/aboute.htm> accessed 10 December 2013.

494 CAREWIB 2008 Progress Report (CAREWIB Tashkent/Arendal/Geneva 2009). Online: <http://cawater-info.net/library/eng/carewib/report2008en.pdf> accessed 10 December 2013.

water-related data about this riparian country to the Amudarya basin.[495] Article 3 of the CIS Informational Cooperation Agreement seeks to provide another platform for the wide exchange of environmental information among the Commonwealth of Independent States through an interstate environmental information system.[496]

In addition to information exchange, riparian countries are also required to enter into consultations with each other with respect to their shared waters. As a matter of customary law, the 1997 UN Watercourses Convention strictly requires countries to consult each other at least in two instances: (i) when planned measures in one country may cause significant transboundary effect in another, and (ii) when it is necessary to achieve and maintain equitable and reasonable use.[497] The former case will be considered in the section on notification on planned measures and other related obligations below. As far as the latter is concerned, the Convention states, 'In the application of article 5 [on Equitable and reasonable utilization and participation] or paragraph 1 of [Article on factors relevant to equitable and reasonable utilization], watercourse States concerned shall, when the need arises, enter into consultations in a spirit of cooperation'.[498]

The Convention also requires countries to consult each other, directly or indirectly,[499] in other circumstances, including negotiations on watercourse

495 CAWATERInfo – Portal of Knowledge for Water and Environmental Issues in Central Asia. Database on Water resources of Afghanistan. Online: <http://www.cawater-info.net/afghanistan/data/indexe.htm> and Knowledge Base on Afghanistan. Online: http://www.cawater-info.net/afghanistan/knowledge-basee.htm> accessed 10 December 2013.

496 1998 CIS Agreement on Informational Cooperation, art 3 states,

> To ensure coordinated policy in the field of ecology and environmental protection, the High Contracting Parties recognise as necessary [...] to set up and maintain an interstate environmental information system and provide information at the disposal of other High Contracting Parties [...].

497 McCaffrey, *The law of international watercourses – Non-navigational uses* at 477.

498 1997 UN Watercourses Convention, art 6 (2). McCaffrey states that 'it might be argued, with some force, that regular consultations are indirectly required by the very nature of the obligation of equitable and reasonable utilization, namely, that it is a process premised on regular communication between states sharing an international watercourse'. McCaffrey, *The law of international watercourses – Non-navigational uses* at 478.

499 1997 UN Watercourses Convention, art 30 sets forth,

> In cases where there are serious obstacles to direct contacts between watercourse States, the States concerned shall fulfil their obligations of cooperation provided for in the present Convention, including exchange of data and information, notification, communication, consultations and negotiations, through any indirect procedure accepted by them.

agreements,[500] harm elimination or mitigation,[501] pollution control measures,[502] the management of an international watercourse,[503] and the safe operation, maintenance and protection of installations.[504] Moreover, Article 4 sets forth an entitlement of every watercourse state 'to participate in the negotiation of and to become a party to any watercourse agreement that applies to the entire international watercourse, as well as to participate in any relevant consultations'.[505]

In similar fashion, the 1992 UNECE Water Convention prescribes in forceful terms that consultations between the Riparian Parties 'shall be held [...] on the basis of reciprocity, good faith and good-neighbourliness' and 'aim at cooperation regarding the issues covered by the [...] Convention'.[506] It further assigns

---

500 Ibid, art 3 (5) states,

> Where a watercourse State considers that adjustment and application of the provisions of the present Convention is required because of the characteristics and uses of a particular international watercourse, watercourse States shall consult with a view to negotiating in good faith for the purpose of concluding a watercourse agreement or agreements.

501 Ibid, art 7(2) reads,

> Where significant harm nevertheless is caused to another watercourse State, the States whose use causes such harm shall, in the absence of agreement to such use, take all appropriate measures, having due regard for the provisions of articles 5 and 6, in consultation with the affected State, to eliminate or mitigate such harm and, where appropriate, to discuss the question of compensation.

502 Ibid, art 21(3) provides,

> Watercourse States shall, at the request of any of them, consult with a view to arriving at mutually agreeable measures and methods to prevent, reduce and control pollution of an international watercourse, such as: (a) Setting joint water quality objectives and criteria; (b) Establishing techniques and practices to address pollution from point and non-point sources; (c) Establishing lists of substances the introduction of which into the waters of an international watercourse is to be prohibited, limited, investigated or monitored.

503 Ibid, art 24(1) states,

> Watercourse States shall, at the request of any of them, enter into consultations concerning the management of an international watercourse, which may include the establishment of a joint management mechanism.

504 Ibid, art 26(2) reads,

> Watercourse States shall, at the request of any of them which has reasonable grounds to believe that it may suffer significant adverse effects, enter into consultations with regard to: (a) The safe operation and maintenance of installations, facilities or other works related to an international watercourse; and (b) The protection of installations, facilities or other works from wilful or negligent acts or the forces of nature.

505 Ibid, art 4.

506 1992 UNECE Water Convention, art 10.

an important role to river basin commissions by requiring that '[a]ny such consultations shall be conducted through a joint body [...] where one exists'.[507]

To date, the agreements concluded under the umbrella of the Commonwealth and within the Aral Sea basin make no direct reference to regular consultations. The only exception is Article 3 of the 1998 CIS Agreement on Transboundary Waters, which requires the Parties to enter into mutual consultations when they develop water protection measures.[508] For the rest, these agreements encompass consultation mainly as a means of dispute settlement.[509] Therefore, by joining to the 1997 UN Watercourses Convention, the countries would have clearer guidelines on consultations with each other with respect to their shared waters.

Finally, the forceful language of the Ramsar Convention explicitly requires the Parties to 'consult with each other about implementing obligations arising from the Convention especially in the case of a wetland extending over the territories of more than one Contracting Party or where a water system is shared by Contracting Parties'.[510]

5.3 Prior Notification on Planned Measures and other Related Obligations

International water law provides for a definite procedural framework to aid countries in maintaining an equitable balance between their respective uses, when the need to consider new uses occurs.[511] Riparian countries have the obligations to exchange information, to conduct an environmental impact assessment, to give prior notification and to consult each other on possible effects of planned measures that may have a significant adverse effect.[512] Discussions in this section are centered on the obligation to give prior

507 Ibid.

508 1998 CIS Agreement on Transboundary Waters, art 3.

509 See eg 1999 IFAS Agreement, art 14; Agreement between the Government of the Republic of Kazakhstan and the Government of the Kyrgyz Republic on the Use of Water Management Facilities of Intergovernmental Status on the Rivers Chu and Talas, Astana (signed 21 January 2000). Online: <http://cawater-info.net/library/eng/chu_talas_e.pdf>, art 12; Agreement on Hydromet, art 7; 1998 CIS Agreement on Transboundary Waters, art 13 and 1998 CIS Informational Cooperation Agreement, art 7.

510 Ramsar Convention, art 5(1).

511 ILC Commentary to 1994 Draft Articles at 111, para 1.

512 See eg McCaffrey, *The law of international watercourses – Non-navigational uses* at 409 (discussing 'the procedural system applicable in respect of planned measures').

notification as the core of the procedural system applicable with respect to planned measures, while pointing out the principal terms of other related obligations.

The obligation to prior notification on planned measures is well recognised as part of customary international law, as evidenced by international agreements,[513] decisions of courts and tribunals,[514] and in the writings of publicists.[515] As a reflection of the customary law, Article 12 of the 1997 UN Watercourses Convention forcefully states, 'Before a watercourse State implements or permits the implementation of planned measures which may have a significant adverse effect upon other watercourse States, it shall provide those States with timely notification thereof'.[516] As it follows from this and other relevant provisions, there are at least two preconditions for a duty of prior notification to arise. First, there shall be 'planned measures'. The 1994 ILC's Commentary explains that the phrase 'planned measures' is employed in its broader sense and includes 'new projects or programmes of a major or minor nature, as well as changes in exiting uses of an international watercourse'.[517] Using slightly different language, the 1991 Espoo Convention defines 'proposed activity' as to include both a new activity and change to an activity, conditioning that change should be 'major'.[518] The terms of both instruments do not make difference on the location of a planning state in a watercourse – upstream, midstream or downstream – to trigger the obligation.[519] Second, only planned measures, 'which may have a significant adverse effect upon other watercourse States', is a subject to prior notification under this customary norm. In

513 See eg Agreement (with final protocol) regulating the withdrawal of water from Lake Constance (signed 30 April 1966, entered into force 25 November 1967) 620 UNTS 191; Convention and Statutes relating to the Development of the Chad Basin (signed 22 May 1964, entered into force 15 September 1964); Agreement concerning the River Niger Commission and the navigation and transport on the River Niger (signed 25 November 1964, entered into force 12 April 1966) 587 UNTS 19.

514 See eg *Lake Lanoux Arbitration*, *Gabčíkovo-Nagimaros* case, and *Pulp Mills* case.

515 See eg McCaffrey, *The law of international watercourses – Non-navigational uses* at 409, Birnie, Boyle and Redgwell, *International law and the environment* at 567,

516 1997 UN Watercourses Convention, art 12.

517 ILC Commentary to 1994 Draft Articles at 111 para 4.

518 Espoo Convention, art 1 defines 'proposed activity' as 'any activity or any major change to an activity subject to a decision of a competent authority in accordance with an applicable national procedure'.

519 McCaffrey, *The law of international watercourses – Non-navigational uses* at 407, M.A. Salman Salman, 'Downstream riparians can also harm upstream riparians: the concept of foreclosure of future uses' (2010) 35 Water International 350–364.

McCaffrey's word, '[t]he duty to provide notification under the Convention arises when the planning state has reason to believe that the measures in question may have a "significant adverse effect" upon other states'.[520] The threshold of '*likelihood* of significant adverse effect' – which is lower that standard of 'significant harm' – is employed here to prevent a breach of the no-significant harm obligation by triggering the procedural system concerning planned measures.[521] Given that the obligation relies on the qualifier of 'significant', which is not without ambiguity, a certain level of indeterminacy is unavoidable and plays its role in the operation of this procedural norm.[522]

Two interrelated questions of how a planning state has to go about determining whether planned measures may have a significant adverse effect upon other watercourse states and what should constitute the content of notification are in order. McCaffrey and others stress that a determination of a likelihood of significant adverse effect is best made through an impact assessment.[523] Supported by widespread states practice, environmental impact assessment

520 McCaffrey, *The law of international watercourses – Non-navigational uses* at 406.

521 ILC Commentary to 1994 Draft Articles at 111, para 2. See also Dissenting Opinion of Gavan Griffith QC in Dispute Concerning Article 9 of the OSPAR Convention (Ireland/UK) which states, that [...] 'likely' in its ordinary meaning means 'probable' as something expected but not certain to happen. The result of 'likely adverse effect' is not a fact that is required to be proven empirically, but is merely to be recognised as a possibility as something may, but not necessarily will happen. Perhaps the phrase 'reasonably to be expected' accurately expresses the standard.[...] In other words, when qualifying an activity as potentially harmful the Tribunal must be guided by the word 'likely' that applies a lower threshold of proof for satisfaction at the level that is not 'adverse effect' that must be established, but merely the likelihood of such adverse effect. *OSPAR Award* at 89 para 81–82.

522 Frederic L. Kirgis, *Prior consultation in international law: A study of state practice* (Univeristy Press of Virginia 1983) at 41 argues that 'Any reasonable doubt must be resolved in favour of notification'. This problem is partially resolved by the customary duty to each party to act in good faith. See Birnie, Boyle and Redgwell, *International law and the environment* at 567 stating that the principle of good faith imports some limit of reasonableness in unilateral assessments by the proposing state, and in the *Lac Lanoux* arbitration, the tribunal observed:

> A state wishing to do that which will affect an international watercourse cannot decide whether another state's interests will be affected; the other state is sole judge of that and has the right to information on the proposals.

523 McCaffrey, *The law of international watercourses – Non-navigational uses* at 475. See also Craick, *The international law of environmental impact assessment: Process, substance and integration* at 95 arguing that 'Where the UNEP EIA Goals and Principles advance the development of international EIA obligations is that they make explicit what was until that time largely presumed – that notification, exchange of information and consultation shall be undertaken on the basis of the information contained within the EIA document'.

(EIA) became an essential part of interstate cooperation on planned measures. Given that impact assessment has evolved to include different interrelated procedures and seems to go beyond *ad hoc* assessment for planned measures, it is considered in more detail in the following section. It is sufficient to note here that the results of EIAs are to be included in the package of notification documents, according to Article 12 of the 1997 UN Watercourses Convention.[524] The terms of the 1991 Espoo Convention are more detailed with the respect to the content of notification by prescribing that the notification shall contain, *inter alia*, information on the proposed activity and its possible transboundary impact, the nature of the possible decision, and the indication of a reasonable timeframe for a response by a notifying country, and may include relevant information regarding the environmental impact assessment procedure.[525]

As far as timeframe concerned, the notification shall be made *before* implementation or authorisation of the planned measure (prior notification) and '*sufficiently early* in the planning stages to permit meaningful consultations and negotiations' ('timely notification').[526] The 1991 Espoo Convention adds some clarification by prescribing that a notification shall be sent 'as early as possible and no later than when informing its own public about that proposed activity'.[527] This indication can reduce uncertainty around the determination

524 1997 UN Watercourses Convention, art 12 requires that 'notification shall be accompanied by available technical data and information, including the results of any environmental impact assessment, in order to enable the notified States to evaluate the possible effects of the planned measures'.

525 Espoo Convention, art 3(2) sets forth that

> This notification shall contain, *inter alia*: (a) Information on the proposed activity, including any available information on its possible transboundary impact; (b) The nature of the possible decision; and (c) An indication of a reasonable time within which a response under paragraph 3 of this Article is required, taking into account the nature of the proposed activity; and may include the information set out in paragraph 5 of this Article.

Accordingly, art 3(5) reads,

> Upon receipt of a response from the affected Party indicating its desire to participate in the environmental impact assessment procedure, the Party of origin shall, if it has not already done so, provide to the affected Party: (a) Relevant information regarding the environmental impact assessment procedure, including an indication of the time schedule for transmittal of comments; and (b) Relevant information on the proposed activity and its possible significant adverse transboundary impact.

526 ILC Commentary to 1994 Draft Articles at 111 para 3–4.

527 Espoo Convention, art 3.1.

of 'timely notification' by linking it to domestic EIA procedures, which are usually defined in more details.

The 1997 UN Watercourses and 1992 UNECE Water Conventions, as a reflection of a customary law on notification, leave it to the riparian states to decide *how* to notify other international watercourse states either through diplomatic channels or through an institutional mechanism, although the language of 1992 UNECE Water Convention seems to favor the latter option.[528] In contrast, the language of the decision of the 1991 Espoo Convention's Meeting of the Parties is undisguised:

> Notifications of proposed activities likely to cause significant adverse transboundary impact shall be transmitted to the relevant points of contact [...] unless otherwise provided for in bilateral or multilateral agreements or other arrangements. Where no point of contact has been nominated, the notification shall be transmitted to the Ministry of Foreign Affairs of the affected Party or Parties.[529]

The 1997 UN Watercourses Convention and the 1991 Espoo Convention envisage a set of provisions on reply or absent of reply to notification.[530] Importantly, the obligation to notify is closely related to the duties to exchange information, consult and negotiate on the possible effects of planned measures as a part of the overall consultation system. These requirements help establish the process of a two-way communication between the parties concerned and 'avoid problems inherent in unilateral assessments of the actual nature of such effects'.[531] The 1997 UN Watercourses Convention establishes a six-month period within which the notified state is expected 'to study and evaluate the possible effects of the planned measures and to communicate the findings' to the states implementing

528 1992 UNECE Water Convention, art 9(2)(h).

529 Espoo Convention, Decision I/3, UN Doc ECE/MP.EIA/2, annex III at 17 para. 1. Online: <http://www.unece.org/env/documents/1998/eia/decision.I.3.e.pdf> accessed 22 December 2013.

530 1997 UN Watercourses Convention, art 13 (Period for reply to notification), art 14 (Obligations of the notifying State during the period for reply), art 15 (Reply to notification), art 16 (Absence of reply to notification). Article 3 of the Espoo Convention. See also Birnie, Boyle and Redgwell, *International law and the environment* at 567 (stating that 'the decision is not one the proposing state alone to take once the possibility of adverse effects is foreseen. The affected state is itself entitled to initiate the process of notification and consultation, if the proposing state does not act').

531 ILC Commentary to 1994 Draft Articles at 111, para 3.

the measure.[532] The 1991 Espoo Convention requires the notified state to reply within 'a reasonable time'.[533] Moreover, the 1991 Espoo Convention specifies that notification shall be given 'for the purpose of ensuring adequate and effective consultations' between affected parties,[534] lays down the possible content of consultations,[535] and requests consultations on the revision of the decision on the proposed activity[536] and during the post-project analysis.[537]

In the context of the Aral Sea basin, the riparian countries have not agreed on detailed procedures to be invoked in case of planned measures on their international watercourses. The language of sub-regional agreements only goes as far as to suggest that water management projects are subject to 'joint consideration' by the parties concerned.[538] The preambular recitals of the 1992 Almaty Agreement refers to the need for 'coordinated and organised solution to the issues' and 'unified and coordinated actions', but the operative part of the agreement falls short to specifying those procedures. Similarly, while the terms of Article 10 of the 1998 Syrdarya Agreement clearly endorses that such matters as the construction of new water facilities, dam safety, water conservation issues and wastewater disposal are subject to joint consideration by the countries, the procedures for such consideration remains to be defined. The 1998 Environmental Cooperation Agreement between Kazakhstan, the Kyrgyz Republic and Uzbekistan stipulates that the parties cooperate in the coordination of actions on building new facilities in frontier zone as well as facilities that may have transboundary adverse effect irrespective of their geographical location, but again the treaty is silent about how this coordination should take place.[539] Article 19 of the 1958 Soviet-Afghan Frontier Treaty requires prior agreement between the parties for the construction of new facilities or the introduction of any changes that are 'likely to hinder navigation or influence the flow of water' or 'may affect the flow of water and the state of the banks, and also cause damage thereto'.[540] Finally, the 2006 Framework Convention on Sustainable Development is more detailed in this regard, but it is not yet in force. It determines that the principle that transboundary harm and other adverse effects are to be prevented and reduced

532 1997 UN Watercourses Convention, art 13.

533 Espoo Convention, arts 3(2)(c) and 5.

534 Espoo Convention, art 3(1).

535 Espoo Convention, art 5.

536 Ibid, art 6.

537 Ibid, art 7.

538 Afghanistan is not a party to these agreements.

539 1998 Environmental Cooperation Agreement, art 2 (z).

540 1958 Soviet-Afghan Frontier Treaty, arts 19(2) and 19(3).

among others through the 'prior, timely and accompanied by appropriate information notification of the Parties exposed to the danger of adverse effect and consultations in the spirit of good will' should 'guide' the Parties in their relations.[541]

Existing joint bodies also lack a clear mandate that would stipulate their role in procedures concerning planned measures. The 1992 ICWC Statute gives the Commission the mandate to 'coordina[te] implementation of large water-related works and joint use of existing water management potential of the countries'.[542] Although positive *in abstracto*, this provision carries little legal weight in the absence of relevant procedural obligations and agreed timetables. Therefore, the 1997 UN Watercourses Convention and the 1991 Espoo Convention, with their sound and detailed procedural framework to guide countries in the case of planned measures, are of exceptional relevance for the countries in the Aral Sea basin.

Finally, global MEAs such as the Ramsar Convention and the Convention on Biodiversity also contain relevant provisions. The Convention on Biodiversity is characterised by vague language in setting forth obligations on notification and consultation by anticipating that these procedures will be formulated in other arrangements.[543] In contrast, the language of the Ramsar Convention is more stringent, although still very general.[544]

5.4 Transboundary Impact Assessment

Transboundary impact assessment has become an essential part of the procedural system of transboundary water cooperation out of recognition that

541 2006 Convention on Sustainable Development in CA, art 4.

542 1992 ICWC Statute, para 2.5.

543 Convention on Biodiversity, art 14 (c) requires the Parties to

> Promote, on the basis of reciprocity, notification, exchange of information and consultation on activities under their jurisdiction or control which are likely to significantly affect adversely the biological diversity of other States or areas beyond the limits of national jurisdiction, by encouraging the conclusion of bilateral, regional or multilateral arrangements, as appropriate.

544 Ramsar Convention, art 5(1) reads,

> The Contracting Parties shall consult with each other about implementing obligations arising from the Convention especially in the case of a wetland extending over the territories of more than one Contracting Party or where a water system is shared by Contracting Parties. They shall at the same time endeavour to coordinate and support present and future policies and regulations concerning the conservation of wetlands and their flora and fauna.

understanding the consequences of a state's activities is a necessary preliminary to meeting the due diligence obligation of the no-significant harm and the duty to cooperate, exchange information, consult and notify.[545] In general terms, impact assessment refers to the process of identifying the future consequences of a current or proposed action, such as a policy, plan, program, or project.[546] It seeks to ensure that such interventions are economically viable, socially equitable and environmentally sustainable.[547] The applicable law sets forth several interrelated procedures by which impact assessment for activities that may cause transboundary effects shall be conducted in the Aral Sea basin, including 'environmental impact assessment', 'strategic impact assessment', 'environmental expert review' and 'continuous assessment'.

Environmental Impact Assessment

Environmental impact assessment (EIA), the oldest and best-established assessment procedure, is defined as 'a national procedure for evaluating the likely impact of a proposed activity on the environment'.[548] Typically, the

545 See eg Request for an Examination of Situation in Accordance with Paragraph 63 of the Court's Judgment of 20 December 1974 in the *Nuclear Tests* (New Zealand vs France) Case, 1995 ICJ 228 a 344; Günther Handl, 'The environment: International rights and responsibilities' (1980) 74 American Society of International Law Proceedings 223–242; Günther Handl, 'Environmental security and global change: The challenge to international law' in W. Lang, H. Neuhold and K. Zemanek (eds), *Environmental protection and international law* (Graham & Trotman/Martinus Nijhoff 1991) at 76–77; Johan G. Lammers, 'International and European Community Law Aspects of Pollution of International Watercourses' in W. Lang, H. Neuhold and K. Zemanek (eds), *Environmental protection and international law* (Graham & Trotman/Martinus Nijhoff 1991) 131 at 131; Craick, *The international law of environmental impact assessment: Process, substance and integration* and ILA's 2004 Berlin Rules that states 'Implementation of the precautionary principle requires careful planning and the evaluation of the likely effects of significant actions before the action is implemented. The primary, but not the only, method that this will occur is through the impact assessment process that is now part of the requirements for the protection of the environment under international law'. Cf John H. Knox, 'The myth and reality of transboundary environmental impact assessment' (2002) 96 American Journal of International Law 291–319 who views transboundary EIA as 'an offshoot of domestic EIA laws extended in accordance with the principle of non-discrimination'.

546 International Association for Impact Assessment, What Is Impact Assessment? Online: <http://www.iaia.org/publicdocuments/special-publications/What%20is%20IAweb.pdf≥ accessed 22 December 2011. See also Convention on Biodiversity, Impact Assessment Programme. Online:<http://www.cbd.int/impact/≥accessed 22 December 2013.

547 Ibid.

548 Espoo Convention, preamble.

impact on the environment in this context should be understood in a broader sense to take into account interrelated socio-economic, cultural and human-health impacts.[549] The primary objectives of EIA are to aid well-informed decision-making and provide a forum for public participation and a meaningful dialogue about the benefits and costs of planned interventions.[550]

EIA initially emerged within a national context. As early as 1969, the United States National Environmental Policy Act[551] introduced the concept, which rapidly spread around the world[552] and was widely promoted in various soft law instruments at the international level.[553] In recent decades, the need to perform EIAs for activities that may affect the environment within a national jurisdiction and beyond has been recognised in a range of treaties,[554] judicial decisions,[555] declarations,[556] works of

---

549 See Espoo Convention, art 1(vii) that reads,

> 'Impact' means any effect caused by a proposed activity on the environment including human health and safety, flora, fauna, soil, air, water, climate, landscape and historical monuments or other physical structures or the interaction among these factors; it also includes effects on cultural heritage or socio-economic conditions resulting from alterations to those factors.

550 Aarhus Convention.

551 National Environmental Policy Act of 1969 (NEPA) § 102, 42 USC § 4332 (2000).

552 Jane Holder and Donald McGillivray (eds), *Taking stock of environmental assessment: Law, policy and practice* (Routledge-Cavendish 2007).

553 UNEP, Governing Council Decision: Goals and Principles of Environmental Impact Assessment, principle 4, UNEP/GC.14/17 Annex III, UNEP/GC/DEC/14/25 (17 June 1987); Rio Declaration, principle 17; *Agenda 21: A Programme for Action for Sustainable Development* (Rio de Janeiro 13 June 1992) *in Report of the United Nations Conference on Environment and Development* Annex II UN Doc A/Conf.151/26 (Vol II) (1992), Rio de Janeiro; World Charter for Nature, GA Res 37/7, UN GAOR 37th Sess, Agenda Item 21, UN Doc A/Res/37/7 (1982).

554 See eg Espoo Convention; 1992 UNECE Water Convention; North American Agreement on Environmental Cooperation, (signed 14 September 1993, entered into force 1 January 1994) 32 ILM 1480 (1993), arts 2(1)(e) and 10(7)(a); United Nations Convention on the Law of the Sea, (adopted 18 December 1982, entered into force 16 November 1994) 21 ILM 1261(1982), arts 204–206; Agreement between the Government of the Republic of Latvia and the Government of the Republic of Estonia on Environmental Impact Assessment in a Transboundary Context (signed 14 March 1997) 1986 UNTS 116; and European Council Directive 85/337 OJ 1985 L175/40 amended by EC Council Directive 97/11 OJ 1997 L73/5 and by EC Council Directive 03/35.

555 *Gabčíkovo-Nagymaros case* and *Pulp Mills case*.

556 Rio Declaration, principle 17 and *Agenda 21: A Programme for Action for Sustainable Development* (Rio de Janeiro 13 June 1992) *in Report of the United Nations Conference on Environment and Development* Annex II UN Doc A/Conf.151/26 (Vol II) (1992).

publicists[557] and authoritative international organisations,[558] and development banks' operational policies.[559] Consequently, this distinct form of public decision-making has reached the status of a customary obligation for activities that may have a transboundary impact.[560] In clarifying the legal nature of EIA in an international domain, the ICJ stated in the recent *Pulp Mill* case,

---

557 See eg Birnie, Boyle and Redgwell, *International law and the environment* 169; Beyerlin, 'Different types of norms in international environmental law: Policies, principles, and rules' at 440 states 'the EIA norm not only may be binding as a matter of treaty law but also may have grown, at least in the European context, to a (regional) customary legal rule'. Handl, 'Environmental security and global change: The challenge to international law' notes that 'in light of recent state practice, [...] it will be increasingly difficult to maintain that states are not (yet) obliged under customary international law to assess potential transboundary effects'. Günther Handl, 'Transboundary impacts' in Daniel Bodansky, Jutta Brunnée and Ellen Hey (eds), *The Oxford Handbook of International Environmental Law* (Oxford University Press 2007) at 541.

558 ILC Commentary to 2001 Draft articles, art 7; ILA's 2004 Berlin Rules, UNEP Governing Council: Goals and Principles of Environmental Impact Assessment, principles 4, 11 and 12, UNEP/GC.14/17 Annex III, UNEP/GC/DEC/14/25 (17 June, 1987); World Charter for Nature, GA Res 37/7, UN GAOR 37th Sess, Agenda Item 21, UN Doc A/Res/37/7 (1982). OECD Recommendation C(74)216 on the Analysis of the Environmental Consequences of Significant Public and Private Projects (1974); OECD Recommendation C(79)116 on the Assessment of Projects with Significant Impacts on the Environment (1979); OECD Recommendation C(85)104 on Environmental Assessment of Development Assistance Projects and Programmes (1985); OECD Joint Recommendations on the Environmental Assessment of Development Assistance Projects and Programmes (1985 and 1986) in OECD, OECD and the Environment (Paris: OECD, 1986).

559 See eg World Bank's Operational Policy 4.01. Online: <http://www.env.go.jp/earth/coop/coop/document/10-eiae/10-eiae-7.pdf> accessed 22 December 2013; Asian Development Bank's Environmental Policy and Operations Manual (OM) 20: Environmental Considerations in ADB Operations and the 2003 Environmental Assessment Guidelines.

560 Have considered implicitly the issue of transboundary EIAs in a few previous cases, the ICJ has stated in the recent Pulp Mill case,

> [I]t may now be considered a requirement under general international law to undertake an environmental impact assessment where there are a risk that the proposed industrial activity may have a significant adverse impact in a transboundary context, in particular, on a shared resource.

Pulp Mills case at 61 para 204. See also Request for an Examination of Situation in Accordance with Paragraph 63 of the Court's Judgment of 20 December 1974 in the Nuclear Tests (New Zealand vs France) Case, 1995 ICJ 228 at 344 (Separate Opinion of Justice Weeramantry). Weeramantry states that the principle of TEIA was 'gathering strength and international acceptance, and [had] reached the level of general recognition [such that the] Court should take notice of it'; *Gabčíkovo-Nagymaros case.*

> [D]ue diligence, and the duty of vigilance and prevention which it implies, would not be considered to have been exercised, if a party planning works liable [to] affect the régime of the river or the quality of its waters did not undertake an environmental impact assessment on the potential effects of such works.[561]

In addition to a customary obligation to perform an EIA for activities that may have a transboundary impact, a range of water-specific and general environmental treaties at global, regional, and basins levels contain EIA related requirements.

The 1997 UN Watercourses Convention, rather than actually imposing an independent obligation to conduct EIAs, considers EIA as a source of 'available technical data and information' under a general obligation to notify and exchange information on planned measures.[562] As McCaffrey, one of the 1997 UN Watercourses Convention architects, explains, this wording was the result of a compromise between government delegations, which either supported or opposed the idea of including EIA as a separate requirement.[563]

Two conventions under the auspices of UNECE formulate EIA provisions in a more robust way by requiring state parties to take real actions to undertake EIAs. The 1992 UNECE Water Convention requires its parties, including Kazakhstan, Turkmenistan and Uzbekistan in the Aral Sea basin, to take measures to ensure that an EIA and 'other means of assessment' applied by the parties in order to 'prevent, control and reduce transboundary impact'.[564] The

561 *Pulp Mills case* at 61 para 204. See also Judge Weeramantry's separate opinion.

562 1997 UN Watercourses Convention, art 12 reads,

> Before a watercourse State implements or permits the implementation of planned measures which may have a significant adverse effect upon other watercourse States, it shall provide those States with timely notification thereof. Such notification shall be accompanied by available technical data and information, including the results of any environmental impact assessment, in order to enable the notified States to evaluate the possible effects of the planned measures.

563 McCaffrey, *The law of international watercourses* 408.

564 1992 UNECE Water Convention, art 3(1)(h) reads,

> To prevent, control and reduce transboundary impact, the Parties shall develop, adopt, implement and, as far as possible, render compatible relevant legal, administrative, economic, financial and technical measures, in order to ensure, *inter alia*, that environmental impact assessment and other means of assessment are applied.

See also 'UNECE *Guide to Implementing the Convention*' at 69 para 199 states that 'While the SEA Protocol is not yet in force, SEA is relevant nonetheless for the implementation of article 3 (1(h)) of the Water Convention, insofar as it falls within the scope of the expression "other means of assessment" contained in the provision under review'.

1991 Espoo Convention, a regional stand-alone procedural mechanism on EIA, obliges its parties, including Kazakhstan and Kyrgyzstan, to assess the transboundary environmental impact of specified activities and to notify and consult with potentially affected parties about those effects by prescribing the detailed provisions for such an assessment.

EIA related commitments in the 1992 CIS Agreement on the Environmental Interaction, the 1998 CIS Agreement on Informational Cooperation Waters, and the 2006 Framework Convention on Sustainable Development in CA are also couched in mandatory terms by requiring parties to conduct assessments, harmonise national EIA procedures, and exchange information about those assessments.[565]

However, some level of legal uncertainty with respect to these assessments remains, given that these agreements envisage diverse thresholds of harm potential to trigger the obligations to conduct EIA. Customary law and the 1991 Espoo Convention require a likelihood of *significant* adverse impact/harm to be foreseen for conducting a transboundary EIA.[566] The 2006 Framework Convention on Sustainable Development in CA, the 1992 CIS Agreement on the Environmental Interaction and the 1998 Environmental Cooperation Agreement lower the threshold of risk by requiring the likelihood of *adverse* impact or *any* impact that potentially may cross a border when deciding whether a transboundary EIA is required.[567] While the presence of different standards does not help to increase consistency and coherence of the legal frameworks in general, the threshold of significant harm seems to be the minimum which the Aral Sea basin countries have to respect according to customary law requirements.

---

565 1992 CIS Agreement on the Environmental Interaction, arts 2 and 3; 1998 CIS Agreement on Informational Cooperation, arts 2(1) and 3 and 2006 Framework Convention on Sustainable Development in CA, arts 2(b), 4(6) and 7.

566 See eg Rio Declaration, principle 17; Article 7 of the ILC's 2001 Article and ILC Commentary to 2001 Draft articles at 157 para 1.

567 2006 Framework Convention on Sustainable Development in CA, art 2(b) reads,

> [The Parties] shall ensure that any plans, strategies, projects and activities that may have adverse affect on natural resources and the environment as a whole are subject to appropriate impact assessments at early stages; and that ecological monitoring and audit of these are conducted regularly.

The 1992 CIS Agreement on Environmental Interaction uses the expression 'affect or may affect the interest' and the 1998 CIS Environmental Cooperation Agreement – 'have or may have impact'.

Strategic Impact Assessment

Unlike an EIA, which deals with projects, strategic impact assessment (SEA) operates at strategic levels of decision-making and seeks to evaluate the likely environmental consequences of draft plans and programs and, to the extent appropriate, policies and legislation. It is designed to be undertaken earlier in the decision-making process than the EIA of projects.

Legal provisions for SEA are slowly emerging in the Aral Sea region, albeit neither the Central Asian countries nor Afghanistan are parties to the SEA Protocol to the 1991 Espoo Convention, which provides for the most detailed provisions of such assessments.[568] The 2006 Framework Convention on Sustainable Development in CA,[569] a treaty pending its entry into force, prescribes that its would-be parties 'ensure that any plans, strategies, projects and activities that may have adverse affect on natural resources and the environment as a whole are subject to appropriate impact assessments at early stages'.[570] Legally binding requirements to evaluate the environmental consequences of their plans, programs, and strategies arise for the Central Asian republics under the scope of an environmental expert review.

Environmental Expert Review ('Ecological Expertise')

The concept of an environmental expert review (or 'ecological expertise') was introduced in the Soviet time and referred to as a determination whether a planned or existing activity meets ecological and human security requirements, and whether this activity may be allowed to be undertaken or continue. An environmental expert review anticipates an EIA as a mandatory procedure to lay the groundwork for making its decisions. It also comprises elements of SEA by requiring mandatory assessment for plans, programmes, and draft laws.[571] Only those activities that have obtained a positive evaluation from an

568 Protocol on Strategic Environmental Assessment to the Convention on Environmental Impact Assessment in a Transboundary Context, Kyiv (adopted 21 May 2003, entered into force 11 July 2010).

569 2006 Framework Convention on Sustainable Development in CA.

570 2006 Convention on Sustainable Development in CA, art 2(b).

571 The CARs list 'the objects of environmental expert review', ranging from plans, programmes, draft laws, and projects, in specialised laws on the environmental protection and environmental expert review that are supplemented by a range of secondary regulations. See arts 35–44 of the Environmental Code of the Republic of Kazakhstan; arts 16–17 of the Law on the Environmental Protection of the Kyrgyz Republic (Bishkek, 16 June 1999); arts 33–37 of the Law on Nature Protection of the Republic of Tajikistan (Dushanbe, 27 December 1993); arts 13–16 of the Law on Nature Protection of Turkmenistan; arts 24–27 of the Law of the Nature Protection of the Republic of Uzbekistan.

expert commission are allowed to be implemented. While procedures for an environmental expert review are generally stipulated in national legislation, some regional treaties, like the 1992 CIS Agreement on the Environmental Interaction, call on its parties to 'undertake the environmental expert review of programmes and the development forecasts of industrial forces, investment and other projects',[572] to 'be guided by common methodological standards in undertaking environmental expert review',[573] and to cooperate 'in conducting joint environmental expert reviews of facilities that have or may have transboundary impact'.[574] The 1992 Almaty Agreement contains a rather soft provision inviting countries to facilitate a wider information exchange regarding expertise of water management projects.[575]

Continuous Monitoring and Other Means of Assessment

As a result of increased understanding of the systemic nature of environmental changes and the extended consequences of any intervention, the scope of impact assessment is gradually broadening and other means of assessment have begun to emerge. Among these are procedures for the monitoring and mitigation of adverse effects as well as integrated assessments to better accommodate diverse environmental, economic, social and cultural impacts.

The need for both prior and on-going assessments of activities on transboundary waters finds support in regional treaty practice. The 2006 Framework Convention on Sustainable Development in CA goes beyond the requirement of *ad hoc* assessment by prescribing that its would-be parties 'shall ensure that ecological monitoring and audit of [any plans, strategies, projects and activities that may have an adverse affect on natural resources and the environment as a whole] are conducted regularly'.[576] This provision, combined with the requirement to 'cooperate in establishing regional mechanisms for monitoring

572 1992 CIS Agreement on the Environmental Interaction, art 2.

573 Ibid, art 3.

574 Within the Aral Sea Basin context, art 2 (l) of the 1998 Environmental Cooperation Agreement between Kazakhstan, the Kyrgyz Republic and Uzbekistan stipulates that the Parties cooperate 'in conducting the joint environmental expert review of facilities that have or may have transboundary impact'.

575 1992 Almaty Agreement, art 5.

576 2006 Framework Convention on Sustainable Development in CA, art 2(b) reads, the Parties 'shall ensure that any plans, strategies, projects and activities that may have adverse affect on natural resources and the environment as a whole are subject to appropriate impact assessments at early stages; and that ecological monitoring and audit of these are conducted regularly'.

of basic parameters and indicators of the environment status',[577] echoes the requirements of other instruments related to joint monitoring and joint or coordinated assessments of the conditions of transboundary waters (1992 UNECE Water Convention),[578] a common monitoring system of water bodies (1998 CIS Agreement on Transboundary Waters),[579] post-project analysis (1991 Espoo Convention),[580] and the management of an international watercourse (1997 UN Watercourses Convention).[581] This provision is also consistent with the decisions of international courts and tribunals emphasizing that the no-harm and equitable and reasonable use principles anticipate the obligation of continuous monitoring.[582]

Since impacts not only on the environment, but also on persons and property fall within the scope of the obligation of no-significant harm, other means of assessment may be required to evaluate the risks. With respect to the 1997 UN Watercourses Convention, McCaffrey notes that its terms are restricted in a sense that refers to '*environmental* impact assessment' rather than the more

577 Ibid, art 7.

578 1992 UNECE Water Convention, art 11.

579 1998 CIS Agreement on Transboundary Waters, art 4.

580 Espoo Convention, art 7.

581 1997 UN Watercourses Convention, art 24 reads,

1. Watercourse States shall, at the request of any of them, enter into consultations concerning the management of an international watercourse, which may include the establishment of a joint management mechanism.
2. For the purposes of this article, 'management' refers, in particular, to: (*a*) Planning the sustainable development of an international watercourse and providing for the implementation of any plans adopted; and (*b*) Otherwise promoting the rational and optimal utilization, protection and control of the watercourse.

See ILC Commentary to 1994 Draft Articles at 125 para 3 that explains,

Together, subparagraphs (*a*) and (*b*) would include such functions as: planning of sustainable, multi-purpose and integrated development of international watercourses; facilitation of regular communication and exchange of data and information between watercourse States; and *monitoring of international watercourses on a continuous basis* [emphasis added].

582 See eg *Gabčíkovo-Nagymaros case* (Separate Opinion of Judge Weeramantry); *Pulp Mills case* para 281; *Case concerning Land Reclamation by Singapore in and around the Straits of Johor (Malaysia v. Singapore)* Reports of International Arbitral Awards, Vol XXVII pp. 133–145, UN (2008) International Tribunal for the Law of the Sea; Espoo Inquiry Commission. Report on the Likely Significant Adverse Transboundary Impacts of the Danube – Black Sea Navigation Route at the Border of Romania and the Ukraine (July, 2006). See also ILA's 2004 Berlin Rules, art 29(1) provides that 'States shall undertake prior and continuing assessment of the impact of programs, projects, or activities that may have a significant effect on the aquatic environment or the sustainable development of waters'.

general and unqualified term 'impact assessment'.[583] In contrast, 'impact assessment' as one of 'appropriate methods' shall be employed by the parties to the Convention on Climate Change 'taking into account their common but differentiated responsibilities' and 'with a view to minimizing adverse effects on the economy, on public health and on the quality of the environment, of projects or measures undertaken by them to mitigate or adapt to climate change'.[584] In a similar fashion, the 2006 Framework Convention on Sustainable Development in CA prescribes the duty to conduct 'impact assessments' in order to take environmental, social and cultural considerations into account.[585]

The practices of international financial institutions (IFIs) illustrate a more inclusive approach to impact assessment. For instance, the World Bank is presently supporting the preparation of an Assessment Study for the proposed Rogun HPP in Tajikistan to assess its (a) techno-economic/dam safety, and (b) environmental/social impacts.[586] The Techno-Economic Assessment Study (TEAS) conducts the analysis of techno-economic aspects of the construction of the Rogun HPP, including dam type, dam height, construction phasing, reservoir operations and dam safety issues, and the entire Vaksh River Development Masterplan.[587] Environmental and Social Impact Assessment (ESIA) addresses environmental, socio-economic and cultural situation at the

583 McCaffrey, *The law of international watercourses* at 475.

584 Convention on Climate Change, art 4.

585 2006 Framework Convention on Sustainable Development in CA, art 6.

586 The Assessment Studies are being supported by the World Bank in response to a request from the Government of Tajikistan, and include the Techno-Economic Assessment Study (TEAS) and Environmental and Social Impact Assessment (ESIA) for the proposed Rogun Hydropower Project (Rogun HPP) based on the current international standards and practices. The Assessment Studies started in March 2011. For more information see World Bank, 'Assessment Studies for Proposed Rogun Regional Water Reservoir and Hydropower Project in Tajikistan' <http://go.worldbank.org/ZQXIA8J0H0> and 'World Bank Update on the Status of the Rogun Assessment Studies' (Washington, 18 October 2011). Online: <http://go.worldbank.org/ZFMIHFM760> accessed 22 December 2013.

587 Techno-economic Assessment Study (TEAS) for the Rogun Hydroelectric Power Plant Construction Project. Terms of Reference, (3 April 2010) World Bank. The Study will include the assessment of the construction work on the Rogun HPP done to date and future works. The Rogun HPP Project is based mainly on estimates calculated back in 1978, in particular the technical and engineering estimates of the geological, hydrological and seismological elements of its construction. Today the project needs additional and updated documentation, namely engineering specifications, financial analyses, additional safety audits, and environmental impact assessments for all countries of the river basin. For more information about the Rogun Assessment Studies visit online: <http://www.worldbank.org/eca/caewdp/rogun> accessed 22 December 2013.

project site, identify potential impacts, including the cumulative impact of the entire Vakhsh river cascade on the relevant areas of Tajikistan and all the riparian states.[588] Among others, the ESIA will assess Tajikistan's energy policy from environmental and social perspectives (strategic impact assessment),[589] and in terms of riparian and cross-border impacts (regional impacts).[590] The Assessment Studies will be undertaken separately, but in parallel, and the recommendations of the TEAS will include possible trade-offs between techno-economic issues and the safeguard issues of dam safety, environmental, social, resettlement and impacts on other riparian states.[591] Assessments will be based on Tajik laws and regulation, international good practices and the World Bank's Safeguard Policies, which are to be consistent with relevant customary and treaty law.[592]

The foregoing analysis shows that the Aral Sea basin countries have expressed their intentions to conduct transboundary EIAs in forceful language, however specific and clear procedures on water-related assessments are still lacking in the sub-region. The content and process of transboundary EIA have not been set out in a single instrument that would be applicable to all countries of the Aral Sea basin. The 1991 Espoo Convention's requirements on the type of information to be included in transboundary EIA and the procedures to follow are obligatory only for Kazakhstan and the Kyrgyz Republic as its parties. The Guidelines on EIA in a Transboundary Context for the CARs developed by the countries' experts on the basis of the 1991 Espoo Convention provide a good starting point, but cannot substitute binding commitments.[593]

588 Environmental and social impact assessment study (ESIA) for the Rogun Hydroelectric Power Plant Construction Project. Terms of Reference, (3 April 2010) World Bank.

589 Ibid, paras 21–22.

590 Such regional impacts might include, but not limited to the impacts (during the construction and operating phases of Rogun HPP) on irrigation, agriculture, drinking and industrial water supplies, sanitary flows, sedimentation, flooding etc. in the downstream countries, as well as impact on the agreed flow of water to Aral Sea and impacts on the downstream countries relating to the safety of the dam. ToR for the Rogun TEAS at 4 TEAS. See also ToR for the Rogun ESIA, para 27 and also paras 16, 33, 44, 47, 51, 52, 55, 56, 58, and 60.

591 ToR for the Rogun TEAS.

592 As an organisation with international legal personality, the World Bank committed to pursue its activities in compliance with international environmental instruments. World Bank Operational Manual, Operational Policies OP 4.01, para 3 states 'The Bank does not finance project activities that would contravene [the obligations of the country, pertaining to project activities, under relevant international environmental treaties and agreements]'.

593 'UNECE Draft Guidelines on EIA in a Transboundary Context for Central Asian Countries' (2007) Meeting of The Parties to the Convention on Environmental Impact Assessment

The lack of clarity on the content and procedure for transboundary EIA in the applicable treaty and customary law can partly be filled up by domestic requirements. It appears that the evidence from the analysis of contemporary state practice and *opinio juris* did not allow the International Law Commission to specify the content of the assessment in the 2001 Draft Articles on harm prevention. Instead, the issue has been referred to the domestic laws of the state conducting such assessment, with only guidelines that it should include an evaluation of the possible harmful impact of the activity on persons, property and the environment of other states.[594] The ICJ in the *Pulp Mills* case has taken a similar approach, when stating,

> [...] it is the view of the Court that it is for each State to determine in its domestic legislation or in the authorization process for the project, the specific content of the environmental impact assessment required in each case, having regard to the nature and magnitude of the proposed development and its likely adverse impact on the environment as well as to the need to exercise due diligence in conducting such an assessment.[595]

Thus, the domestic EIA systems form a fundamental part of international EIA obligations. In the Aral Sea basin, EIA as a national procedure to ensure environmentally informed decision-making has been established in each country, although consistence and comprehensiveness of its requirements as well as the reflection of the transboundary aspects of EIA vary significantly.

The national laws of Kazakhstan, the Kyrgyz Republic and Tajikistan scantly capture transboundary impacts in the domestic EIA systems. The 1997 Regulation on EIA in the Kyrgyz Republic requires the EIA documentation to include 'analysis of ecological information, including consideration of cumulative and synergistic effects and any kind of transboundary impact'.[596] In Kazakhstan, the 2003 Rules on EIA for national, sectoral and regional programmes echoes this provision by requiring the content of EIA to embody

---

in a Transboundary Context Working Group on Environmental Impact Assessment, 10th Session Geneva 21–23 May 2007 Item 4(d) of the provisional agenda UN Doc ECE/MPEIA/WG1/2007/6. See also Environmental Impact Assessment in a Transboundary Context: Pilot Project in Central Asia. Project Report 2010. Online: <http://www.osce.org/documents/eea/2010/02/42814en.pdf> accessed 22 December 2013.

594 Commentary to Article 7 of the ILC's 2001 Articles (2001), paras 6–8.

595 *Pulp Mills case*.

596 1997 Regulation on EIA in the Kyrgyz Republic, para 8(d). See also Annex 2 Terms and definitions which include term 'transboundary impact'.

'possible significant transboundary environmental impacts'.[597] The Environmental Code of Kazakhstan states, however, that the specifics of EIA for 'objects with transboundary impact' shall be found in international agreements ratified by the Republic of Kazakhstan,[598] while the Law on Environmental Expert Review of the country introduces a definition of 'transboundary object' and assigns to the central executive body in the environmental field the task of performing a state environmental expert review of 'strategic, transboundary and ecologically hazardous objects;' and according and approving the documentation that regulates the activity of 'strategic, transboundary and ecologically hazardous objects' with a view to ensuring 'full consideration of ecological requirements'.[599]

Unlike Kazakhstan and the Kyrgyz Republic, Tajikistan did not complete the ratification procedure to become a party to the 1991 Espoo Convention yet. Nonetheless, this country's national regulatory framework on EIA refers to the provisions of this treaty. Thus, the Regulation on EIA of 3 October 2006 states that its provisions have been designed taking into account the legal and regulatory framework of the Republic of Tajikistan as well as international experiences, including the 1991 Espoo Convention.[600] The 2003 Tajik Law on Environmental Expert Review states that 'feasibility studies and projects of economic activities that may have an adverse effect on the environment of neighbouring countries or the implementation of which necessitates the use of shared natural resources; or which affect the interests of neighbouring countries, as defined in the international legal acts recognised by the Republic of Tajikistan', are subject to a mandatory environmental expert review.[601] This

597 Decree 129-п of the Ministry of the Environmental Protection of the Republic of Kazakhstan of 9 June 2003 on Rules for environmental impact assessment of proposed activities within preparation of the national, sectoral and regional programmes on development of economic sectors and of schemes for the location of industry, appendix 1 para 10.

598 Environmental Code of Kazakhstan, art 43. See also Decree №204-п of the Ministry of the Environmental Protection of the Republic of Kazakhstan of 28 June 2007 on Instruction on the environmental impact assessment of proposed economic and other activities within preparation of pre-planned, pre-project and project documentation (as amended on 26 March 2010).

599 Law on Environmental Expert Review of the Republic of Kazakhstan.

600 Procedure on EIA of 3 October 2006 approved by Resolution of the Government of the Republic of Tajikistan.

601 2003 Law of Tajikistan on Environmental Expert Review, art 7. See also 1993 Law of Tajikistan on the Nature Protection, art 88 stating as one other principle of international cooperation that 'economic activity carried out on the territory of the state must not harm the natural environment within its jurisdiction and beyond'.

requirement is further supported in the 2006 Procedure on EIA in Tajikistan which states that an EIA is a mandatory procedure for planned activities that may have a transboundary impact and should be conducted in accordance with the provisions of the 1991 Espoo Convention as well as bilateral and multilateral agreements to which Tajikistan is a party.[602] The Procedure also requires information about all sources of possible adverse impact on the environment, including one in a transboundary context, to be gathered, and the affected public, including in the areas of transboundary impact, are to be informed.[603]

The 2007 Environmental Law of Afghanistan does not contain separate provisions on a transboundary EIA, but states that 'Where there are environmental issues of a regional or transboundary nature, the Islamic Republic of Afghanistan shall cooperate with other States to resolve these issues'.[604]

The above provisions of the national laws do not provide precise methodologies for *how* transboundary EIA should be carried out. In particular, these fall short of specifying detailed procedures to ensure that the transboundary effects of the project are examined and taken into due account, and to collect and disseminate information on transboundary effects. Certain minimal standards on these matters can be found in the 1991 Espoo Convention to which Kazakhstan and the Kyrgyz Republic are parties, and to which Tajikistan explicitly stated its adherence. In contrast, Turkmenistan and Uzbekistan are neither parties to the 1991 Espoo Convention nor have been designated any provisions on transboundary aspects of EIA in their respective legislations. Hence, accession to the 1991 Espoo Convention or adoption of a specific regional agreement would help countries to harmonise their laws at the transboundary level and to address the problem of reciprocity by binding all parties to the same minimum standards with respect to the activities that might have transboundary impacts.

5.5 Emergency Cooperation

The devastating effects of natural and human-induced disasters on people and the environment ignore political boundaries and call for active cooperation

602 Procedure on EIA in Tajikistan, Chapter 3.

603 Dmitriy Skrylnikov, *A review of the national legislation of the Republic of Tajikistan on environmental impact assessment in the context of implementation and application of the Espoo Convention. In Russian* (Bureau of Environmental Investigation, 2010) at 11, para 64.

604 2007 Environmental Law of Afghanistan, art 5.

between the countries in order to prevent, reduce and eliminate the harmful effects of these events. The 1997 UN Watercourses Convention treats these cases as a matter of 'emergency', understood as 'a situation that causes, or poses an imminent threat of causing, serious harm to watercourse States or other States and that results suddenly from natural causes, such as floods, the breaking up of ice, and slides or earthquakes, or from human conduct, such as industrial accidents'.[605] Accordingly, what distinguishes 'emergency' from other situations or activities that may have transboundary effects is that it involves 'imminent threat' and results 'suddenly'.[606] The need for cooperation throughout all phases of emergency situations, such as prevention, preparedness, response and restoration, gains even greater significance in the light of continuing extreme climatic and other events.

Today, the general duty to notify each other and cooperate in cases of emergencies is widely endorsed in state practice.[607] Its application to transboundary waters, as a matter of customary law, finds reflection in the forceful and precise language of Articles 27 and 28 of the 1997 UN Watercourses Convention and Articles 3(j) and 14 of 1992 UNECE Water Convention. These obligations set forth both anticipatory and responsive actions for states.

The anticipatory actions have to deal with the prevention of and preparedness to emergencies. In particular, the Article 27 of the 1997 UN Watercourses Convention provides that

> [States] shall, individually and, where appropriate, jointly, take all appropriate measures to prevent or mitigate harmful conditions related to an

---

605 1997 UN Watercourses Convention, art 27. 1992 UNECE Water Convention, arts 14–15 deals with a 'critical situation that may cause transboundary impact'. Tanzi and Arcari, *The un Convention on the Law of International Watercourses* at 224 explains that the term 'critical situation' used in Articles 14 and 15 of the 1992 UNECE Water Convention enables the scope of these provisions to cover at the same time situations that in the present 1997 UN Watercourses Convention are covered separately by Articles 27 and 28, i.e. harmful conditions, on the one hand, and emergency situations, on the other.

606 See *Corfu Channel* on the discussion of 'imminent threat'.

607 Birnie, Boyle and Redgwell, *International law and the environment* at 571 (stating that 'The general principle that states must notify each other and cooperate in cases of emergency to avert harm to other states applies also to international watercourses'); Handl, 'Transboundary impacts' at 542 ('the case for the obligation to notify in emergency situations might arguably be strongest in terms of international support in practice'); ILA's 2004 Berlin Rules (stating that articles 27 and 28 of the 1997 UN Watercourses Convention reflects customary international law expressed in numerous international environmental instruments). Rio Declaration, principle 18.

> international watercourse that may be harmful to other watercourse States, whether resulting from natural causes resulting from natural causes or human conduct, such as flood or ice conditions, water-borne diseases, siltation, erosion, salt-water intrusion, drought or desertification.[608]

As the 1994 ILC Commentary explains, this wording is an application of the general obligation of equitable participation that received a special consideration due to the severity of these problems.[609] The 1997 UN Watercourses Convention is also clear in setting another preventive norm that requires states to develop contingency plans to be prepared for responding to emergencies when these occur.[610] Similarly, the 1992 UNECE Water Convention prescribes its Parties to ensure that contingency planning is developed[611] and the Riparian Parties to 'set up, where appropriate, and operate coordinated or joint

608 1997 UN Watercourses Convention, art 27.

609 ILC Commentary to 1994 Draft Articles at 129 para 2. See also Tanzi and Arcari, *The UN Convention on the Law of International Watercourses* at 222 (discussing complementary role of the Article 27 with respect to Article 7 together with other provisions, namely, with respect to Article 9, on regular exchange of data and information, to Part III on planned measures, to Articles 5(2), 20 and 21 on protection and preservation of the ecosystems of international watercourses, to Article 24 on the obligation of consultation on management, and to Articles 25 and 26, insofar as they provide, respectively, the obligation to co-operate in the regulation of the flow and in the operation, maintenance and protection of installations). Cf. Vinogradov, Wouters and Jones, *Transforming potential conflict into cooperation potential* at 25 (arguing that 'However, there is no international customary legal obligation that would require a state to prevent or mitigate natural conditions on its territory, which contribute to naturally occurring hazards, such as flooding').

610 1997 UN Watercourses Convention, art 28(4) reads,

> When necessary, watercourse States shall jointly develop contingency plans for responding to emergencies, in cooperation, where appropriate, with other potentially affected States and competent international organizations.

See also 2001 ILC Draft Articles, art 16 (Emergency preparedness) which states, The State of origin shall develop contingency plans for responding to emergencies, in cooperation, where appropriate, with the State likely to be affected and competent international organizations.

611 1992 UNECE Water Convention, art 3(1)(j) reads,

> To prevent, control and reduce transboundary impact, the Parties shall develop, adopt, implement and, as far as possible, render compatible relevant legal, administrative, economic, financial and technical measures, in order to ensure, *inter alia*, that: (j) Contingency planning is developed.

communication, warning and alarm systems with the aim of obtaining and transmitting information'.[612]

In responding to an actual emergency situation, according to the 1997 UN Watercourses Convention, a state bears the strict obligation to notify, 'without delay and by the most expeditious means available, [...] other potentially affected states and competent international organisations of any emergency originating within its territory'.[613] The 1992 UNECE Water Convention imposes the similar obligation to 'without delay inform [...] about any critical situation that may have transboundary impact', but only on the Riparian Parties vis-à-vis each other.[614] Both provisions establish a rather low threshold to trigger the obligation to notify – the imminent threat of 'serious harm' and the critical risk of 'any significant adverse effect' respectively – to allow states notify each other on a wider range of situations.[615] Neither of these conventions specifies the content of notification, but useful guidelines on the information to be provided in notification can be found in the OECD Guiding Principles on the Environment.[616] Finally, the requirement to prevent, mitigate and eliminate harmful effects of emergency is couched in the 1997 UN Watercourses Convention in forceful language as a standard of due diligence by requiring a

---

612 Ibid, art 14.

613 1997 UN Watercourses Convention, art 28(2). See also 2001 ILC Draft Articles, art 17.

614 1992 UNECE Water Convention, art 14.

615 The fact that these provisions leave certain discretion to a state in which emergency occurs to determine whether the threshold is reached might raise questions on the norm determinacy. However, these claims might be dismissed by a convincing argument set forth by Nollkaemper that setting up a threshold '[i]nduced by the (in itself) legitimate objective not to overburden states with unnecessary notification requirements'. Nollkaemper, *The legal regime for transboundary water pollution* at 173. Cf. 'UNECE *Guide to Implementing the Convention*' at 106 para 299 (stating that 'This requirement does not fix the threshold or scale of possible transboundary impact. The lack of any threshold together with a reference to "any" critical situation serve to ensure that the Riparian Parties avoid losing time and inform each other about wider range of situations at the earliest stage'.).

616 An OECD Council Decision, OECD, Guiding Principles on the Environment, annex, tit A (1972), usefully suggests the information to be provided in notifying of harmful conditions: 1. The location and general description of the harmful condition or of a hazardous installation; 2. General information regarding the nature, extent, and likely effects on human health or well-being or on the environment generally arising from the harmful condition; 3. The common chemical names or the generic names or the general danger classifications of any substances likely to cause transfrontier harm; 4. The legislative, regulatory, and administrative requirements affecting the harmful condition; and 5. Information on any emergency plans relevant to the exposed country.

state within whose territory an emergency originates, 'in cooperation with potentially affected states and, where appropriate, competent international organizations, [...] take all practicable measures necessitated by the circumstances' to do so.[617]

Given that these provisions mainly concerned with the obligations imposed on a state within whose territory an emergency originates, the question may arise whether there are any normative requirements with the respect to the conduct of a potentially affected state (or other states) in responding to emergencies. In this regard, Bourne argues that 'the neighbouring state exposed to the danger is itself under a duty to use reasonable care to ensure its own safety; if it does not do so, it may be held to have contributed to its own injury and thus be wholly or partly responsible for it'.[618] In certain extent, this argument seems to find its reflection in Article 28 (3) of the 1997 UN Watercourses Convention requiring a state within whose territory an emergency originates, 'in cooperation with potentially affected States and, where appropriate, competent international organizations, [...] take all practicable measures necessitated by the circumstances to prevent, mitigate and eliminate harmful effects of the emergency'.[619] However, the terms of the 1998 CIS Agreement on Transboundary Waters are more straightforward in stating that parties (not only a state of origin) assume the due diligence obligation to take measures, individually or when necessary in concurrence with other interested parties, to reduce and eliminate the effects of natural and human-induced emergencies,[620] such as floods, ice drift and accidental pollution.[621]

Similar emergency related obligations, with different degree of specificity and stringency, are contained in global and regional MEAs that deal with water-related issue, such as biodiversity or wetlands, or particular types of emergencies, such as industrial accidents. The terms of the Convention on Biodiversity are stringent with respect to the obligation to notify, prevent and

---

An exposed State would be required to provide the following information: 1. The distribution of its population, including any particularly sensitive groups; 2. The location and general description of any properties likely to be affected adversely; and 3. The location of natural resources, protected areas, sensitive ecosystems, and historical monuments that could be damaged.

617 1997 UN Watercourses Convention, art 28(3).

618 'Procedure in the Development of International Drainage Basin: Notice and Exchange of Information' in Patricia Wouters (ed) *International water law: Selected writings of Professor Charles B. Bourne* (Kluwer Law International 1997) at 156.

619 1997 UN Watercourses Convention, art 28(3).

620 1998 CIS Agreement on Transboundary Waters, art 1.

621 Ibid, art 6.

minimize imminent or grave danger or damage to biological diversity and rather weak in requesting the Parties to 'promote' national arrangements for emergency responses and 'encourage' international cooperation.[622] Although the text of the Ramsar Convention does not contain provisions dealing with emergencies, the Contracting Parties to the Convention adopted resolutions to address impacts associated with natural disasters.[623] The 1992 UNECE Convention on the Transboundary Effects of Industrial Accidents, to which Kazakhstan is a party, is designed to protect human beings and the environment against industrial accidents.[624] It specifies in great details the measures

---

622 Convention on Biodiversity, arts 14(1)(d) and (e) reads,

> Each Contracting Party, as far as possible and as appropriate, shall [...i]n the case of imminent or grave danger or damage, originating under its jurisdiction or control, to biological diversity within the area under jurisdiction of other States or in areas beyond the limits of national jurisdiction, notify immediately the potentially affected States of such danger or damage, as well as initiate action to prevent or minimize such danger or damage; and [...p]romote national arrangements for emergency responses to activities or events, whether caused naturally or otherwise, which present a grave and imminent danger to biological diversity and encourage international cooperation to supplement such national efforts and, where appropriate and agreed by the States or regional economic integration organizations concerned, to establish joint contingency plans.

623 In 2002, the Contracting Parties to the Ramsar Convention adopted Resolution VIII.35 on 'The impact of natural disasters, particularly drought, on wetland ecosystems', requesting monitoring and assessment of the impact of drought and other natural disasters on the ecological character of wetlands and on the livelihoods of local communities. In 2005 Resolution IX.9 on 'The role of the Ramsar Convention in the prevention and mitigation of impacts associated with natural phenomena, including those induced or exacerbated by human activities'. See also Agreement on Interface Procedures between the Secretariat of the Ramsar Convention on Wetlands (Ramsar Secretariat) and The Joint UNEP/OCHA Environment Unit of the UN Office for the Coordination of Humanitarian Affairs (OCHA) (17 January 2007).

624 UNECE Convention on Industrial Accidents, art 2 sets the scope of the Convention as follow,

> 1. This Convention shall apply to the prevention of, preparedness for and response to industrial accidents capable of causing transboundary effects, including the effects of such accidents caused by natural disasters, and to international cooperation concerning mutual assistance, research and development, exchange of information and exchange of technology in the area of prevention of, preparedness for and response to industrial accidents.
>
> 2. This Convention shall not apply to: (a) Nuclear accidents or radiological emergencies; (b) Accidents at military installations; (c) Dam failures, with the exception of the effects of industrial accidents caused by such failures; (d) Land-based transport

to be taken in order to establish an active international cooperation between countries before, during and after an industrial accident. The Convention seeks to prevent such accidents as far as possible, by reducing their frequency and severity and by mitigating their effects and spells out the obligations imposed on its Parties in stringent language of affirmative actions towards an objective ('shall take appropriate measures', 'shall cooperate', 'shall ensure', 'shall enter into discussions', 'shall apply', 'shall inform', 'shall provide', 'shall exchange', 'shall keep', 'shall report', or 'shall endeavour').

Treaty law under the umbrella of the Commonwealth also envisages preventive and responsive obligations that deal with emergencies situations in forceful language. In the 1998 CIS Agreement on Transboundary Waters, parties assume the due diligence obligation to take measures to reduce and eliminate the effects of natural and human-induced emergencies, such as floods, ice drift and accidental pollution.[625] The 1992 CIS Agreement on Environmental Interaction obliges its parties to set up and maintain special forces and assets in order to prevent ecological disasters and accidents as well as eliminate their effects.[626] It is a main task of the parties to the 1998 CIS Agreement on Informational Cooperation to alarm about environmental emergencies, accidents and hazardous waste transfers.[627]

In the context of the Aral Sea basin, Kazakhstan, Kyrgyzstan, Tajikistan and Uzbekistan must cooperate to ensure timely forecasting of natural hydrometeorological events and provide assistance to each other on the basis of international law in case of their occurrence.[628] Under the Agreement on the Parallel Operation of the Energy System, these four countries must provide mutual assistance in the cases of emergencies for implementing remedial actions on energy facilities and restoring normal energy supply for consumers.[629] In their efforts to prevent emergencies arising from the possible breakdown of tailings and rock dump due to adverse natural, climatic and hydrometeorological conditions, Kazakhstan, Kyrgyzstan and Uzbekistan

accidents with the exception of: (i) Emergency response to such accidents; (ii) Transportation on the site of the hazardous activity; (e) Accidental release of genetically modified organisms; (f) Accidents caused by activities in the marine environment, including seabed exploration or exploitation;(g) Spills of oil or other harmful substances at sea.

625 1998 CIS Agreement on Transboundary Waters, arts 1 and 6.

626 1992 CIS Environmental Interaction Agreement, arts 2–4.

627 1998 CIS Informational Cooperation Agreement, art 3.

628 1999 Agreement on Hydromet, preambular recitals and art 3 on the forms of cooperation.

629 1999 Agreement on the Parallel Operation of the CARs' Energy System, art 8.

agreed to assess the danger, prepare tailings deactivation and closure projects, and undertake activities on rock dump reclamation.[630] Further, the 1996 Agreement on the Use of Fuel and Energy Resources and Water Resources, Construction and Operation of Gas Pipelines requires these three countries to nominate the ministries and agencies in charge of information exchange on the occurrence or likelihood of occurrence of contingency situations on reservoir cascades, hydropower stations and interconnection lines and to participate jointly in their prevention and elimination.[631] Finally, the 1958 Soviet-Afghan Frontier Treaty prescribes parties to exchange information in order to avert danger or damage from flooding, and alert each other during periods of high water.[632]

5.6 Compliance Review

This section examines whether the treaties under consideration provide for a compliance review procedure and assign institutions devoted to monitoring compliance in a determinate and precise manner.

The regional and global water-related conventions contain some provisions to monitor and facilitate compliance. The 1997 UN Watercourses Convention does not require compliance monitoring *per se*, but it does establish various provisions to facilitate it. These include Articles 8 on general obligation to cooperate, Article 9 on regular exchange of data and information, Articles 11–19 on planned measures, and Article 24 on management.

630 Agreement between the Government of the Republic of Kazakhstan, the Government of the Kyrgyz Republic, the Government of the Republic of Tajikistan and the Government the Republic of Uzbekistan on Joint Activities on the Rehabilitation of the Tailings and Rock Dump that have Transboundary Effect, Tashkent (signed 5 April 1996), arts 1–5.

631 Agreement between the Government of the Republic of Kazakhstan, the Government of the Kyrgyz Republic and the Government of the Republic of Uzbekistan on the Use of Fuel and Water Resources, Construction and Operation of Gas Pipelines in Central Asian Region, Tashkent (signed 5 April 1996). Online: <http://www.cawater-info.net/library/rus/gov5.pdf>, art 1.

632 1958 Soviet-Afghan Frontier Treaty, art 17 reads,

> The competent authorities of the Contracting Parties shall exchange as regularly as possible such information concerning the level and volume of water in frontier rivers and also concerning precipitation in the interior of the territory of the two Parties as might avert danger or damage from flooding. The competent authorities shall as necessary also agree on a mutual system of signals during periods of high water.

Another issue is the lack of governing mechanisms under the Convention, such as the Meeting of the Parties or the Secretariat, to facilitate and review compliance. In his 6th Report, the Special Rapporteur had proposed a draft article on the Conference of the Parties that would provide for 'institutionalized and regular collective action by the contracting parties', and 'permit the parties to review, on a regular basis, the effectiveness of the convention in question and monitor its performance'. The Special Rapporteur was hesitant to propose the establishment of the Secretariat 'in connection to what is envisaged as a framework agreement'.[633] However, this does not preclude the parties to the Convention establishing such institutions in the future if they so decide, following, for instance, the model of the Ramsar Convention[634] or conventions under the umbrella of the UNECE which provide a sound institutional support to facilitate implementation and compliance with their requirements through the Meetings of the Parties, secretariats, implementation and compliance committees, and various working groups and boards.[635] Various suggestions have been raised recently on the possible housing for the 1997 UN Watercourses Convention, mostly among UN agencies such as UNEP, UNESCO or UNECE.[636]

---

633 *Sixth Report on the Law of the Non-Navigational Uses of International Watercourses, by Mr Stephen C. McCaffrey, Special Rapporteur,* [*1990*] *2*(*10*) *YB Int'l L Comm'n, 41* [6th Report by McCaffrey], 64 para 1 and 65 para 3.

634 Second Meeting of the Conference of the Contracting Parties (May 1984, Groningen, Netherlands) established the framework for implementing the Ramsar Convention. Online: <www.ramsar.org> accessed 3 July 2013.

635 See eg 1992 UNECE Water Convention, arts 17 and 19; Espoo Convention, arts 11 and 13 and Decision II/4 of the 2nd Meeting of the Parties revised as Decision III/2.

636 See eg 'Bangkok Declaration of African Basin Organizations', First International Environment Forum For Basin Organizations, African Basin Organizations Consultative Meeting Pre-Session Event, 24–25 October 2011, Bangkok ('There is a need for an agency to champion the implementation of the 1997 UN Convention and the ILC Draft Articles on the Law of Transboundary Aquifers, probably appointing relevant UN agencies, in particular UNEP and UNESCO, to take up that role'); UNEP's solution for Solutions for Water platform – 6th World Water Forum in Marseille, 12–17 March 2012 'Facilitating the implementation of international water law principles by utilizing UNEP's extensive experience and institutional capacity administering multilateral environmental agreements'. Online: <http://www.solutionsforwater.org/solutions/facilitating-the-implementation-of-international-water-law-principles-by-utilizing-uneps-extensive-experience-and-institutional-capacity-administering-multilateral-environmental-agreements> accessed 22 December 2013. The representative of the Bureau of 1992 UNECE Water Convention, Sibylle Vermont, during one of the panels at the 6th World Water Forum suggested to consider UNECE as a possible secretariat, given its extensive

Such institutional support is capable even in the absence of explicit provisions regarding compliance review, as it is the case for the 1992 UNECE Water Convention. The framework nature of the Convention implies that detailed compliance control provisions are subject to basin specific agreements.[637] Nonetheless, a number of the articles of the 1992 UNECE Water Convention are used as a foundation for building a cooperative framework to facilitate compliance, including Article 10 on consultations, Article 11 on joint monitoring and assessment, Article 12 on common research and development, Article 13 on exchange of information, Article 15 on mutual assistance, Article 16 on public information, and Article 17 on the Meeting of the Parties. The latter article that entrusts the Meeting of the Parties to 'keep under continuous review the implementation of this Convention',[638] has served the Meeting of the Parties to initiate a preparatory work for establishment a specific mechanism under the Convention through which problems related to implementation and possible differences on the Convention's interpretation could be addressed. This endeavor sought to address concerns raised by a number of countries that Parties 'do not have a clear and permanent forum to resort to for advice and support in the case of a specific potential or ongoing problem of a procedural, legal and/or technical nature'.[639] With this in mind, the Meeting of the Parties has authorised the Legal Board of the Convention to explore options for the establishment of a mechanism to support implementation and

experience in administering multilateral environmental agreements, including the 1992 UNECE Water Convention, which may soon become the only global water instrument in force.

637 The Protocol on Water and Health to the UNECE Water Convention (London 17 June 1999) ECOSOC Doc MPWAT/AC1/1999/1 (signed 24 March 1999, entered into force 4 August 2005) takes another step forward and includes several compliance review provisions. See UNECE and WHO Regional Office For Europe 'Report of the Meeting of the Parties to the Protocol on Water and Health' (Meeting of the Parties 1st Sess 17–19 January 2007 Geneva) UN Doc ECE/MP WH/2/Add3 EUR/06/5069385/1/Add3. The protocol's compliance mechanism is not covered here in detail as none of the CARs is a party to it.

638 1992 UNECE Water Convention, art 12(2).

639 'UNECE Facilitating and supporting implementation and compliance: A needed step in the Convention's evolution. Background document' (2009) Meeting of the Parties to Convention on the Protection and Use of Transboundary Watercourses and International Lakes 5th Session Geneva 10–12 November 2009 UN Doc ECE/MPWAT/2009/3. UNECE Highlights Meeting of the Parties to Convention on the Protection and Use of Transboundary Watercourses and International Lakes 5th Session Geneva 10–12 November 2009. Online: <http://www.unece.org/env/water/mop5.htm> accessed 20 April 2013.

compliance. Based on results of this work, the Meeting of the Parties, at its sixth session in 2012, established the Implementation Committee with the aim to facilitate, promote and safeguard the implementation and application of and compliance with the 1992 UNECE Water Convention.[640]

Other UNECE conventions also set up compliance review and monitoring systems.[641] Under the 1991 Espoo Convention, implementation is reviewed through periodic national reports submitted by parties completing a questionnaire.[642] This Convention also envisages two specific institutional mechanisms to facilitate implementation and compliance: the implementation committee, and an inquiry commission. Parties are invited to make submissions to the implementation committee if they have concerns about their own or another party's compliance with obligations under the convention.[643] An inquiry procedure allows parties to make a submission to an inquiry commission to 'advise on the likelihood of significant adverse transboundary impact' if they cannot reach agreement between themselves.[644]

Finally, the compliance mechanism of the Aarhus Convention, another UNECE instrument, is frequently referred to as unique.[645] Kravchenko defines three significant features of this mechanism: '(i) the ability of nongovernmental organisations to nominate experts for possible election to the Compliance Committee; (ii) the requirement that all Committee members be independent experts rather than representatives of state Parties to the Convention; and (iii) the right of any member of the public and any NGO to file a "communication" with the Committee alleging a Party's noncompliance'.[646] The Aarhus Convention also requires regular reporting on the implementation of the convention.[647]

640 1992 UNECE Water Convention, Decision VI/1 on support to implementation and compliance (Meeting of the Parties 6th Sess 28–30 November 2012 Rome) UN Doc ECE/MP.WAT/37/Add.2.

641 See eg Espoo Convention, Decision II/10 on the review and Aarhus Convention, art 10(2).

642 Espoo Convention, Decision II/10 on the review.

643 Espoo Convention art 11(2) and Decision II/4 of the 2nd Meeting of the Parties revised as Decision III/2.

644 Espoo Convention, art 3 and app IV.

645 Aarhus Convention, art 15 on review of compliance and Decision I/7 on review of compliance adopted at the First Meeting of the Parties to Aarhus Convention (21–23 October 2002).

646 Kravchenko, 'The Aarhus Convention and innovations in compliance with multilateral environmental agreements' at 1.

647 Aarhus Convention, art 10(2).

Four of the global MEAs – the Ramsar Convention, the Convention on Biodiversity, the Convention on Desertification and the Convention on Climate Change – enjoy a developed compliance review system. These conventions provide for some form of general reporting and monitoring to which all parties are subject (performance review information), and non-compliance response information, designed for those parties found to be in non-compliance. Performance review information is gathered through national self-reporting in the Ramsar Convention,[648] the Convention on Biodiversity,[649] the Convention on Desertification,[650] and the Convention on Climate Change.[651] The Ramsar Convention includes a template review format while the Conventions on Biodiversity, Desertification and Climate Change provide detailed guidelines.[652] Third party monitoring of the national reporting system and third party verification of national performance review can be respectively undertaken under the Ramsar Convention and the Convention on Climate Change.[653] The Ramsar Convention also provides for third party monitoring of degraded wetlands as a non-compliance response.[654]

In 2007, the UNEP analysed compliance mechanisms under selected MEAs and found promising opportunities for links between their compliance review

648 Ramsar Convention, art 6 established a Conference of the Contracting Parties (COP) to review and promote its implementation. COP 2 (1984) recommended that all parties submit reports to the bureau six months before each ordinary COP. Ramsar Recommendations 2.1 and 4.3.

649 Convention on Biodiversity, art 26 calls upon parties to present to the Conference of the Parties, reports on measures which it has taken for the implementation of the provisions of this Convention and their effectiveness in meeting the objectives of this Convention.

650 Convention on Desertification, art 26(1) states that 'each party shall communicate to the Conference of the Parties [...] reports on the measures which it has taken for the implementation of the Convention'. For more information see online: <http://www.cbd.int/reports/>accessed 22 December 2013.

651 There exist different reporting obligations for Annex I and non-Annex I Parties. Convention on Climate Change, art 7 provides for regular self-reporting by Annex I Parties. Online: <http://unfccc.int/nationalreports/items/1408.php> accessed 22 December 2013.

652 For more information on the Convention on Biodiversity guidelines see online: <http://www.cbd.int/reports/guidelines/≥; on the Convention on Desertification see online: <http://www.unccd.int/cop/cric5/helpguides.php≥; see also Convention on Climate Change, Decisions 22/CP.7 and 22/CP.8 and Online: <http://unfccc.int/nationalreports/items/1408.php> accessed 22 December 2013.

653 Convention on Climate Change, art 8 establishes a third-party process for independent review of self-reported information. The Convention on Climate Change Secretariat conducts on-site verifications, mainly to obtain performance information.

654 Ramsar Convention, annex 1 to recommendation 4.7.

requirements.[655] The study also pointed out the importance of links between subject-related global, regional and bilateral MEAs, but to date research efforts have not focused on the water-related cluster of international agreements.

At the basin level, beyond the basic procedural norms related to notification, consultation and exchange of information, specific legal norms related to implementation and compliance are relatively limited. The sub-regional agreements do not provide for a compliance review procedure. Article 2 of the 1992 Almaty Agreement prescribes in forceful language that parties shall ensure that the agreed regime is 'strictly observed', but it remains unclear how non-compliance shall be detected and monitored.[656] The same agreement stipulates that, by 1992, parties should have elaborated economic and other measures to deal with the cases of non-compliance with the established regime and limits of water use; however, such mechanisms are still lacking.[657] Some disjointed attempts to monitor and facilitate compliance have been undertaken under the 1998 Syrdarya Agreement. Article 5 stipulates that parties shall take appropriate measures to ensure compliance with the provisions of the agreement through various forms of guarantees, such as credit lines, security deposits and others.[658] Article 7 of the 2001 Protocol adopted to implement the 1998 Syrdarya Agreement states that, when necessary, the parties shall allow observers from other contracting parties access to water management facilities in the Syrdarya river basin operation area.[659]

Although a compliance control system is yet to be established in the sub-region, the activities of the ICWC and its executive bodies appear to provide a basis on which such a system can be built. Although the ICWC does not have a mandate to monitor compliance, its practice helps to establish a collective and transparent forum for preventing and addressing controversies. A recent development of sub-regional and national information systems on water and environmental issues under the aegis of the ICWC (discussed above) is one such example.

---

655 UNEP 'Compliance Mechanisms under Selected Multilateral Environmental Agreements' (UNEP Nairobi 2007) at 13.

656 1992 Almaty Agreement, art 2.

657 Ibid, art 12.

658 1998 Syrdarya Agreement, art 5.

659 Protocol between the Governments of the Republic of Kazakhstan, the Kyrgyz Republic, and the Republic of Uzbekistan on the Use of Water and Energy Resources of the Naryn-Syrdarya Cascade in 2001, Bishkek (signed 20 May 2001).

5.7 Dispute Settlement

Finally, in line with Article 2(3) of the UN Charter states are under an obligation to settle their disputes, if these arise, by peaceful means. At the global level, the 1997 UN Watercourses Convention echoes this requirement. In addition to traditional means of negotiation, the good offices, mediation or conciliation, arbitration or adjudication, the Convention provides for the possibility to establish an impartial fact-finding commission to resolve a dispute.[660] The relevant provisions reiterate the residual character of the 1997 UN Watercourses Convention by stating that its dispute settlement provisions can be invoked in the absence of an applicable agreement between the parties.[661] Further, the Convention requires that the parties concerned shall seek a settlement of the dispute by peaceful means. Such means may include negotiations, good offices, mediation or conciliation by a third party, or joint watercourse institutions. The parties may also agree to submit the dispute to arbitration, according to the procedure established in the Annexes to the Convention, or to the International Court of Justice. What is more, the Convention provides an innovative mechanism of an impartial fact-finding commission to resolve a dispute, which can be triggered if the parties concerned have not been able to settle their dispute through negotiation or any other means within six months from the time of the request for negotiations.[662] Upon completion of its investigation, the Commission issues report with 'its findings and the reasons therefor and such recommendations as it deems appropriate for an equitable solution of the dispute, which the parties concerned shall consider in good faith.'[663]

The 1992 UNECE Water Convention is less detailed regarding dispute resolution. Article 22 makes a concise reference to 'seek a solution by negotiation or by any other means of dispute settlement acceptable to the parties to the dispute'.[664] The possibility to refer a dispute not resolved by the above means to the judicial and arbitral bodies is optional for the parties. The parties may accept such dispute settlement means as compulsory when signing, ratifying, accepting, approving or acceding to the Convention.[665] For such cases, the Convention specifies arbitration procedures in its annex.[666]

---

660 1997 UN Watercourses Convention, art 33.

661 Ibid, art 33(1).

662 Ibid, art 33(3–10).

663 Ibid, art 33(8).

664 1992 UNECE Water Convention, art 22 (1).

665 Ibid, art 22(2).

666 Ibid, annex IV (arbitration).

Dispute settlement mechanisms relating to transboundary waters are largely undeveloped in the Aral Sea basin treaties. The 1992 Almaty Agreement refers any dispute that could arise between the parties to the Ministers of Water Resources for the five CARs. In other words, disputes shall be resolved internally within the ICWC, the body responsible for the implementation of this agreement. As such, the ICWC acts to prevent and resolve emerging controversies and provides a forum where representatives of the five basin states can meet, discuss, and make binding decisions on contentious issues. The 1992 Agreement further states that 'if necessary, an impartial third party can be involved',[667] but fails to detail the procedure for such a dispute settlement, and further measures if a dispute cannot be resolved in this manner. Article 9 of the 1998 Syrdarya Agreement use the stringent language to prescribe that 'Any dispute or controversy under this agreement is subject of negotiation and consultations. If the dispute cannot be resolved in this manner, the issue shall be submitted to an *ad hoc* arbitral tribunal'. However, the agreement does not specify the rules and procedures by which such a tribunal shall operate.

Conclusion

This chapter has explored the norms that form the procedural system of transboundary water cooperation in the Aral Sea basin and compliance and dispute settlement mechanisms through the lenses of determinacy and stringency.

The analysis has shown that for the most part customary and treaty law creates for the Aral Sea basin countries obligations to establish joint bodies, to exchange information with riparian states, to consult with each other, to notify regarding proposed activities, to conduct transboundary impact assessments, and to work together in emergency situations in stringent terms; while leaving the content of these obligations as applied to the transboundary waters in the basin less defined. For example, a general minimum requirement on information exchange is set forth clearly as a matter of customary law, whereas the sub-regional agreements seem to fall short of indicating detailed provisions on information about specific characteristic of the region's watercourses that would enable more effective implementation of the equitable and reasonable use principle in the basin. Similarly, the sub-regional treaties, which are mostly framework agreements, impose a set of obligations for the parties to exercise

667 1992 Almaty Agreement, art 13.

'coordinated management' and prevent them from acting unilaterally rather than specifying a procedural system concerning planned measures in the basin. More consistent endeavours are required to ensure that impact assessment procedures for activities that may have transboundary impacts are set up on a reciprocal and equivalent basis either in national laws or in international instruments, such as the 1991 Espoo Convention, that would allow the countries to have the same minimum standards to be followed in the case of planned measures.

It is unfortunate that relevant procedural provisions, if these exist, are scattered in various instruments, which are poorly connected to each other on their own. Inconsistencies in the formulation of the obligations are also widespread, that does not help increase the clarity of the norms. The different thresholds to trigger the obligations of notification and impact assessment, and the lack of clarity and coherence in the documents defining an institutional structure of cooperation are illustrative in this regard. These shortcomings impede the ability of the countries to ascertain the required standards of their conduct and, ultimately, the ability of the law to generate behavioural (normative) expectations as its core function.

Beyond the basic procedural norms related to notification, consultation and exchange of information, specific legal norms related to compliance and dispute settlement are relatively limited in the Aral Sea basin. A review of the compliance provisions embedded in sub-regional, regional, and global water-related agreements shows that much remains to be done if a sound compliance regime for transboundary water resources management is to be developed. Useful lessons can be learned from MEAs, especially under the UNECE umbrella, but care should be taken to avoid 'blind' transplantation. As Beyerlin reminds us, 'every single MEA needs its own tailor-made compliance control mechanism [...and] choosing the "right" [one] depends on the type of obligations contained in each particular treaty'.[668] The same stands for dispute settlement provisions of the sub-regional agreements.

This having been said, it will be misleading to dismiss the existing system of procedural cooperation in relation to transboundary waters in the Aral Sea basin as weak on these only grounds. It remains to be considered whether and

668 Ulrich Beyerlin, Peter-Tobias Stoll and Rudiger Wolfrum, 'Conclusions drawn from the Conference on Ensuring Compliance with MEAs' in Ulrich Beyerlin, Peter-Tobias Stoll and Rudiger Wolfrum (eds), *Ensuring compliance with multilateral environmental agreements: Academic analysis and views from practice* (Koninklijke Brill NV 2006). Online: <http://www.umweltbundesamt.de/umweltrecht/conclusions.pdf> accessed 22 December 2013.

how well the existing legal regime reflects the process characteristics of inclusiveness, transparency, discursiveness, and coherence that are essential to generate, elaborate and refine shared understandings and collective expectations about the meaning and implementation of the norms. The next chapter will explore this question.

CHAPTER 6

International Water Law in the Aral Sea Basin

Process Properties

The creation and maintenance of international law requires a commitment to communication, a willingness to listen, and openness to reciprocal modification of outlook.[669]

The preceding two chapters have illustrated that there exists an extensive body of legal norms applicable to transboundary waters in the Aral Sea basin, characterised by the various degree of stringency and determinacy and standing in need for constant process of interactions about their meaning and implementation. This chapter looks at international water law as constituted by and enabling continuous process of interactions among actors, serving to generate, elaborate and refine shared understandings and collective expectations about the meaning and implementation of the norms.

The central argument of the chapter is that the work of international law is the work of building and maintaining transboundary water relationships, which is best done if legal processes are inclusive, transparent, discursive and integrative. The theoretical underpinnings of the argument rest on the understanding of law as a system of legal relations built through the continuous process of interactions in law making, interpretation, and implementation.[670] On this account, a right or duty represents a legal relation, which is to be built and maintained. Reframing analysis in this way gives a more dynamic picture of international law and its role in building transboundary water relationships that allows for adaptability, flexibility and learning, while also substantially anchored by the requirements of clarity, predictability and stability in legal relationship.

To advance the argument, international legal interactions relevant to transboundary waters in the Aral Sea basin is scrutinised through the lens of four process features, namely inclusiveness, transparency, discursiveness and

669 Brunnée and Toope, *Legitimacy and legality* at 353.

670 Allott, 'The concept of international law' at 36: 'Law is not, as so often supposed, a system of legal rules. Law is a system of legal relations. A legal system is infinite number of interlocking legal relations forming a network of infinite density. A legal relation (right, duty, power, freedom, liability, immunity, disability) is a pattern of potentiality into which actual persons and situations may be fitted'. See also Deidre Curtin and Andre Nollkaemper, 'Conceptualizing accountability in international and European Law' (2005) 36 Netherlands Yearbook of International Law 3–20 at 8.

 | DOI 10.1163/9789004274266_007

coherence; each contributing to a more effective interaction on its own way, but all of them being interrelated to each other.

6.1 Inclusiveness

Inclusiveness refers to a process of taking part, but also of relating to others. It helps to unfold what actors are involved in international legal interactions, in what capacity, and how they relate to and connect with each other. The very idea of transboundary water management, with its political, socio-economic, environmental and technical complexities, calls for the engagement of the broadest spectrum of actors, including diverse governmental and non-governmental agencies as well as the general public and individuals within and across national borders. However, the degree of participation in transboundary water interactions and inputs from these actors varies, contingent to political and legal environment as well as the nature and scope of an issue at stake or activity under consideration.

Nation states, represented by the heads of the states, diplomats or top officials from water, energy and environmental authorities, remain the main actors in the transboundary water interactions in the Aral Sea basin. Such interactions take forms of political, professional, and even personal communications that at different degrees influence transboundary water management in the basin. There exists a rather unique example of leadership that has been demonstrated by water professionals in establishing the current water management framework in the sub-region. In their capacities as the heads of water authorities within the structure of the Ministry of Land Reclamation and Water Recourses of the USSR, five top officials from the CARs' water ministries adopted a statement of 12 October 1991, in which they expressed their professional concerns with the growth of water deficit and the environmental tension in the Aral Sea basin and stated that a coordinated and joint response from all Central Asian republics is the only way to addressing water problems in the region.[671] Four months later, on 18 February 1992, the then-heads of water authorities of already new Central Asian republics – N. Kipshakbaev (Kazakhstan), M. Zulpuev (Kyrgyzstan), A. Norov (Tajikistan), A. Ilamanov (Turkmenistan), and R. Ginyatullin (Uzbekistan) – signed the 1992 Almaty Agreement, which still remains the foundational treaty governing relations of the five countries in the field of joint use and conservation of water resources

671 1991 Statement of the Heads of the CARs' water authorities.

diverted from transboundary rivers.[672] This leadership serves as a remarkable illustration of personal responsibility and wisdom of water professionals of the basin, the need for which is acute again.[673]

Interstate organisations provide a platform for institutionalised interactions on transboundary waters in the basin; yet these have been heavily criticised for the failure to include main stakeholders into their decision-making frameworks, among other things.[674] The fact that Interstate Commission for Water Coordination (ICWC) in Central Asia has no representatives either from energy or environmental sectors and insufficiently coordinates its activity with other sub-regional organisations seems to undermine its ability to take a strategic and integrated approach to transboundary water management in the Amudarya and Syrdarya basins. Intentions to establish a basin-wide advisory body, bringing together all stakeholders, for each river basin organisation incorporated into a new draft agreement on organisational structure,[675] and efforts to restructure the existing institutional framework led by EC IFAS and UNECE[676] seek to address some of these shortcomings.

Despite these deficiencies, the contribution of the sub-regional institutions such as ICWC and IFAS to transboundary cooperation is significant. In addition to providing a forum for information exchange, capacity building, conducting research and joint projects, these institutions have played a profound role in law development and implementation in the years after independence.

---

672 The heads of states has approved the signing of the 1992 Almaty Agreement by heads of water authorities in the 1995 Nukus Declaration.

673 Dukhovny and de Schutter, *Water in Central Asia: Past, present, future*.

674 See eg 2010 Discussion paper on Strengthening the institutional and legal frameworks of the International Fund for Saving the Aral Sea: Review and proposals.

675 Draft Agreement on Strengthening the Organisational Structure for Transboundary Water Management, Protection and Rational Use in the Aral Sea Basin (Version 1/2007) (on file with author), art 6(7) states that 'ICWC establishes a Basin Water Users Supervisory Board for each basin, which serves as a public consultation body to Basin Water Organisations'. See also Dukhovny and Sokolov, *Lessons on cooperation building to manage water conflicts in the Aral Sea basin* at 20 stating that 'The strategy prepared by ICWC envisages public participation developing from the basin level through the medium of basin committees, which should bring together representatives of different provinces, economic sectors (especially hydropower, ecology, agriculture, and water supply), along with government bodies and NGOs. Some proposals in the form of interstate agreements were suggested by IFAS and ICWC'.

676 Project 'Regional Dialogue and Cooperation on Water Resources' Management in Central Asia' implemented by the IFAS Executive Committee and UNECE, financed by the Government of Germany through GIZ. Online: <http://unece.org/env/water/cadialogue/cadwelcome.htm> accessed 9 April 2013.

Thus, protocols adopted in ICWC quarterly meetings not only set up water allocation quotas for each country and the Aral Sea, but also tried to accommodate irrigation and hydropower requirements to the extent possible. Those protocols also gave a green light to introducing contemporary approaches to water management such as integrated water resources management, strengthening informational cooperation, decision support systems and automation of head water facilities.[677]

Active involvement of the public in transboundary water interactions is not yet widespread in the region. Some commentators observe that basin-wide public engagement usually follows the progress on public participation at national level, which is still to be enhanced in the countries.[678] Still, non-governmental actors, affected groups and individuals are finding roles in the new multilateral and multilevel setting of transboundary interactions. Under the Aarhus Convention, which addresses environmental decision-making more generally, when activities listed under Annex I to the Convention are proposed, the state of origin is required to notify and extend participation rights to the public regardless of whether the proposed activity is likely to have a significant adverse transboundary impact. Arguably, the latter provision includes the involvement of 'external' public in a case of transboundary environmental impact assessment (EIA). The 1991 Espoo Convention clearly envisages this possibility, by requiring concerned Parties to ensure that the affected public is informed about proposed activities (Article 3(8)), receives documentation on the EIA (Article 4(2)), and has an opportunity to participate in the EIA procedures to the same extent as the public located in the Party of origin (Article 2(6)). Still, there exists no right under the 1991 Espoo Convention for foreign citizens to request information held by another state.[679]

In practical terms, there exists a range of examples in the countries of the Aral Sea basin to involve broader public participation as part of the efforts to

677 Information about the meetings of ICWC is available online: <http://www.icwc-aral.uz/meetings.htm> accessed 20 April 2013.

678 See eg Barbara Schreiner, Amos Mtsweni and Guy Pegram, *An institutional framework for stakeholder participation in transboundary basins* (Water Research Commission, 2010).

679 See also ILC Commentary to 2001 Draft articles 'Inspired by new trends in international law, in general, and environmental law, in particular', the ILC included in its Draft Article a requirement on providing information to 'the public likely to be affected'. Art 13 on information to the public reads,

> States concerned shall, by such means as are appropriate, provide the public likely to be affected by an activity within the scope of the present articles with relevant information relating to that activity, the risk involved and the harm which might result and ascertain their views.

implement IWRM principles. Participatory water management at water users association and main canals levels has been introduced in the pilot areas of the IWRM in Fergana Valley project implemented in Kyrgyzstan, Tajikistan and Uzbekistan.[680] There is some progress in introducing public participation into the activities of joint bodies for the Chu and Talas Rivers shared by Kazakhstan and the Kyrgyz Republic. In 2010, a Draft Statute of the proposed international (transboundary) basin council for the Chu and Talas Rivers was prepared and discussed at the 9th session of the Commission of the Republic of Kazakhstan and the Kyrgyz Republic on the Use of Water Management Facilities of Intergovernmental Status on the Rivers Chu and Talas.[681]

Science and scientists have an important role to play in transboundary water management. The complexity and interconnectivity of transboundary water issues calls for scientific inputs from diverse disciplines, requiring fruitful interaction between scientists across disciplines and countries as well as between scientific community and decision-makers; a challenging task on its own. Experts' contribution to informing *meaningful* notification, consultation and negotiation processes is fundamental for substantive reasons as those who have a special knowledge, expertise or skill can advance scientifically informed outcomes.[682] However, every effort should be taken to avoid the problem of 'advocacy science', 'in which disputing parties use hired experts to undercut

However, this innovative development did not find support of the ICJ in the *Pulp Mills* case, which found 'no legal obligation to consult the affected populations arises for the Parties from the instruments invoked by Argentina'. *Pulp Mills case*. See also McIntyre, 'The proceduralisation and growing maturity of international water law' 496.

680 Integrated Water Resources Management in Fergana Valley (IWRM-Fergana) project was implemented by national water authorities of Kyrgyzstan, Tajikistan and Uzbekistan in coordination with Scientific Information Centre of Interstate Commission for Water Coordination (SIC ICWC) and International Water Management Institute (IWMI) with financial support of the Swiss Agency for International Development and Cooperation (SDC). The Project sought to improve effectiveness of water resources management through introduction of IWRM principles in Fergana Valley. Online: <http://iwrm.icwc-aral.uz/index_en.htm> accessed 15 March 2013 .

681 See UNECE, 'Strengthening water management and transboundary water cooperation in Central Asia: The role of UNECE envrionmental conventions' (2011) United Nations, Geneva UN Doc ECE/MPWAT/35 at 109.

682 See eg Bodansky, 'Legitimacy' (suggesting three alternative bases of legitimacy comprised of democracy, public participation and expertise). See also Water Policy and Strategy of UNEP for 2007–2012. Online: <http://www.unep.org/Themes/freshwater/Documents/WaterPolicyStrategy.pdf> accessed 22 December 2013 (stating that 'To inform stakeholders, assessments must be clear and tailored to specific audiences while maintaining their scientific integrity. The information flowing from assessments must facilitate and enable

each other's claims' and '[i]nstead of being examined and resolved, legitimate scientific and technical differences are exaggerated, as each side attempts to bolster its position by attacking the validity of the information provided by others'.[683]

In the current structure of transboundary water management in the Aral Sea basin, the Scientific Information Centers under the ICWC and the Interstate Commission for Sustainable Development in Central Asia (ICSD) have been established to provide continuous scientific and information support for these regional bodies.[684] As was noted in Chapter 5, the domestic legislation of Tajikistan and the Kyrgyz Republic contains provisions on the interaction of experts from other countries in conducting environmental expert reviews.[685] Another matter is to ensure the neutrality of expertise, which usually is upheld by the separation of evaluative and decision-making functions and making it subject to public scrutiny and control. This issue is especially sensitive for transboundary EIAs. Thus, the World Bank seeks to uphold the independence of expertise in assessing the possible impacts of the proposed Rogun HPP by involving independent consultants to conduct studies and then making the studies subject to peer review by international independent panels of experts.[686]

These actors, being directly responsible for transboundary water management in the sub-region, and many others, being engaged in professional activities associated with the practice or issues related to transboundary waters, make for increasingly complicated interactions that influence formation, interpretation and application of legal frameworks in the Aral Sea basin. A broader circle of actors who have weight in transboundary water interactions in the sub-region includes, but not limited to UN agencies, MEAs bodies, multilateral development banks, and various regional integration institutions.

---

interaction and participation by all sectors of society in the making of informed choices and decisions about managing water resources').

683 Lawrence Susskind and Jeffrey Cruikshank, *Breaking the impasse: Consensual approaches to resolving public disputes* (New York, Basic Books 1987) at 29.

684 Interstate Commission for Sustainable Development (ICSD) established the Scientific Information Centre (SIC) on 10 August 1995. See the Statute of SIC ICSD of 12 April 2001. Interstate Commission for Water Coordination (ICWC) in Central Asia established the Scientific Information Centre (SIC) on 5 December 1993. See the Statute of SIC ICWC of 1996.

685 2003 Law of Tajikistan on Environmental Expert Review, art 11 and 1999 Law of the Kyrgyz Republic on Environmental Expert Review, art 7.

686 World Bank, 'Assessment Studies for Proposed Rogun Regional Water Reservoir and Hydropower Project in Tajikistan'. Online: <http://go.worldbank.org/ZQXIA8J0H0> accessed 22 December 2013.

The UNECE is constantly engaged in maintaining a transboundary water dialogue in the Aral Sea region, *inter alia*, by supporting the countries' efforts in reforming their policy, legal and institutional frameworks. Acting as the secretariat to the conventions elaborated under its auspices, the UNECE administers the implementation of the countries' commitments, but also drives normative development through the scientific and technological apparatus of its treaty systems. Similarly, the secretariats of other MEAs, such as the Convention on Biodiversity, the Ramsar Convention, the Convention on Climate Change, are considered to be dynamic and influential actors in their own rights; although their water-related activities are rather limited in the sub-region.

Development banks seek to play active roles in framing the processes of law making and implementation in the Aral Sea region. Most recently, the Asian Development Bank (ADB) has been actively involved to facilitate collaboration on transboundary water issues in the Amudarya, Syrdarya and Chu-Talas rivers through technical assistance projects, focused, *inter ilia*, on the negotiation of new water agreements.[687] It was argued elsewhere that multilateral development banks can play a more prominent role in promoting and supporting the development and maturity of environmental commitments and serve as 'informal agents for compliance' with international obligations.[688]

Finally, a host of institutions for economic and political cooperation in Central Asia and beyond as well as a number of partnerships and initiatives, often with overlapping mandates, influence the process of interactions in the region in one way or another. Agenda of the key regional economic integration institutions, such as Eurasian Economic Community (EurAsEC),[689] Shanghai

---

687 See ADB TA 6163-REG: Improved Management of Shared Water Resources in Central Asia. Online: <http://cawater-info.net/reta/documents/index_e.htm> accessed 22 December 2013.

688 For the examples of EIA related obligations see eg Mehrdad M. Nazari, 'The transboundary EIA convention in the context of private sector operations co-financed by an International Financial Institution: two case studies from Azerbaijan and Turkmenistan' (2003) 23 Environmental Impact Assessment Review 441–451 and McIntyre, 'The proceduralisation and growing maturity of international water law' 497. In his analysis of the *Pulp Mills* case, McIntyre observes,

> In the absence of the [sic] guidance from the Court, the content of an EIA will often be dictated by the safeguard policies of multilateral development banks and other international financial institutions involved in funding projects with the potential to cause transboundary harm, thus cementing the well-established role of such institutions as informal agents for compliance with international environmental law.

689 The Eurasian Economic Community (EurAsEC) originated from the CIS customs union between Belarus, Russia and Kazakhstan from 1996. Kyrgyzstan joined in 2000 and

Cooperation Organisation (SCO),[690] Central Asia Regional Economic Cooperation (CAREC) Program,[691] and Economic Cooperation Organisation (ECO),[692] includes water-related issues. Yet, insufficient coordination of their activities and unstable membership or participation of individual countries in these institutions remains a challenge. Attempts to initiate international negotiations over transboundary water controversies in the Aral Sea region under the umbrella of these organisational settings have not being successful so far. Given the countries' diverging interests, forum shopping and overlapping negotiations come as no surprise. For example, in 2006–2007 negotiations over water and energy issue in the Syrdarya river basin had been undergoing in parallel within the frameworks of the EurAsEC and the ADB. Whereas potentially discussions in different institutional settings may give rise to new opportunities for cooperation, desired outcomes have not been reached in the case of the Aral Sea basin.

Central Asian countries make efforts to address transboundary water issues in different forums and through different institutions. While nation states constitute these international organisations and play the dominant role

---

Tajikistan and Uzbekistan in 2005 (Uzbekistan suspended its membership in 2008). EurAsEC aims to provide the countries with a single economic space for coordinating approaches to the international trading system. Online: <http://www.evrazes.com/>accessed 25 December 2013.

690 The Shanghai Cooperation Organisation is an intergovernmental mutual security organisation founded in 2001 by China, Kazakhstan, Kyrgyzstan, Russia, Tajikistan and Uzbekistan. Formerly all countries with the exception of Uzbekistan were parts of the Shanghai Five formed in 1996. Besides the work on security related issues, the organisation works also to address socio-economic development issues. A framework on economic cooperation was agreed in 2003. The organisation promotes bilateral cooperation where multilateral cooperation is not politically feasible. Online: <http://www.sectsco.org> accessed 25 December 2013.

691 The Central Asia Regional Economic Cooperation (CAREC) Program was initiated in 1997. CAREC's goal is to improve living standards and to reduce poverty in CAREC countries through more efficient and effective regional economic cooperation. To date, the programme has focused on financing infrastructure projects and improving the region's policy environment. The members of CAREC are Afghanistan, Azerbaijan, China, Kazakhstan, Kyrgyzstan, Mongolia, Pakistan, Tajikistan, Turkmenistan and Uzbekistan. Online: <www.carecprogram.org/>accessed 25 December 2013.

692 The Economic Cooperation Organisation (ECO) is an intergovernmental regional organisation established in 1985 by Iran, Pakistan and Turkey for the purpose of promoting economic, technical and cultural cooperation. ECO is the successor organisation of the Regional Cooperation for Development (RCD). Online: <www.ecosecretariat.org/>accessed 25 December 2013.

in their operation, it worth noting that each institution has its specific composition, mandate, agenda and organisational culture that frames the issues and perspectives differently. Institutions can hardly be conceived as neutral organisational structures through which nation states interact; they are increasingly considered as 'incubators of coalitions' comprised of international civil servants, experts and activists.[693] These factors combined with the current geopolitical realities inject an additional dynamics in the countries relations and choice of forums.

Finally, interactions with Afghanistan, a riparian country to the Amudarya basin, are mostly taking place in a bilateral basis and coloured by the issues of trust and political stability. No institutionalised framework for interstate water cooperation that would involve also Afghanistan currently exists. Afghanistan and the CARs share a membership only in organisations with the main mandate on economic rather than water or environmental issues (e.g. ECO).[694]

The characteristic of inclusiveness demonstrates that a range of actors take part in interactions related to transboundary water management in the Aral Sea basin. But can a multitude of the actors in the current legal and institutional landscape of this basin be considered as forming a normative community, which sets the parameters of legal discourse in the sub-region? The answer to this question requires an investigation of other properties of processes, such as transparency, discursiveness and coherence.

6.2 Transparency

The feature of transparency seeks to disclose whether a process by which information about existing conditions, decisions and actions related to transboundary waters of the Aral Sea basin is made accessible, visible and understandable to all actors involved or that should be involved. As such, it can be determined through its textual and substantive elements.

---

693 See discussion in Chapter 2.

694 Michael Renner, *Water and energy dynamics in the Greater Himalayan region: Opportunities for environmental peacebuilding* (Norwegian Peacebuilding Resource Centre Report, 2011). United Nations Regional Office for Preventive Diplomacy in Central Asia (UNRCCA) that tasked with assisting the governments of Kazakhstan, Kyrgyzstan, Tajikistan, Turkmenistan and Uzbekistan in building capacities to peacefully prevent conflict, in facilitating dialogue, and in catalysing international support behind projects and initiatives makes efforts involve in its activities also Afghanistan. Online: <http://unrcca.unmissions.org/> accessed 20 August 2013.

The idea of textual transparency or transparency of commitments is well established in law with its requirements of promulgation and clarity that enable its addresses to know and understand what the law requires.[695] The analysis of norms through the lenses of norm stringency and determinacy undertaken in the previous chapters helps to elucidate that the specificity of international commitments with respect to transboundary waters in the Aral Sea basin can be further strengthened. In some instances, riparian parties and other actors cannot gain the full understanding of the relevant provisions to take advantage of their normative requirements. This is especially so for sub-regional agreements, which lack precision in establishing the required standard of conduct for the basin states.

The textual transparency of the exiting legal framework can be increased through legal arrangements at the regional and global levels. UNECE Conventions, as a source of more detailed rules on transboundary harm prevention and cooperation, further supported institutionally, can contribute significantly to the degree of openness of applicable legal frameworks in the basin. Recently, the Meeting of the Parties to the 1992 UNECE Water Convention has adopted a Guide to Implementing the Convention, which seeks to provide further clarification of this treaty's provisions.[696] At the global level, the 1997 UN Watercourses Convention helps to increase transparency of international law by codifying and crystallising customary legal norms in the field. The Convention makes it easier for riparian countries to consult the written text and rely on its specific language in interpreting their customary rights and obligations. The relative clarity of language of the *jus scriptum* and a universal reference to the 1997 UN Watercourses Convention makes international law 'more easily accessible and more transparent' and provides 'a more reliable knowledge of the scope of their rights and obligation'[697] which is an essential prerequisite for building trust among the countries.

Substantive transparency takes place when a legal framework accommodates provisions for information exchange and information disclosure to the public as well as requires accessibility and clarity with regard to implementation of and compliance with commitments through visible monitoring or compliance review systems and openness in the work of institutions and decision-making processes. The degree of substantive transparency depends on quality and frequency of data and information exchange.

---

695 See eg Fuller, *The morality of law*, Franck, *The power of legitimacy among nations*, and Brunnée and Toope, *Legitimacy and legality*.

696 'UNECE *Guide to Implementing the Convention*'.

697 Dinstein, 'The interaction between customary international law and treaties' at 365.

As was illustrated in Chapter 5, transparency provisions form part of most global, regional and sub-regional water-related agreements applicable to transboundary waters in the Aral Sea basin; yet the existing legal framework would benefit from more specificity about the relevant data to be shared, according to the characteristics and needs of the basin. In addition to regular exchange of information, the greater specification of a procedural system of cooperation, such as environmental impact assessments, consultations and notifications on planned measures, would increase significantly transparency of decision-making in the sub-region. With respect to information disclosure to the public, the 1998 Aarhus Convention lays the necessary transparency requirements for environmental decision-making in the basin; yet the implementation of those provisions remains challenging and still need to be improved.[698] MEAs under the umbrella of the UNECE offer a promising avenue to increase transparency setting up the requirements of reporting, compliance review and monitoring[699] as well as implementation or compliance committees,[700] but not all basin states are parties to these instruments. Openness of the existing regulatory framework in the Aral Sea basin is further diminished by the fact that a compliance review system at the sub-regional level is largely absent.[701]

More transparency in the work of the joint commissions in the basin would also appear to be required.[702] In practical terms, the CARs have established the Central Asia Regional Water Information Base, with the aim of ensuring more transparency and public awareness on regional water management issues as

---

698 See national implementation reports submitted by Parties to the Aarhus Convention. Online: <http://live.unece.org/env/pp/reportsimplementation2011.html> accessed 20 August 2013, the Synthesis report on the status of implementation of the Convention, ECE/MP.PP/2011/7. Online: <http://live.unece.org/env/pp/mop4/mop4.doc.html> accessed 20 August 2013 and NGO's opinion on implementation of the Aarhus Convention in Tajikistan. Online <http://live.unece.org/fileadmin/DAM/env/pp/reporting/NIRs2011/Tajikistanngocommente.pd> accessed 20 August 2013.

699 See eg Espoo Convention, Decision II/10 on the review and Aarhus Convention, art 10(2).

700 See eg 1992 UNECE Water Convention, arts 17 and 19; Espoo Convention, arts 11 and 13 and Decision II/4 of the 2nd Meeting of the Parties revised as Decision III/2.

701 See Ziganshina, 'International water law in Central Asia: Commitments, compliance and beyond'.

702 'UNECE Finalization of the second Assessment of transboundary rivers, lakes and groundwaters in the United Nations Economic Commission for Europe region. Major findings of the assessment for Central Asia' (2011) Convention on the Protection and Use of Transboundary Watercourses and International Lakes, Working Group on Integrated Water Resources Management 6th Meeting Geneva 4–5 May 2011 UN Doc ECE/MPWAT/WG2/2011/4–ECE/MPWAT/WG1/2011/4.

well as support decision-making in the water sector.[703] Not only does this project seek to provide raw data and information, but also analytical materials to facilitate better understanding and knowledge. Despite its positive contribution, the project was also heavily criticized for not being able to achieve better results in terms of transparency, national ownership and financial sustainability.[704] Recently, a range of proposals have been put forward aimed at modernizing this regional information system in organizational, political, substantive, technical and financial terms.[705] Putting all these requirements into practice in light of very limited funds available will require serious commitments and dedication from regional organizations and nation states.

These practical efforts are further complicated by the fact that the monitoring of water resources has significantly deteriorated over the past 20 years, with the quality and reliability of hydrometeorological data declining and the monitoring of water quality almost absent.[706] Besides, the countries are still protective over their own data and credibility to each other in the delivery of information is still to be established.[707] Such credibility, substantially depending on the reliability and accuracy of information that countries bring into the decision-making process, can yield positive outcomes in terms of increased trust that might ease future interactions. In addition to trust building, more transparent process of transboundary water management in the Aral Sea basin can mitigate power asymmetry between the countries by providing for

703 The project was funded by the Swiss Agency for Development Cooperation and implemented by the Scientific Information Centre of the ICWC with the assistance of UNECE and the UNEP/GRID-Arendal Office in Geneva, in close cooperation with five national water management organisations. For more information see online: <www.cawater-info.net/aboute.htm> accessed 4 April 2011.

704 Discussions during a special session on the future of the CAREWIB project organized by the Executive Committee of the Interstate Fund for the saving Aral Sea on 18 September 2012.

705 See eg Nikolay Denisov & Bo Libert, 'Vision for Water Information in Central Asia' (2012) Online: <cawater-info.net/concept/files/vision_for_water_information_in_central_asia_eng.pdf>accessed 30 January 2014.

706 'UNECE Finalization of the second Assessment of transboundary rivers, lakes and groundwaters in the United Nations Economic Commission for Europe region. Executive summary of the second Assessment' (2011) Convention on the Protection and Use of Transboundary Watercourses and International Lakes, Working Group on Integrated Water Resources Management Working Group on Integrated Water Resources Management 6th Meeting Geneva 4–5 May 2011 UN Doc ECE/MPWAT/WG2/2011/3-ECE/MPWAT/WG1/2011/3 para 89.

707 See eg Kai Wegerich, 'Hydro-hegemony in the Amu Darya Basin' (2008) 10 Water policy 71–88.

openness and accessibility to different actors of rules, procedures and settings of international legal interactions.

Transparency along with inclusiveness of law making, interpretation and implementation can therefore lay a necessary foundation for political dialogue and joint water resources management in the Aral Sea region. Of essential relevance is to keep procedural frameworks for transboundary water interactions in the basin open for the public and a broader interpretive community, if the potential of international law to operate through discursive process in which norms are invoked to explain, defend, justify and persuade is to be taken seriously, and trust and confidence are to be built.[708]

In summary, a process by which information about existing conditions, decisions and actions related to transboundary waters of the Aral Sea basin can only partly be considered as accessible, visible and understandable.

6.3 Discursiveness

As used in this study, discursive process in law refers to a fusion of argumentation, deliberation and communication that allows participants to exchange reasons and search for intersubjective meaning in law making, interpretation, implementation and application. This section considers whether international law as applied to transboundary waters in the Aral Sea basin provides for a dialogical process of exchange of reasons in which actors generate, elaborate and refine shared understandings and expectations and whether discourse about the meaning and implementation of legal norms actually takes place in the sub-region.

The problems to be resolved in transboundary water management require stakeholders to work constantly in problem-solving governance regimes. Transboundary water management is an on-going process in which decisions are made in response to changing circumstances and needs. As discussed in the section on inclusiveness, the interests of various stakeholders must be considered together if an optimal decision to be achieved. Because significant differences exist among stakeholders as to objectives and preferences in water use and allocation in the Aral Sea basin, reasoned justification for proposed

708 Johnstone, 'Security Council deliberations' at 463 (stating that 'the impact of the broader, outer circle of the interpretive community can only be felt if the debates are public. [...] This would give the interpretive community better opportunity to assess and judge the claim. [...] Allowing more opportunity for the voice of civil society to be heard would have a similar impact'.).

modifications would allow actors to present proofs and arguments according to their legal entitlements. Transboundary water management is therefore an inherently rational process that can give effect to the claims of parties advanced in a reasoned and informed process.

Existing sub-regional agreements in the Aral Sea basin acknowledge this need by seeking to establish 'joint management' for shared waters. However, the laudable intentions calling for 'joint management' and 'joint consideration' can hardly be realised without the mechanisms for making 'joint' or 'collective' decisions, which would be acceptable by all actors who are governed by them.[709] To be deemed truly 'collective', a decision must be a product of reciprocal deliberative exchange and 'reasoned consensus' rather than political compromise.[710] The structure and mandate of current interstate institutions, however, do not allow establishing such a platform for joint decision-making. Having a framework within which to make reasoned decisions would allow stakeholders to be more effective in managing their shared waters.

Within the existing legal framework in the Aral Sea basin, environmental impact assessment (EIA) comes closest to the idea of deliberative process by enabling participatory and reasoned decision-making. EIA seeks to shift discussions from positions and interests to reasons on which decisions are based by requiring the reasoned argumentation of its decisions.[711] By providing a forum, although temporary, for communication and dialogue, exchange of views and, more importantly, reasons between experts, stakeholders, and the public, EIA may help to promote shared understandings and consider alternatives to what has been proposed.[712] With respect to transboundary EIA, the national laws of the Aral Sea basin states do not allow for another state's participation in a transboundary EIA procedure, but provide for possibility to consult (Tajikistan and the Kyrgyz Republic), or conduct join or international EIAs. In contrast, the 1991 Espoo Convention extends the passive right to be notified about the results of EIAs by allowing the affected Party to participate

709 Cohen, 'Procedure and substance in deliberative democracy' at 407.

710 Risse, '"Let's argue!"'.

711 See Weber, *Economy and society: An outline of interpretive sociology* 979 (stating 'The only decisive point for us is that in principle a system of rationally debatable "reasons" stand behind every act of bureaucratic administration, namely, either subsumption under norms, or a weighing of ends and means'). See also Steffek, 'The legitimation of international governance: A discourse approach' at 262.

712 See Hugh Wilkins, 'The need for subjectivity in EIA: Discourse as a tool for sustainable development' (2003) 23 Environmental Impact Assessment Review 401–414.

in EIAs.[713] In this regard, joint EIAs carried out in a systematic and all-encompassing manner are desirable for the countries in Aral Sea region. It is worth noting that transboundary EIA is only a part of a wider system of procedural cooperation over shared waters and, by requiring decisions to be reasoned and justified, EIA enables states to fulfil their obligation of *meaningful* consultation, notification and negotiation *in good faith*.[714]

A duty to consult each other and negotiate in good faith is another promising avenue to strengthen the deliberative account of transboundary interactions in the Aral Sea basin. As Chapter 5 has shown, the agreements concluded under the umbrella of the Commonwealth and between CARs make no direct reference to regular consultations or negotiations, leave alone laying down its procedures. Not only do the customary norms as reflected in the 1997 UN Watercourses Convention and 1992 UNECE Water Convention prescribe these obligations, but also require that consultations and negotiations are to be pursued in a specific way: in 'good faith'. A recent legal memorandum summarises extensive international case law and scholarly writings on the meaning of good faith in the context of negotiations as follow:

> Good faith constitutes a 'fundamental principle' of international law. It is associated with building trust and stabilizing relationships by preserving the legitimate interests and expectations of parties. [...] Several international tribunals, including the ICJ, have illuminated fundamental elements of good faith negotiation: meaningful negotiations, willingness to compromise, compliance with temporal and procedural requirements, and serious efforts to reach an agreement.[715]

Such considerations concur closely with the deliberative account of international interactions, providing a basis for sustained meaningful negotiations for trust and consensus building.[716]

---

713 Espoo Convention, arts 3(3)–(6) on the notification stage and art 4(2) on preparation of EIA documentation.

714 Birnie, Boyle and Redgwell, *International law and the environment*, Craick, *The international law of environmental impact assessment: Process, substance and integration.*

715 *Good faith negotiations leading to the total elimination of nuclear weapons. Request for an Advisory Opinion from the International Court of Justice. Legal Memorandum* (International Association of Lawyers Against Nuclear Arms; International Human Rights Clinic, Human Rights Program, Harvard Law School, 2009).

716 Such considerations related to meaningful negotiations, willingness to compromise, respect to procedural requirements, and serious efforts to reach an agreement are also supported by consensus building scholarship highlighting the importance of trust

In the Aral Sea basin, formal negotiations conducted with financial and technical support from the donor community have been taking place since 1990s. These negotiations fell short of producing new water agreements – with the exception of the USAID-led negotiation resultant in the 1998 Syrdarya Agreement, which proved to be short-lived – yet they gave rise to a nascent form of deliberation on shared waters in the sub-region. An example of the countries' negotiations on transboundary water issues under the umbrella of ICWC and with the support of the ADB conducted in 2005–2008 is illustrative. The ADB regional technical assistance (RETA) was aimed to encourage a transboundary water dialogue, which would lead to crafting new agreements, with the revision of the 1998 Syrdarya Agreement being a priority issue.[717] The project offers a few insights and lessons to be learned from the standpoint of a deliberative interaction and good faith negotiation.

First of all, the project sought to bring to the negotiation table key stakeholders and decision-makers by establishing national working groups represented by water, energy, environmental agencies and foreign affairs officials, and a regional working group constituted of regional organisations. Designed as a formal process of negotiation, the groups did not include representation from the public, although the results of the discussion were widely disseminated and available online. This fact might have partly undermined the success of the negotiation because the groups could not fully benefit from the public inputs, but could have been open for critiques and attacks from their domestic constituencies if they were willing to switch from the discussion of their positions towards seeking the maximization of joint gains. The frequent change in the composition of national working groups did not contribute to the efficiency of the process either.[718]

Secondly, continuous efforts have been deployed to make the negotiation meaningful, starting from its preparatory work, which sought to accumulate previous draft agreements and analytical documents to avoid duplications and ensure the continuity of efforts, to the course of the negotiation itself.

---

building for successful negotiations. See eg Susskind and Cruikshank, *Breaking the impasse: Consensual approaches to resolving public disputes* and Lawrence Susskind, *The consensus building approach: Water diplomacy* (2011).

717 ADB TA 6163-REG: Improved Management of Shared Water Resources in Central Asia. Online: <http://cawater-info.net/reta/documents/index_e.htm> accessed 22 December 2013.

718 With regards to procedural and temporal requirements of good faith, see eg *Lake Lanoux Arbitration* (*France v. Spain*) 24 International Law Reports 126 (1957) at 281 (where the Arbitral Tribunal ruled that good faith would be violated 'in case of unjustified breaking off of talks, of abnormal delay, [or] of failure to follow agreed procedures').

The national working groups prepared reports to elucidate the shortcomings of the existing legal framework from the perspective of national interests. The representatives of the countries tried to engage in meaningful negotiations by 'declare[ing] their positions and rationale for those positions openly, so as to identify points of conflict and to facilitate an exchange of views'.[719] National and regional experts worked together in five subgroups on specific technical issues.[720] Yet, it appears that the negotiation fell short of developing 'common knowledge' about the situation and defining the situation in 'collective' terms[721] to break the impasse of framing issues in terms of established positions of the countries and bargaining. Moreover, a lack of local capacity in legal issues was obvious and hindered the opportunities to engage fully into *legal* deliberations. International legal experts were invited to build capacity on international water law, but this could not fill the gap in available legal expertise in the countries themselves. As a result, the discussion of complex technical issues overthrew the attention to the language and coherence of the draft agreements. More to the point, working groups have failed to develop shared understanding and intersubjective interpretation of the key substantive norms of international water law – the principle of equitable and reasonable use and no significant harm rule – as applied to the Aral Sea basin.

719 Good faith negotiations leading to the total elimination of nuclear weapons. Request for an Advisory Opinion from the International Court of Justice. Legal Memorandum at 30. See also *North Sea Continental Shelf* (where the ICJ stated that negotiating parties should 'not merely [...] go through a formal process of negotiation' but rather 'are under an obligation so to conduct themselves that the negotiations are meaningful').

720 Five working sub-groups include: (1) Sub-group on development of rules for implementation of procedural obligations and preparation of recommendations on improving rules for regulation and management of water and energy resources of Syrdarya river basin; (2) Sub-group on clarification of river losses in the midstream and downstream part of Amudarya river basin; (3) Sub-group on development of detailed methodological recommendations on assessment of basin-wide expenditures, data collection and assessment of actual damages from different regimes of water use; (4) Sub-group on finalization of a draft Agreement on strengthening of organisational structure for management, protection and development of transboundary water resources; and (5) Sub-group on preparation of inventory of interstate water facilities and improvement of draft Agreement on the use of water and energy resources of Syrdarya river basin. ADB TA 6163-REG: Improved Management of Shared Water Resources in Central Asia. Online: <http://cawater-info.net/reta/documents/index_e.htm> accessed 22 December 2013.

721 Risse, '"Let's argue!"' at 20.

Thirdly, the national working groups made efforts to reach a compromise,[722] which was initiated by a strong desire to speak common language within the group composed of experts from a diverse professional background. For this end, the glossary of terms was developed to facilitate discussions. However, the consideration of other parties' interests, as required by the good faith negotiation, appeared to be constrained by too strict mandates given to the members of the national working groups.[723] In other words, commitments made to home constituencies and high political sensitivity of the issues at stake made it difficult to be flexible and creative for the sake of consensus building.

Finally, despite sharply contradicting positions of the countries, the national working groups made efforts to reach an agreement. A resultant revised draft agreement on the Syrdarya was developed in 2007, but its wider discussion within individual countries and adoption is still pending.

Overall, such negotiations seem to help maintain relationships through on-going process of dialogue, even not having a signed agreement as its outcome. This is not to say that the maintenance of any interaction is a necessarily good thing, on the contrary 'mutual engagement can be a vehicle for sharing ownership of meaning, it can also be a vehicle for denying negotiability and can thus result in non-participation'.[724] In this respect, the accent of transboundary interactions has to be on the imperative of *the good faith* as a legal basis for building trust and confidence.

---

722 With respect to the requirement of willingness to compromise in the good faith negotiations, see eg Genevieve Guyomar, Arbitration Panel/Tribunal of the Agreement on German External Debt AFDI, in XIX Recueil des Sentences Arbitrales [Report on International Arbitration Awards] 27–64 (1973) stating that 'parties must make every effort [...] to reach a mutually satisfactory compromise, even going so far as to abandon previously inflexibly held positions'. See also *North Sea Continental Shelf* holding that compromise requires flexibility by all parties and an understanding that no party insists upon its own position without contemplating any modification of it. See also Good faith negotiations leading to the total elimination of nuclear weapons. Request for an Advisory Opinion from the International Court of Justice. Legal Memorandum at 30.

723 See eg Susskind, McKearnan and Thomas-Larmer, *The consensus building handbook: A comprehensive guide to reaching agreement* at 277 (stating 'The more specific your mandate is, the sharper the tension between your view and your constituents is likely to be. If you go to the table with specific demands and limits on what you can agree on, you will either have a hard time negotiating with other representatives or quickly find yourself at odds with your own mandate. You should expect and even favour a mandate that requires interpretation. At the same time, you should treat interpretation as a process of renegotiating your mandate with your group'.).

724 Wenger, *Communities of practice*.

In addition to formal negotiations, deliberations take the form of 'diffuse communication in the public sphere that generates public opinion that can in turn exercise political influence'.[725] The wider public forum that includes various regional and international organisations, governmental and non-governmental bodies is largely used in the Aral Sea basin to declare the countries' positions on the issues and falls short of producing the reciprocal exchange of well-elaborated justificatory (legal) reasons behind them. Public debate in the media and meetings is influenced by 'the sovereignty contest' that appears to be inescapable in a highly politicised nature of transboundary water management in the Aral Sea region, as in many other basins.[726] In these settings, reference to international law is often made strategically to push policy agendas and national interests, while the ability of international law to serve as a forum 'in which actors argue over, and seek to reach a common understanding of, the validity claims that they reciprocally make' is neglected.[727]

Nonetheless, the mere fact that the countries of Central Asia do make a reference to international law, even if mostly in strategic terms, is already an encouraging sign.[728] Echoing Risse's point that this in turn can lead to 'argumentative self-entrapment', Johnstone asserts that '[o]nce governments accept a legal norm rhetorically, they begin to argue over its interpretation and its application to the particular case at hand, rather than the validity of the law itself'.[729] It appears to be happening in the sub-region where debates around international water law can be framed as disputes over meaning of the norms rather than their validity or relevance.[730] The countries' different interpretations (and sometimes misinterpretations) of international water law have

725 Dryzek, *Deliberative global politics: Discourse and democracy in a divided world.*

726 Ibid, 66.

727 Pulkowski, 'Universal international law's grammar' at 153.

728 Risse, '"Let's argue!"' at 4–5. Johnstone, 'Security Council deliberations' at 453.

729 Johnstone, 'Security Council deliberations' at 454.

730 See eg Dinara Ziganshina, 'The role and relevance of the UN Watercourses Convention to the countries of Central Asia and Afghanistan in the Aral Sea Basin' (2011) Thematic and Regional Assessments of the Relevance and Applicability of the 1997 UN Convention on the Law of the Non-navigational Uses of International Watercourses (stating that 'Misperceptions about the normative requirements imposed by the UN Watercourses Convention are still present in the region. The provisions of the UN Watercourses Convention have been interpreted as giving preferential treatment to the interests of wealthy and powerful states, ignoring the situation in water-stress countries, leaving too much discretion on individual states to interpret its provisions on their own benefits, and being vague and imprecise in defining the rights and obligations imposed on riparian countries'.).

already been discouraged by a broader interpretive community; yet the intersubjective interpretation of relevant legal norms can be reached only through the mutual engagement of the countries in a legal discourse.[731] To benefit from this process, the Aral Sea basin countries have to be active participants in and contributing to the practices of communities, which seek to gain shared understanding of the meanings of legal norms. Being involved in the activities of such interpretive communities, the countries will go away from auto-interpretation of the legal norms as an exercise of unilateral sovereign will towards a process of intersubjective interpretation, in which participants ascertain what the norms mean to the parties collectively rather than individually, taking due care of collective expectations and interests of all parties.

Law, as an important form of argumentative action, has a potential to contribute to more effective interactions between the countries by promoting legal discourse to create shared understandings in various forums, such as the activities of international organisations, treaty bodies, expert bodies, and academia. The authority of expert bodies, set up and entrusted with certain tasks by states or international organisations, can play a valuable role. The International Law Commission (ILC), International Law Association, and the committees established under the various multilateral environmental and human rights treaties are the most notable examples. They provide a forum where different views can be discussed and partial consensus may be reached. Meanwhile, the representatives of the Aral Sea basin countries have not been actively involved in such legal forums so far.

The countries did not participate actively in the preparation of the draft articles on international watercourses by the ILC in 1974–1994 nor in the negotiation of the Convention in the Sixth (Legal) Committee of the General Assembly in 1996–1997.[732] The fact that five CARs were part of the USSR until 1991 explains partly their absence in the ILC's work. It is less obvious why the countries of the sub-region did not participate actively in the deliberations that took place in the Sixth Committee and in the Working Group of the Whole

731 See eg UNECE, 'The role of UNECE environmental conventions' at 133 ('While the rules of international customary law and selected soft-law instruments could be applied to govern the relations of Central Asian States on the protection and management of water resources, they are often differently interpreted by Central Asian countries').

732 These countries did not submit written replies to the ILC's questionnaire designed to elicit the views of states on international watercourses use and management with a view to facilitating the future study of the topic by the ILC. No reply was received from the USSR to the ILC's questionnaire before 1991; neither comments nor observations were submitted by the newly independent CARs after gaining independence or by Afghanistan.

in 1996–1997.[733] Most likely, the participation of Afghanistan was hampered by a continuous state of war in this country since the late 1970s.[734] The non-participation of the CARs may be explained by a number of reasons, such as the unpreparedness or unwillingness of the countries to engage in active international negotiations at that stage, the lack of interest in the issue at the time, or the treatment of transboundary water issues as a concern to be resolved within the sub-region through basin agreements.[735] The latter point is evident in a large number of treaties concluded between the CARs or within the Commonwealth in the 1990s. Nonetheless, during the Convention's adoption at the UN General Assembly in 1997, no country from the Aral Sea region voted against it.[736]

The CARs are more active in the work of UNECE Conventions bodies. Still, their underrepresentation in the 'legal' bodies of the conventions, in contrast to 'technical' bodies, is apparent. For instance, the Legal Board under the 1992 UNECE Water Convention has been established in 2003 to deal with legal questions related to the work under the Convention, but no official representative from the CARs attended its meetings till 2008.[737] Sporadic attendance in the following meetings could not ensure effective engagement of legal experts from the sub-region in the work of the Legal Board. In addition to task forces and working groups, UNECE Conventions, as well as other MEAs, also envisages the governing body such as a Meeting of the Parties (or a Conference of the Parties) to provide the Parties a platform to meet regularly and 'deliberate on scientific, policy and legal issues [...] doing so on the basis of, and continuously

733 The summary records of the meetings of the Sixth (Legal) Committee of the General Assembly conducted in 1996–97 contain no reference to the comments from the countries.

734 The same may be at least partially true for Tajikistan, where the civil war took place from 1992 till 1997.

735 Second report on the law of the non-navigational uses of international watercourses, by Mr Stephen C. McCaffrey, Special Rapporteur, [1986] 2(1) Y B Int'l L Comm'n, 87 at 97 para 51.

736 Kazakhstan was in favour of the Convention, Uzbekistan abstained from voting, Afghanistan, the Kyrgyz Republic, Tajikistan and Turkmenistan were absent during the voting procedure. See UN General Assembly, 51st Session, 99th plenary meeting, Agenda item 144 Convention on the law of the non-navigational uses of international watercourses, 21 May 1997 (A/51/PV.99). Official Records.

737 See the records of the Legal Boards' meetings on 1 September 2004, 3 December 2004, 13–14 June 2005, 20–21 June 2006, 2–3 October 2008, 23–30 April 2009, 15–16 April 2010, and 24–25 February 2011. Online: <http://live.unece.org/index.php?id=3033> accessed 20 August 2013.

reinforcing, the substantive and procedural requirements'[738] and therefore advance implementation of the agreements through the decisions taken on these meetings.[739] The Aral Sea basin countries, even those that are not parties to these MEAs yet, can benefit from discussions and negotiations in these meetings, which 'partially transform intergovernmental bargaining into deliberative transnational problem-solving processes'[740] by fostering interlocking engagement between technical experts, lawyers, and policy-makers.

Importantly, the Aral Sea basin countries' participation in these deliberative forums has to take a form of mutual engagement, with transformative potential going both ways, allowing the countries to learn from others, but also feed their own experiences into the practice of the communities. Weigner, a social anthropologist who advanced a social theory of learning, observes on this point,

> [L]earning depends on our ability to contribute to the collective production of meaning because it is by this process that experience [as a resource for the production of meaning] and competence pull each other. When, in a community of practice, the distinction between the production and adoption of meaning reflects enduring patterns of engagement among members – that is, when some always produce and some always adopt – the local economy of meaning yields very uneven ownership of meaning. This situation, when it persists, results in a mutually reinforcing condition of both marginality and inability to learn.[741]

Then, social learning aspect of discourse and deliberation can lead to the reconstruction of relationships.[742] Deliberative processes where shared understandings are generated through 'contestations of meanings' help to create 'ownership of meaning', connect participants of a joint exercise and, ultimately,

738 Brunnée and Toope, *Legitimacy and legality* at 144.

739 See Jutta Brunnée, 'Reweaving the fabric of international law? Patterns of consent in environmental framework agreements' in Rudiger Wolfrum and Volker Roben (eds), *Developments of International Law in Treaty Making* (Berlin, Heidelberg, New York, Springer 2005) and Pulkowski, 'Universal international law's grammar' at 143.

740 Gehring, 'Treaty-making and treaty evolution' at 496.

741 Wenger, *Communities of practice* at 203.

742 Dryzek, *Deliberative global politics: Discourse and democracy in a divided world* at 28 (stating that 'deliberation on the public sphere can also involve the reconstruction of relationships'). See also Weiner at 9 (stating that 'social learning remains a process that exclusively involves the participating elites within the environment of international organization').

shape relationships among them.[743] The goal of such exercise is to gain mutual understanding. As Brunnée and Toope points out '[e]pistemic communities or norm entrepreneurs initiate and shape debates, but only a community of practice can instantiate and sustain the background knowledge, norms and practices that nourish a regime'.[744]

A special attention has been paid to mutual learning of water specialists from five CARs since the establishment of Interstate Commission for Water Coordination in Central Asia in 1992. The joint implementation of water-related projects can be seen as one of the best mutual learning mechanisms used in the sub-region that allowed water professionals from various countries to work together on practical – not political – matters and share experiences and concerns.[745]

In 2000, with the generous support from Canadian International Development Agency (CIDA), Training Centre under Scientific Information Center of ICWC has been established to build capacity of water professionals on a constant basis.[746] Five year training project on water resources management in the Aral Sea basin funded by CIDA in 2000–2005 helped to create a sub-regional training network on water-related issues. Capacity building activities were continued in cooperation with the IHE-UNESCO Institute for Water Education in 2009–2012, when a more systematic approach to water professionals training has been taken. These projects has played an important role in providing a platform for exchanging views between trainees from five CARs and talking through the differences in such an informal setting.

Also, a range of modeling and decision support tools linked to a regional data base has been developed in the region to allow researchers, water managers, planners and decision makers to assess and simulate various development options that assist to create mutually acceptable and sustainable solutions. For instance, the Aral Sea Basin management model (ASBmm) has been developed by the UNESCO-IHE Institute for Water Education and SIC ICWC. This

743 Wenger, *Communities of practice* at 76.

744 Brunnée and Toope, *Legitimacy and legality* at 144.

745 The key projects implemented within the umbrella of the ICWC include, but not limited to: Water Use and Farm Management Survey (WUFMAS) (European Union, 1996–1999), Integrated Water Resources Management in the Fergana Valley (Swiss Development Cooperation, 2001–2012), Fergana Valley Canal Automation Project (SDC), Asian Development Bank Regional Technical Assistance Improvement of Shared Water Resources Management in Central Asia (2005–2010), and Central Asia Regional Water Information Base Project (CAREWIB) (SDC, 2003–2012).

746 For more details see SIC ICWC Training Centre. Online: <http://tc.icwc-aral.uz/>accessed 23 March 2013.

model is an useful tool for the development of mutually acceptable ways of water resources development and use in the basin that takes into account climate change implications and environmental needs and can simulate different scenarios of socio-economic, water management and agricultural developments. Using this model, it is possible and desirable to develop a coordinated strategy of water resources development in the basin.[747]

A process of social learning towards building normative consensus is especially powerful within treaty regimes. Bodansky, for instance, observes that international environmental regimes 'can change a state's perceptions of its own interests through a process of social learning'.[748] UNECE institutional landscape supports such learning process for the CARs through a series of workshops and dialogues, among other things. In 2012, the Meeting of the Parties to the 1992 UNECE Water Convention established a new mechanism to facilitate and support implementation and compliance with – the Implementation Committee, which can fortify processes of social learning and deliberation for the CARs. Two features of this facilitative mechanism are especially appealing from a discursive point of view. First, the mechanism can provide a forum for the Parties to the 1992 UNECE Water Convention to get *competent* advice from the Committee for any request relating to specific issues concerning difficulties in implementing the Convention vis-à-vis each other, other Parties and/or non–Parties.[749] The members of the Implementation Committee are elected by the Meeting of the Parties from among candidates nominated by the Parties, with the consideration of the geographical distribution of membership and to the diversity of experience and expertise. The members have to be persons with experience and recognized expertise in the fields related to the Convention, including legal and/or scientific and technical expertise and serve in their personal capacity and objectively, in the best interest of the Convention.[750] This new mechanism may allow the Parties (and no-Parties) involved to consider themselves as a collective of solution seekers rather than defenders of individual interests or positions. Second, the Committee is envisaged to operate in a transparent way and provide the *reasoning* for its decisions. The fact that reasoned decisions are expressly required is of particular relevance, given the advisory nature of the mechanism.

747 Online: <www.asbmm-uz> accessed 30 January 2014.

748 Bodansky, *The art and craft of international environmental law* at 152.

749 1992 UNECE Water Convention, Decision VI/1 on support to implementation and compliance (Meeting of the Parties 6th Sess 28–30 November 2012 Rome) UN Doc ECE/MP.WAT/37/Add.2.

750 Ibid.

Transparent reasoning adds significantly to the persuasive power of the decision. Moreover, the Committee's decisions, by the reasons of composition, recognised expertise and its reasoning, may have broader implications beyond a case at stake.

In sum, there exists some evidence that discursive processes of exchange of views and reasons in which actors generate, elaborate and refine shared understandings and expectations about the law are available to the Aral Sea basin countries. But these processes are rather weak and need to be strengthened substantially.

6.4 Coherence

This section examines whether the Aral Sea basin countries benefit from integrative processes that are enabled through normative and institutional connections between different norms, legal regimes and between national and international law domains.

The perception and interpretation of international water law as an integrated whole, comprised of global, regional, sub-regional and bilateral water-related arrangements and nested in a wider framework of general international law, is still lacking in the Aral Sea region.[751] While the need for well-developed watercourse-specific agreements is indisputable, in the situation of stagnation to proceed with their negotiation, countries may wish to utilize the potential of global and regional framework agreements, which remain largely untapped in the sub-region. A recent study on the role and relevance of the 1997 UN Watercourses Convention for the Aral Sea basin countries illustrates the benefits of such exercise, arguing, *inter alia*, that the 1997 UN Watercourses Convention can serve for the countries as a common platform for the negotiation of future agreements in the basin, supplement existing agreements that do not comprehensively define the right and obligations of the parties, including such provisions as equitable and reasonable use or joint management or serve as a background for their interpretation.[752] Similarly, a new UNECE study that focuses on the role of UNECE conventions in strengthening water

751 1969 Vienna Convention, art 31(1)(c) and Laurence Boisson de Chazournes, 'Freshwater and international law: The interplay between universal, regional and basin perspective' (UN World Water Assessment Programme side publications, 2009).

752 Ziganshina, 'The role and relevance of the UN Watercourses Convention to the countries of Central Asia and Afghanistan in the Aral Sea Basin'.

management and transboundary water cooperation in Central Asia can guide the countries on their potential contribution.[753]

In this context, it is necessary to understand the operation of water treaties within a multilevel governance context. Section 3.2 of this book has demonstrated that the legal architecture of transboundary water cooperation in the Aral Sea basin is composed of numerous agreements at different levels. The abundance of treaties on the subject matter raises the question of their relationship with each other. Although most often treaties complement each other, clarity over their relationship is important in case of conflicting obligations and to ensure coherent interpretation and application.

Water treaties concluded between riparian countries represent *lex specialis*, which means that parties have agreed to regulate their relationships by special norms that override more general norms (*lex specialis derogate generali*).[754] Two considerations should be borne in mind in this regard. First, states cannot, even by agreement and as between themselves, authorise norms contrary to peremptory norms of general international law (*jus cogens*).[755] Second, *lex specialis* is just one principle among others in treaty interpretation and application that seek to elucidate the law as a legal system. This implies, among other things, that no treaty applies in a normative vacuum; rather all norms of international law are applicable against the background of general international law. Because water treaties in the Aral Sea basin do not expressly provide for their relationships with other treaties, whether the specific provisions coexist or exclude norms arising from other treaties or a general international law are to be considered on a case-by-case basis. As per the rights and obligations arising from successive water treaties in the Aral Sea basin, riparian countries should be guided by article 30 of the Vienna Convention on the Law of Treaties, which gives priority, as between the parties, to the rule that is later in time (the principle of *lex posterior*).[756]

By and large, the agreements adopted under the umbrella of the Commonwealth are framework instruments with a minimum intention to change rights and obligations of their parties under other treaties. Thus, Article 6 of the 1992 CIS Agreement on Environmental Interactions clearly states, that

753 UNECE, 'The role of UNECE environmental conventions'.

754 See ILC Report on fragmentation. See also *Gabčíkovo-Nagymaros case* 7 at 76, *Nuclear Weapons* at 240 and *Case Concerning Military and Paramilitary Activities in and Against Nicaragua* (*Nicaragua v. United States of America*) Merits, Judgment of 27 June 1986, [1986] ICJ Reports 14 at 137.

755 1969 Vienna Convention, art 53.

756 Ibid, arts 30 and 59.

countries' participation in the treaty does not affect their rights and obligations arising from earlier and later agreements.[757] Similar provisions are enshrined in the 1998 CIS Agreement on Transboundary Waters.[758]

The 1992 UNECE Water Convention sets out provisions on its relationships with other treaties on the same subject matter in a precise manner. It implicitly requires the Riparian Parties to adapt existing agreements, 'where necessary to eliminate the contradictions with the basic principles of this Convention' and adopt new agreements, where these do not exist, to set up more specific rules.[759] Thus, in the case of conflicting obligations arising from a watercourse specific treaty and the 1992 UNECE Water Convention, the provisions of the latter seems to prevail, but only in regulating relationships between states that are parties to both treaties. The 1992 UNECE Water Convention also introduces the provisions that give priority to more stringent norms on environmental protections, regardless whether these provisions arise from earlier or later agreements.[760] Finally, this Convention – as well as the 1997 UN Watercourses Convention discussed below – can serve for both its parties and for states that are not parties as a background for interpretation of existing watercourse treaties insofar as some of its provisions reflecting customary law on the matter.

The 1997 UN Watercourses Convention – a universal framework instrument – carefully spells out its relationship with existing and future watercourse agreements. The five main pillars of such relationship can be derived from Article 3 of the Convention: it enunciates that the 1997 UN Watercourses Convention does not affect the rights and obligations of a watercourse state arising from existing treaties, unless agreed otherwise.[761] This provision sets forth the complimentary and residual role of the Convention, explicitly stating that if there is a conflict in the provisions of the existing agreements and the 1997 UN Watercourses Convention, the former will prevail. However, the Convention allows watercourse states to decide, on a case-by-case basis, whether they want to give priority to the 1997 UN Watercourses Convention's provisions in their

757 1992 CIS Agreement on the Environmental Interaction, art 6.

758 1998 CIS Agreement on Transboundary Waters, art 12.

759 1992 UNECE Water Convention, art 9, para 1.

760 Ibid, art 2, para 7–8 reads,

> The application of this Convention shall not lead to the deterioration of environmental conditions nor lead to increased transboundary impact.
>
> The provisions of this Convention shall not affect the right of Parties individually or jointly to adopt and implement more stringent measures than those set down in this Convention.

761 1997 UN Watercourses Convention, art 3(1).

relations concerning a particular international watercourse. Referring to the customary law of treaties, Tanzi points out:

> [A]part from the fact that the case-law of the International Court of Justice seems to give prevalence to the principle of the *lex specialis* over that of the *lex posterior*, the fact is that arts. 30 and 59 of the Vienna Convention leave the parties to international treaties free to rule on a case by case basis the legal effects of such treaties between the parties with respect to pre-existing or future treaties on the same subject matter.[762]

The 1997 UN Watercourses Convention, nonetheless, encourages watercourse states to harmonise watercourse agreements with its basic principles, to avoid conflicts.[763] The third pillar relates to the relationship of the 1997 UN Watercourses Convention, as a framework instrument, with future watercourse agreements: the 1997 UN Watercourses Convention may be applied and adjusted to the characteristics and uses of a particular international watercourse or parts thereof, when watercourse states enter into watercourse agreements.[764] The 1994 ILC Commentary explains, '[the 1997 UN Watercourses Convention approach is] that of a framework agreement, which will provide for the States parties the general principles and rules governing the non-navigational uses of international watercourses, in the absence of specific agreement among the States concerned, and provide guidelines for the negotiation of future agreements'.[765]

With a view to avoiding contradictory obligations, the Convention seems to limit the extent of deviation from its provisions by using the words 'apply and adjust'. In this sense, under the 1969 Vienna Convention on the Law of Treaties, the modification of multilateral treaties shall 'not relate to a provision, derogation from which is incompatible with the effective execution of the object and purpose of the treaty as a whole'.[766] Finally, Article 3(6) of the 1997 UN

762 Tanzi, The Relationship between the 1992 UNECE Convention on the Protection and Use of Transboundary Watercourses and International Lakes and the 1997 UN Convention on the Law of the Non Navigational Uses of International Watercourses at 72. See also 1969 Vienna Convention, art 30 deals with application of successive treaties relating to the same subject matter and art 59 regulates termination or suspension of the operation of a treaty implied by conclusion of a later treaty.

763 1997 UN Watercourses Convention, art 3(2).

764 Ibid, arts 3(3) and 3(5).

765 ILC Commentary to 1994 Draft Articles at 92 para 2.

766 1969 Vienna Convention, art 41(1)(b)(ii).

Watercourses Convention articulates the general rule that rights and obligations of third states, namely non-participating watercourse states, shall not be affected by such watercourse agreements.[767]

In addition to coherent interpretation process, it is necessary to ensure coherence in law making in the Aral Sea basin. As was discussed in Section 6.2, the attempts to advance the legal framework for transboundary water cooperation in the Aral Sea basin can be criticised for the lack of coherence. For example, it is unfortunate that relevant procedural provisions of transboundary cooperation, if exist, are scattered in various instruments which are poorly connected to each other on their own. Inconsistencies in the formulation of the obligations are also widespread that does not help increase the clarity of the norms.

The fact that regulation of transboundary waters forms part of a complex system of international environmental governance highlights the need for better linkages within this system. The idea of 'clustering' MEAs by function, such as scientific assessment, monitoring or compliance review, and by issue, such as water, biodiversity or forest, has been proposed to increase the coherence of the system. Some observers consider the prospects of clustering MEAs as a risky endeavor, unless it is done in a pragmatic way by integrating only some elements of certain MEAs, either functional or substantive, on a case-by-case basis.[768]

It was also argued that the overall legal architecture created by MEAs correspond to a legal understating of integrated water recourses management.[769] As a rule, MEAs deal with interrelated issues, water being only one of those, and increasingly MEAs bodies work together to strengthen synergies and promote implementation. Globally, UNEP, as the principal body within the UN system in the field of environment, tries to coordinate the work of the various environmental conventions, particularly those for which it serves as the secretariat, and encourages the secretariats of other MEAs to promote integrated water resources management within their mandate.[770] In 2003, the UN High

767 1997 UN Watercourses Convention, art 3(6).

768 Sebastian Oberthür, 'Clustering of multilateral environmental agreements: Potentials and limitations' in Bradnee W. Chambers and Jessica F. Green (eds), *Reforming international environmental governance: From institutional limits to innovative reforms* (Tokyo, New York, Paris, United Nations University Press 2005) at 59.

769 Laurence Boisson De Chazournes, Christina Leb and Mara Tignino, 'Environmental protection and access to water: The challenges ahead' in van der Michael and Penelope Keenan (eds), *The right to water and water rights in a changing world. Colloquium papers* (Delft, IHP-UNESCO 2011) at 24.

770 See Water Policy and Strategy of UNEP for 2007–2012 at 24.

Level Committee on Programmes established UN-Water, an inter-agency mechanism to strengthen coordination and coherence among UN entities dealing with issues related to all aspects of freshwater and sanitation; yet, the work on water-related synergies and cross-fertilisation in implementing MEAs is not coordinated enough and can be further improved both at international and national levels.[771]

The experience of the Convention on Biodiversity and the Ramsar Convention in establishing extensive institutional links with other MEAs and building partnerships with international organisations, academia and non-governmental organisations can be revealing for strengthening 'water' linkages across water-related treaties.[772] For instance, in 2001 a Joint Liaison Group was established between the Convention on Biodiversity, the Convention on Climate Change and the Convention on Desertification. Importantly, state parties to MEAs themselves, rather than MEAs secretariats, must play more pro-active role in developing cooperative and integrated governance mechanisms in order for these arrangements to be perceived as legitimate.[773] The fact that national focal points for environmental conventions are often in different governmental departments might be one of the obstacles for such integration though.

The experience of UNECE that facilitated the preparation of five MEAs and serves as their secretariats offers a good example of integration at the regional level. The linkages within the UNECE Conventions have been embedded in their texts by introducing similar definitions, couching the rights and obligations in a compatible way, and further strengthened by a strong institutional support for their implementation. UNECE continues the work of promoting

771 See eg 'Implementation of Multilateral Environmental Agreements for Efficient Water Management' (The Foundation for International Environmental Law and Development, 2005) emphasising the need of better co-ordination at all levels for efficient and effective implementation of MEAs.

772 Scott, 'International environmental governance' at 16 and 19 (observing that Convention on Biodiversity, with its 'foreign policy' mandate under article 23(4), has concluded 157 agreements to date with partners that include international organisations, universities, non-governmental organisations, botanic gardens and 18 other MEAs and the Ramsar Convention has developed extensive institutional links with 21 MEAs and the importance of partnership agreements and joint work plans was endorsed in the recently adopted 2009–15 Ramsar Strategic Plan).

773 Ibid, 38 ('The development of cooperative and integrated institutional regimes in pursuit of effectiveness should nevertheless not be pursued at the expenses of legitimacy and accountability'. [...] 'This can be an issue where the cooperative arrangements are comprised of, or largely driven by, treaty secretariats rather than by states'.).

the UNECE Convention in international forums and building synergies with other conventions and international organisations involved in environmental matters. Ideas of closer institutional cooperation, such a harmonised reporting and compatible implementation review, are also taken seriously in the practice of the environmental conventions under the auspices of the UNECE. In the most recent endeavours to introduce reporting mechanisms under the 1992 UNECE Water Convention, reporting requirements under the EU Water Framework Directive has been scrutinised to encourage a harmonised approach and avoid duplications.[774] This adds to continuous developments within individual treaty regimes. Thus, it was argued that the 1992 UNECE Water Convention supplemented by two protocols and a range of basin agreements constitutes an example of institutional nesting on its own.[775]

In addition to institutional connections, the possibility of doctrinal 'borrowing' of similar legal concepts from one regime to another helps to establish links among different subject-specific treaty regimes, even though the terms of these agreements might not be perfectly tuned with each other. Pulkowsky observes that similarities in legal concepts that are deployed in different international regimes 'can serve as anchor points for rational practical discourse'.[776] The co-evolution of 'impact assessment' in various environmental regimes is illustrative.

Another area that requires greater coherence is informed by the fact that transboundary water issues are increasingly intertwined with other traditional areas of international relations such as trade, investment and military security. Integrating water-related concerns into these areas is essential for addressing the problems in the Aral Sea region. Acknowledging this fact, the 2001 US Senate report 'Avoiding Water Wars' states,

> The impact of our actions to address water extends far beyond a country's border, as water transcends political boundaries. This means U.S.

774 'Overview of existing reporting requirements of relevance for the UNECE Water Convention – Challenges and advantages related to the introduction of reporting under the convention' (2011) Convention on the Protection and Use of Transboundary Watercourses and International Lakes, Legal Board 8th meeting Geneva 24–25 February 2011 Item 2 (c) of the provisional agenda UN Doc LB/2011/INF1.

775 Patricia Wouters and Sergei Vinogradov, 'Analysing the ECE Water Convention: What lessons for the regional management of transboudary water resources' in Olav Schram Stokke and Øystein B. Thommessen (eds), *Yearbook of International Co-operation on Environment and Development 2003/2004* (Earthscan Publications 2003–2004) and Scott, 'International environmental governance' at 11.

776 Pulkowski, 'Universal international law's grammar' at 145.

> actions centered on only one part of a river can have unintended consequences either upstream or downstream. For example, water projects are a priority for U.S. assistance in Afghanistan and Pakistan. However, if our assistance is managed or implemented poorly, it may increase tensions over water in the greater region. Our assistance should target comprehensive activities, such as strengthening river basin dialogues and establishing community-level water management projects on shared watersheds. [...] U.S. investment in Afghanistan and Pakistan, which is twelve times greater than what is invested in Central Asia, could have significant unintended consequences.[777]

Transboundary water interactions are also characterised by complex linkages between international and national levels. It has been increasingly acknowledged that international and national law are not two separate systems of law, but rather interact and influence each other in various instances, including norm formation, interpretation, implementation and application.[778] Connections between international and national scenes are therefore inherent in international water law. For instance, the due diligence nature of substantive obligations requires riparian countries to work rigorously at the domestic level, *inter alia*, by adopting relevant legal, administrative, economic, financial and technical measures.[779] In doing so, not only does international law require adopting a more constructive approach to interstate relations, but also recognises that true change begins within the countries when they take leadership in reforming domestic policies and laws. Yet, despite some positive developments in water law and policy, effective implementation of water-related treaties remains limited in the Aral Sea basin.[780] There are also instances when national laws and national organs interpret international obligations in a way that distort their actual meaning, the 2001 Water Law of Kyrgyzstan being just one example.[781] In this respect, Brunnée and Toope argue from an

777 Avoiding water wars at 17.

778 See eg Jonkheer H.F. Panhuys, 'Relations and interactions between international and national scenes of law' (1964) 112 Recueil des Cours 1–88, Koh, 'The 1994 Roscoe Pound lecture: Transnational legal process', Finnemore and Sikkink, 'International norm dynamics and political change'.

779 See eg 1992 UNECE Water Convention, art 3.

780 UNECE, 'The role of UNECE environmental conventions'.

781 Kyrgyz Republic Law on Interstate Use of the Water Bodies, Water Resources and Water Management Facilities of the Kyrgyz Republic (No 73, 23 July 2001) seeking to establish 'procedures for and levels of payments for interstate use of the water resources of the Kyrgyz Republic on the basis of regulations worked out between the parties and taking

interactional law perspective that international law cannot simply be implemented domestically, rather 'it will unfold its obligatory effect only if shared understandings and a practice of legality are extended into the domestic sphere'.[782]

The interplay between international and national actors, processes and institutions are particularly notable in transboundary EIA, which initially evolved through mutually nourishing processes at national and international levels.[783] Today, national EIA systems form a fundamental part of transboundary EIA frameworks due to the very nature of the obligations related to assessments, which require the countries to adopt national EIA systems and trigger them for the activities that may cause transboundary effects.[784] In the context of the Aral Sea basin, more consistent endeavours are required to ensure that impact assessment procedures for activities that may have transboundary impacts are set up on a reciprocal and equivalent basis either in national laws or in international instruments, such as the 1991 Espoo Convention, that would allow the countries to have the same minimum standards to be followed in the case of planned measures.[785]

The interplay of international and national legal frameworks seems to be influenced by a range of factors, including the contextual, historical and temporal dimensions. Thus, in the European context, where the EU Water Framework Directive regulates both transboundary and national waters, at present more emphasis is placed on implementation at national level and harmonisation of the EU member states legislations.[786] Fitzmaurice argues,

---

into account world prices and consumer demand for water resources' has been heavily criticised by other riparian States. See also Kemelova and Zhalkubaev, 'Water, conflict, and regional security in Central Asia revisited' at 483 (arguing that 'While the downstream States have disparaged this law, Kyrgyzstan has not actually undertaken any efforts to implement this law in interstate negotiations, since it is abundantly clear to the government, notwithstanding the legislature's views on the subject, that water negotiations between States must take into consideration the content of international customary law').

782 Brunnée and Toope, *Legitimacy and legality* at 124.

783 Dinara Ziganshina, 'Transboundary impact assessment in the Aral Sea Basin: Interplay of international and domestic laws' (paper presented at International Law: The Trickle Down Effect Symposium, 4–6 May 2011).

784 See eg *Pulp Mills case*.

785 See discussions in Section 5.4 of this thesis.

786 See Strategic document: Common implementation strategy for the Water Framework Directive (European Commission, 2001); Handbook on the implementation of EC environmental legislation (Regional Environmental Centre, The European Communities 2008). Online: <http://ec.europa.eu/environment/enlarg/handbook/handbook.pdf> accessed 02 August 2013.

for example, that successful cooperation between Finland and Sweden over shared rivers is based on the approximation of their national laws.[787] In addition to that, the status and operation of the Finish-Swedish Frontier River Commission is an interesting – and rather unique – example of the interplay between international and national law, since the Commission merges 'certain international and municipal powers of the two states'[788] and grounds its decisions both on international and national law.[789] On the other side, river basins that became 'international' relatively recently[790] appear to refer to regional and global treaties as a reliable framework for their interactions at the first place.[791] In this respect, the role and relevance of the 1997 UN Watercourses Convention and the 1992 UNECE Water Convention for the countries in the Aral Sea basin can scarcely be overestimated.

Finally, linkages between various actors as well as formal and informal processes are instrumental for successful interactions in the Aral Sea basin. As was suggested above, it is not unusual for transboundary water interactions to involve only governmental officials or diplomats, but it is crucial to keep close links with expert communities to make informed decisions as well as other stakeholders and the general public to legitimise decisions taken. This point closely relates to the degree of inclusiveness of international legal interactions.

787 Malgosia Fitzmaurice, 'Finish-Swedish Frontier River Commission – Effective water co-operation' (2003) 3 Non-State Actors and International Law 111–122, 111.

788 Ibid, 117.

789 Agreement between Finland and Sweden Concerning Frontier Waters, (signed 15 December 1971, entered into force 1 January 1972). Online: <http://ocid.nacse.org/tfdd/tfdddocs/340ENG.pdf>, art 8 reads 'In cases where no special provision is made in the Agreement, the laws in force in each State shall apply'.

790 Aaron T. Wolf, Shina B. Yoffe and Mark Giordano, 'International waters: Identifying basins at risk' (2003) 35 Water policy 29–60, 44 (observing that 'The most rapid change institutionally would be associated with "internationalized" basins – i.e. basins whose management institution was developed under one single jurisdiction, but which was dramatically altered as that jurisdiction suddenly became divided among two or more nations'.). See also Sands, *Principles of international environmental law* 227 (who observes with respect to MEAs that 'with regard to implementation, the provision of technical, financial and other assistance to states, particularly developing states, points to the growing "internationalisation" of the domestic implementation and legal process, and an awareness that international environmental law will not achieve its objectives if it does not also take account of the need for and techniques available for improving domestic implementation of international environmental obligations').

791 See eg Musa Abseno, 'How can the work of the General Assembly and the ILC on the Law of Non-navigational Uses of International Watercourses contributes towards basin-wide legal framework for the Nile Basin?' (Unpublished, University of Dundee 2010).

Further, commentators from the public deliberation and dispute resolution fields argue that deliberation (or consensus building efforts) should be kept in some distance from decision (or more formal procedures), but at the same time should not be completely unconnected.[792] In their analysis of the Nile Basin case, Brunnée and Toope argue that law has influenced and been influenced by 'informal interaction' among the basin states and conclude that, 'informal processes, whether conceived as nurturing epistemic communities or building intergovernmental networks, have functioned to allow the sharing of normative knowledge and to build the confidence that permitted the establishment of more formal legal structures for future interaction'.[793]

Based on the recognition of these important interconnections and the increased role of other than states actors, a new understanding of water diplomacy has started emerging and practicing. While traditionally water diplomacy was related only to relations between sovereign states on transboundary waters, nowadays it is transforming and expanding to a broader process that deals with diverse water challenges and involves diverse groups by means of interactions and negotiations. For instance, through the BRIDGE (Building River Dialogue and Governance) Program, IUCN has built a distinctive practice of water diplomacy as a process which operates under the authority of sovereign states, requiring their ultimate involvement, but which also unlocks cooperation among multiple stakeholders, including municipalities, provinces and civil society.[794] Emphasising the important role and contribution of experts and epistemic communities to water diplomacy efforts, the idea of niche diplomacy was put forward by the Netherlands.[795] Building on the internationally renowned Dutch expertise in all issues related to water, the Water

792 Dryzek, *Deliberative global politics: Discourse and democracy in a divided world* argues that for the public deliberation to be effective, government and the public sphere must be loosely connected, or semi-detached (not completely unconnected). In a similar vein, Susskind and other suggest that informal consensus-building forums must have linkages to formal structures. Susskind, McKearnan and Thomas-Larmer, *The consensus building handbook: A comprehensive guide to reaching agreement*.

793 Brunnée and Toope at 155.

794 The IUCN Bridge Program supports the capacities of countries sharing a river basin to implement effective water management arrangements through a shared vision, benefit-sharing principles and transparent, coherent and cost-effective institutional frameworks in the transboundary river basins of South America, Mesoamerica and Mekong. Online: <http://www.iucn.org/about/work/programmes/water/wp_our_work/wp_our_work_bridge/>accessed 30 January 2014.

795 Ruben van Genderen and Jan Rood, 'Water diplomacy: A niche for the Netherlands?' (The Netherlands Ministry of Foreign Affairs and the Water Governance Centre) December 2011.

Diplomacy Consortium has been established to become a knowledge hub for water diplomacy, governance and law, and to contribute to conflict prevention and resolution.[796]

In the Aral Sea basin, informal interactions and networking also constitute a critical component of transboundary water interactions. Informal interactions in the course of joint water-related projects and capacity building initiatives are said to serve as important channels to exchange information and build working relations.[797] To further develop this important area of interactions, Central Asian Regional Water Diplomacy programme to facilitate formal and informal dialogues with a view to strengthening transboundary cooperation is under development now. This programme will seek to promote the regional water dialogue for building consensus on water resources development and management in Central Asia through providing a platform for various actors to come together, understand each others interests and priorities and search for mutually acceptable development options using available information and learning capacity (data, monitoring and modeling tools, scientific research, etc.).

In summary, the Aral Sea basin countries could have used more efficiently normative and institutional linkages that are available to enable a more coherent legal response to transboundary water challenges in the sub-region.

Conclusion

This chapter has illustrated that international water law largely constitutes of and enables inclusive, transparent, discursive and coherent processes; yet this potential of international law to build and maintain transboundary water relationships has not been fully exploited in the Aral Sea basin.

With respect to the inclusiveness of processes, the analysis has shown that interactions over transboundary waters in the Aral Sea basin have not actively involved all riparian countries, all stakeholders and where appropriate the general public into regional decision-making on water issues. In addition to the lack of formal agreements and institutional deficits to do so, this fact can be explained by the unpreparedness of the CARs, in the current geopolitical and social settings, to take active steps to ensure that a new actor (Afghanistan) is

796 See more on the Water Diplomacy Consortium online: <http://www.thehagueinstituteforglobaljustice.org> accessed 31 January 2014.

797 Dukhovny and Sokolov, *Lessons on cooperation building to manage water conflicts in the Aral Sea Basin*. Dukhovny and de Schutter, *Water in Central Asia: Past, present, future*.

effectively included within the sub-regional water management structure and views of stakeholders are fed into official decision-making. More efforts to build trust among the countries, strengthen regional institutions and nourish public involvement are required. Inclusiveness does not require all actors to be included in all interactions, rather it stresses the need to be aware of different actors whose contribution may be useful or necessary in law making and law implementing. In the context of transboundary relations, the form of interaction (from information exchange to joint management, or from norm formation to norm application), the scale of interaction (from local to transboundary) and the scope of interaction (from an individual project to governance regimes) inform the degree of actors involvement, which should be sensitive to the actual needs and serve as a means and not an end itself.[798] The legitimacy that comes with broader participation must be balanced against the need for the process to produce results.[799] The inclusiveness of international legal process also seeks to convey the importance of a sense of community, which allows actors to be part of a joint exercise and relate to others. The Aral Sea basin countries are members of various regional organisations and involved in the activities of different institutions such as development agencies, financial institutions and treaty bodies. Still, how the analysis of the discursiveness of interactions shows, it is important not only belong to a community, but also actively engage in its work, or 'become' the community, which is currently lacking in the sub-region.

The degree of the transparency of international interactions over shared waters in the Aral Sea region may be further improved in textual and substantive terms. Unclear, ambiguous and contradictory provisions of the existing legal instruments decrease the degree of textual transparency and, consequently, appear to impede the ability of the countries to ascertain the required standards of behaviour. More stringent and specific obligations on information exchange coupled with the practical efforts to improve the public access to information and the quality of hydrometeorological data and monitoring stations would contribute significantly to increasing the degree of substantive transparency. Similarly, well-established compliance review systems for basin agreements and effective monitoring of institutions, their activities, expenditure and progress would be add to more open decision-making process in the basin.

798 Schreiner, Mtsweni and Pegram, An institutional framework for stakeholder participation in transboundary basins.

799 Johnstone at 303.

The discursive and deliberative aspect of interactions is also to be realised in the Aral Sea basin, which lacks a culture of reasoning and argumentation. The structure and mandate of existing sub-regional institutions do not allow for the establishment of a deliberative platform for joint decision-making based on 'reasoned consensus' rather than political compromise.[800] Some positive signs for the deliberation on transboundary water issues seem to emerge within an endeavor to establish a platform for a transboundary water dialogue undertaken with the support of the donor community. Yet, international interactions over shared waters in the sub-region largely take a form of strategic rather than communication action, failing short of developing shared understanding and intersubjective interpretation of the relevant legal norms such as equitable and reasonable use and no significant harm for their application in the Aral Sea basin context. More active and informed participation by the Aral Sea basin countries in deliberative forums under existing MEAs appears to be a useful exercise for building legal expertise, nourishing the capacity of strong legal argumentation and reaching shared understanding of the normative meaning of their rights and obligations. These forums should be accessible for the countries of the Aral Sea region, allowing them 'to bring home' and converge general discussion to more focused deliberation on how relevant legal norms can appropriately be related to the specific context of the case before them. The effective forum for collective deliberation and decision-making in the sub-region is crucial to reach the collective understanding of the meaning of equity and reasonableness as applied to transboundary waters in the basin.

With respect to integrative process, legal interactions over transboundary waters break down along different sectorial and spatial axes, posing challenges of complex connections and opening up the opportunities for more enriching interactions. The perception and interpretation of international water law as an integrated whole, comprised of global, regional, sub-regional and bilateral water-related arrangements and being a part of a wider framework of general international law, is still lacking in the Aral Sea region. Hence, the integrative features of international law built on the rules of interpretation and institutional connections may be helpful in the operationalizing international water law for the specific context of the sub-region. In the absence of a well-developed institutional basis for norm interpretation in the basin, the effective implementation and application of open-textured norms is hampered. Meanwhile, the normative reach and institutional platforms of global and regional MEAs, working on enhancing synergies between each other, offer a space for engagement on water-related issues. Stronger linkages between

800 Risse, '"Let's argue!"'.

international and national domains are also needed if transboundary water relationships in the sub-region are to be improved. The due diligence nature of substantive obligations in the field requires the countries to adopt relevant legal, administrative, economic, financial and technical measures at national levels; yet national implementation of these obligations remains challenging. Hence, more active interactions between actors and institutions in national and international domains are essential to unfold the potential of international law.

Overall, the transboundary water relationships in the Aral Sea basin can be further improved if the potential of inclusive, transparent, discursive and integrative interactions is fully realised.

CHAPTER 7

Making Use of International Law in the Aral Sea Basin and Beyond

Main Findings, Recommendations, and Broader Implications

Having used an analytical framework of norm and process properties to assess international water law in the Aral Sea basin, the question now is how these findings can help to understand the work of international law in the sub-region, and beyond. Drawing together the main themes of the book, this chapter suggests that the work of international law in the Aral Sea basin – as anywhere else – is the work of building and maintaining legal relationships through legal norms, legally relevant behaviour and legal consciousness. Conceived as a tripartite of its normative, sociological and psychological facets, international law operates through a system of norms and processes that generate, elaborate and refine shared understandings and collective expectations about the meaning and implementation of norms. In the Aral Sea basin, as the analysis in the previous chapters suggests, this potential of international law has not been fully used and therefore international law does not work as a sound system of norms and processes in addressing transboundary water challenges. At the same time, the findings permit to disregard the claims that international law does not work at all or is too vague to guide the conduct of states with respect to transboundary waters in the Aral Sea basin.

The chapter proceeds in two parts. The first section provides a summary of the main findings of the study of international water law in the Aral Sea basin and offers some recommendations of how to make better use of the potential of international law in building and maintaining peaceful relations over shared waters in the sub-region. The second section outlines the broader implications of the study and identifies possible areas for further research.

7.1 International Water Law in the Aral Sea Basin: Main Findings and Recommendations

The state practice of the Aral Sea basin countries surveyed above demonstrates the important contribution of international law in tackling transboundary water issues in the sub-region, but it also reveals shortcomings that must be addressed in order to invoke more fully the potential of international law.

 | DOI 10.1163/9789004274266_008

Based upon the analysis in the previous chapters, following sub-sections present the key findings of the study and offer some insights and recommendations for policy-makers and practitioners that may help to enable fully the potential of international water law in the sub-region and beyond.

7.1.1 *Improve Treaty System in a Multilevel Governance Context*

The analysis has shown that the Aral Sea basin does not suffer from a lack of regulatory endeavours; the existing legal framework is rather overwhelmed by numerous instruments seeking to govern the countries' relations over the use and protection of shared waters. However, as the study of the legal regime through the matters of scope, substantive and procedural norms, joint bodies, compliance mechanism and dispute settlement suggest, the problem with sub-regional agreements lies in the normative quality of these treaties, most of which have, firstly, been adopted with no links to each other, secondly, fall short of incorporating the contemporary principles of international water law and best water management practice, and thirdly, neglect the significance of establishing a sound procedural and institutional system of transboundary water cooperation. The fundamental principle of equitable and reasonable use has not been operationalised in the region, failing to ensure the sustainable management of the resource and the peaceful change in its regulation when circumstances and needs demand. Similarly, sub-regional treaties impose an obligation to exercise 'coordinated' (or 'joint') management and prevent parties from acting unilaterally, but fail to spell out detailed procedural obligations regarding such coordinated management and planned measures. Hence, sub-regional agreements on their own fall short of providing a comprehensive legal foundation for the peaceful and equitable management of transboundary waters in the Aral Sea basin. Meanwhile, global and regional agreements – reflecting in part customary law in the field – can contribute to strengthening the legal framework in the basin in a number of important ways.

UNECE Conventions, as a source of more detailed rules on transboundary harm prevention and cooperation, further supported institutionally, can contribute significantly to the improvement of the legal framework in the basin. Importantly, the UNECE Conventions share a common normative ground of their key principles and norms such as equitable and reasonable use, transboundary harm prevention and cooperation, which preclude inconsistencies and conflicts in their interpretation and application. The collective body of experience in the form of Meeting of the Parties, task groups, and working groups also seek to diminish cases of biased interpretations of their provisions.

Other advantages arising from the institutional support provided by UNECE treaty bodies include the opportunities of discursive problem solving and mutual learning. The Aral Sea basin countries, even those that are not parties to the UNECE Conventions, can benefit from discussions and negotiations at the meetings under these instruments, which foster interlocking engagement between technical experts, lawyers, and policy-makers to deliberate on scientific, policy and legal issues and therefore advance discursive problem-solving processes rather than intergovernmental bargaining. As per mutual learning, the UNECE Conventions bodies facilitate learning process for the CARs through a series of workshops and dialogues, through exchange of experiences and through guidelines and recommendations. Finally, the UNECE Conventions offer a promising avenue to further fortify processes of social learning and deliberation for the CARs and increase transparency setting up the requirements of reporting, compliance review and monitoring as well as implementation or compliance committees.

The 1997 UN Watercourses Convention can also play various roles. First of all, the relative clarity of language of the *jus scriptum* and a universal reference to the 1997 UN Watercourses Convention's customary provisions helps to increase transparency of international law which is an essential prerequisite for building trust among the countries. The 1997 UN Watercourses Convention codified and crystallised existing customary legal norms in the field. In doing so, the Convention makes it easier for riparian countries to consult the written text and rely on its specific language in interpreting their customary rights and obligations. The Convention made international water law 'more easily accessible and more transparent' and provided riparian countries with 'a more reliable knowledge of the scope of their rights and obligation'.[801] The CARs make use of the Convention's customary provisions when they apply or interpret their international legal rights and obligations vis-à-vis each other and Afghanistan.

Secondly, by joining the 1997 UN Watercourses Convention, the Aral Sea basin countries would benefit from new legal norms for the contracting parties, such as the obligation to protect and preserve freshwater ecosystems and the fact-finding procedure, which did not reach customary status yet and did not receive adequate treatment in the existing legal framework in the basin. Strong endorsement of the 1997 UN Watercourses Convention will also fill loopholes in customary law by providing missing definitions (e.g. 'international watercourse'), prescribing timeframes (e.g. six-month period for reply to notification) and clarifying linkages between norms (e.g. between the equitable and reasonable use principle and no-significant harm rule). Professor Bourne notes on this matter, 'In fleshing out these basic rules, such as

801 Dinstein, 'The interaction between customary international law and treaties ' at 365.

providing for a six-month time limit, the ILC has engaged in beneficial progressive development of the law [...] the new provisions merely elaborate the existing law and will make it more effective'.[802] Hence, by joining the Convention, the CARs and Afghanistan will be able to not only strengthen the legal framework for their shared waters, but also contribute to strengthening international water law at the global level.

Thirdly, not only do individual (customary) provisions, but also the entire text of the Convention that was carefully crafted to provide a system of interacting and mutually supporting rules and procedures provide an additional value to the existing framework in the basin. The substantive and procedural norms of the 1997 UN Watercourses Convention interlaced with one another, make a sound framework for 'the utilization, development, conservation, management and protection of international watercourses and the promotion of the optimal and sustainable utilization thereof for present and future generations'.[803] In this respect, the 1997 UN Watercourses Convention establishes a *regime* that results from all of its provisions in conjunction.

Fourthly, the 1997 UN Watercourses Convention can play a supplementary role to the existing agreements, which do not comprehensively define the rights and obligations of the parties. Given its framework and residual nature, the norms of the 1997 UN Watercourses Convention are mostly couched in broad terms to be applied to a range of different river basins. Nonetheless, as the analysis above has demonstrated, some of its provisions are still more precise and specific than the norms of sub-regional agreements in the Aral Sea basin. The principle of equitable and reasonable use and notification procedure on planned measures, which the sub-regional agreements seem to subsume under 'joint management' and 'joint consideration' provisions, are the most notable examples. In this context, the 1997 UN Watercourses Convention can strengthen the substantive and procedural system of cooperation in the basin.

Fifthly, the 1997 UN Watercourses Convention can serve for the CARs and Afghanistan as a common platform for the negotiation of future watercourse agreements, since this global framework instrument does not preclude or dismiss the need for such agreements.[804] Existing legal arrangements in the basin were not designed to accommodate changing circumstances, nor can they be

802 Charles B. Bourne, 'The International Law Commission's Draft Articles on the law of international watercourse: Principles and planned measures' (1992) 3 Colorado Journal of International Environmental Law and Policy 65–32 at 72.

803 1997 UN Watercourses Convention, preamble.

804 Ibid, art 3(1).

easily amended. As a result, many treaties became stagnant and lost their effectiveness. The negotiations of new agreements have not succeeded so far. Hence, the CARs and Afghanistan may want to join the 1997 UN Watercourses Convention to have an agreed common framework at the global level, and later on they can strengthen their commitments and/or adjust them to the characteristics of their watercourses. It might be also useful to have the 1997 UN Watercourses Convention as a background for interpretation of bilateral treaties and arrangements increasingly emerging in the region.[805]

Sixthly, the 1997 UN Watercourses Convention's entry into force may enhance the collective interest dimension of international water law. Operating at the global scale, the Convention extends concerns about shared waters beyond the interests of riparian countries to the broader interest of the international community in attaining sustainable development and maintaining peace and security. Cooperative conduct from *all* states in ensuring equitable and reasonable use of transboundary waters gains a special relevance and importance in the context of the globalised world that struggles to achieve water security and ensure water for all.[806] Similarly, the 1997 UN Watercourses Convention can contribute to enhancing the domestic dimension of water management by requiring changes within the jurisdiction of individual countries. The domestic application is especially evident in the need for integrated water resources management, ecosystem protection, and establishing 'all appropriate measures' such as relevant legal, administrative, technical and practical mechanisms for the implementation of the Convention.

Further, the 1997 UN Watercourses Convention's contribution to the peaceful settlement of disputes is manifested in its sound procedural system and a range of dispute settlement mechanisms, including an impartial fact-finding commission. Finally, the 1997 UN Watercourses Convention can play an expressive role by signalling the willingness of those countries that join it to actively deploy the rules and principles of international law to deal with the pressing water problems.[807]

805 Granit and others, Regional Water Intelligence Report Central Asia at 17–18.

806 See eg Dukhovny, 'Water and globalization: Case study of Central Asia' Hoekstra and Chapagain, *Globalization of water: Sharing the planet's freshwater resources*, Wouters, Vinogradov and Magsig, 'Water Security' and Patricia Wouters and Dan Tarlock, 'The third wave of normativity in global water law – The duty to cooperate in the peaceful management of the world's water resources: an emerging obligation *erga omnes*?' (2013) 23 Water Law 51–65.

807 Dinara Ziganshina, 'Legal framework governing transboundary waters in the Aral Sea Basin: What is a role for the UNWC?' in A. Rieu-Clarke, and F.R. Loures (eds.) *The UN*

In a concluding note, both the UNECE Conventions and the 1997 UN Watercourses Convention have much to offer to the countries in the Aral Sea basin in addressing their transboundary water problems. Two clarifications are important. First, the affirmative actions from the countries to take an informed decision to join the conventions, if they did not do so yet, and implement their provisions are essential prerequisites. Second, being framework treaties, global and regional water treaties cannot substitute for detailed regulations to be adopted by riparian states with a view of accommodating the needs and circumstances of individual international watercourses. The 1992 UNECE Water Convention explicitly states that its objectives are achieved primarily through the conclusion by the Parties to the Convention of separate bilateral and multilateral agreements with respect to specific transboundary waters.[808] The 1997 UN Watercourses Convention is less strict, stating that watercourse states 'may enter' into agreements to apply and adjust the provisions of the Convention to the characteristics and uses of a particular international watercourse or parts thereof, when watercourse states enter into watercourse agreements.[809]

In this context, the need for the improvement of the existing legal framework in the Aral Sea basin is undeniable. Some insights from a combined reading of normative, sociological and psychological facets of international law that have emerged as a result of this study may be useful for the Aral Sea basin countries in their on-going endeavours to improve the legal and institutional frameworks of transboundary water cooperation in the sub-region.

7.1.2 *Enable the Dual Role of Legal Norms for Stability and Peaceful Change*

The intersubjective basis of international law assigns legal norms the dual role of providing stability and allowing peaceful change in governing transboundary waters in the Aral Sea basin. On the one hand, norms are constructed from collective expectations, meanings and understandings; they only can be changed when these intersubjective understandings – not individually held beliefs – change. As such, norms provide for a stable legal framework within which relations occur. On the other hand, norms do not freeze the situation because stability also requires opening up avenue of change. Collective expectations, meanings and understandings embedded in norms allow a legal regime evolve and nourish, while restraining individualistic behaviour and

---

Watercourses Convention in force: Strengthening international law for transboundary water management (Earthscan, 2013).

808 1992 UNECE Water Convention, art 9.

809 1997 UN Watercourses Convention, arts 3(3) and 3(5).

ensuring a certain degree of stability and predictability in legal relations. In this respect, they give rise to normative development within the existing framework and allow states to introduce necessary changes. This dynamism is necessary to keep international law rooted in actual needs and address effectively emerging challenges. Then, legal norms can be seen not only as constraining, but also constitutive, facilitating and enabling actors to pursue their shared – rather than individualistic – goals in addressing transboundary water challenges within the frame of international law.

This point was illustrated in the book through the analysis of norm determinacy and stringency, used by states to fix the contours of permitted conduct, while keeping control over the refinement and application of norms contingent to time and place considerations. The analysis in Chapter 4 demonstrates that open-textured and elastic substantive norms prevail in the law governing international watercourses as applied to the Aral Sea basin. For the most part, these substantive norms operate within a due diligence framework. The due diligence nature of obligations – along with the corresponding concept of 'appropriateness' of the measures – implies that a significant degree of flexibility and relativity must be applied to both contents and time-frame of the conduct of the parties.[810] Similarly, the requirements of 'equity' and 'reasonableness' leave wide discretion on states to decide on their case-by-case application, in which riparian countries themselves must designate factors and circumstances as 'relevant' and 'important' for a particular situation. Consequently, the determination of a required standard of conduct that flows from the principle of equitable and reasonable use, the no-harm rule, and the obligations to protect international watercourses is tied up with the specific context of the norm application and contingent upon the existence of an adequate procedural and institutional system in place. As per procedural and institutional system, for the most part customary and treaty law establishes for the CARs and Afghanistan the obligations to establish joint bodies, to exchange information with riparian states, to consult with each other, to notify regarding proposed activities, to conduct transboundary impact assessments, and to work together in emergency situations in stringent terms; while leaving the content of these obligations as applied to the transboundary waters in the Aral Sea basin less defined.

These findings suggest that the indeterminacy and softness of substantive norms of international water law as applied to the Aral Sea basin are not adequately backed up with clear and precise procedural and institutional mechanisms to allow the regime to develop and the peaceful change to happen.

810 'UNECE *Guide to Implementing the Convention*'.

Equally, the countries of the sub-region have not benefited so far from the inherently open-textured nature of equitable and reasonable use principle, which permits the accommodation of specific needs and circumstances of each individual international watercourse. Indeterminacy of equitable and reasonable use principle does not make all things possible; it just does not fix or predetermine concrete solutions. Importantly, however, the stringent language of the norm expression ('shall') seeks to ensure that equitable and reasonable outcome is a must. This understanding may help to transform complaints on the vagueness of international water law into more persistent endeavours to operationalise and contextualise its provisions to make them work for the benefit of all riparian states and the environment. A more specific lesson from Chapters 4 and 5 is that the nature of legal norms and the design of a legal regime as a whole matter.

7.1.3 *Make Process Matter*

The failures of the legal framework of transboundary water cooperation in the basin only partly relate to unsatisfactory legal provisions. The study findings suggest that 'better' agreements will not help on their own, unless there exists well-thought treaty making process and a sound follow-up system. Norms and processes are parts of the integral reality of international law. It is only through legal processes that norms emerge, evolve, operate and demise. The processes of law making, development, interpretation, implementation, and application essentially shape international law. More specifically, international water law is one of those areas of international law where the relationship between substantive and procedural law is legally significant. The fundamental principle of international water law – equitable and reasonable use – is essentially process-based, requiring a sound procedural cooperation to enable its successful implementation.

Still, the value of legal processes remains largely unappreciated in the Aral Sea basin. As Chapter 6 demonstrates, transboundary water relationships in the sub-region can be significantly improved if the potential of inclusive, transparent, discursive and integrative interactions is fully realised. It is often overlooked that treaty drafting is the key for the acceptance and implementation of legal provisions. What is required is a change in the ways of how treaty negotiations in the sub-region are taking place. Given that negotiations are often donor-led, part of the problem stems from a fragmentation in donors intervention, absence of long-term commitments and frequent change in donors' priorities. More importantly, national and regional actors and processes need to drive and implement the agenda, with the Aral Sea Basin Programme guiding their endeavours.

7.1.4 *Catalyse Actors*

Norms are as 'good' or 'bad' as actors – predominantly nation states – want them to be. The quality of treaties and norms they prescribe is not something externally given, but collectively constructed. They are designed so as being a product of compromise between actors with divergent understandings of underlying issues and interests at stake. To design 'better' treaties requires therefore both better knowledge and willingness of actors to accept it as a conduct prescribed by law. Yet, even an ideally drafted treaty cannot fulfill the work of the countries to put its provisions into practice because there is also nothing remotely automatic about successful implementation of norms prescriptions. In other words, norms are what actors make of them.[811]

The discussions in Chapters 2 and 6 has shown that there are a multitude of actors involved in international legal interactions related to transboundary water management in the Aral Sea basin, starting from governmental agencies to individuals within and across national borders. The central role of nation states represented by the heads of the states, diplomats or top officials from water, energy and environmental authorities is of particular relevance. The analysis suggests, however, that due to political and legal constraints the balanced and productive engagement of all these entities into sub-regional water-related decision-making has not been achieved yet. More efforts to build trust among the basin countries, strengthen sub-regional institutions and broaden the representation of different sectors and states in the activities of these institutions are required.

Similarly, the more active role of state representatives in the work of treaty bodies can be beneficial in terms of mutual learning and nourishing a sense of belonging to a community that would enable more active and effective interactions. An urge for participation in the work of various international legal forums is dictated by at least two considerations. First, the identities of the Aral Sea basin countries as newly independent states are shaped by both participation and non-participation in communities. In other words, participation (or non-participation) shapes not only what states do, but also who states are and how they interpret their own and others' conduct in international relations. Second, the power relations between countries in the international domain need to be balanced to ensure genuine representation, particularly of countries that gained their independence recently. This point reflects back to the concerns raised by some scholars on the need to ensure that equity of the

811 Brown Weiss and Jacobson, *Engaging countries* at 1 and Wiener and Puetter, 'The quality of norms is what actors make of it' at 4.

'games of rule-making' is secured.[812] Such representation would also help to ensure that norms are indeed 'shared' and therefore accepted in the sub-region.

In addition to states as collectivities, selected individuals and national leaders can make a crucial difference in entering into international agreements and facilitating their implementation and compliance.[813] The role of the then-heads of water authorities of the Central Asian countries in establishing a legal foundation for cooperation in the new reality of independence discussed in Chapter 6 is illustrative. Such leadership can also take a form of political, structural, entrepreneurial or intellectual leadership and represents an interesting area for further research that may explore, for example, the role of individuals and organisations as agents of change.[814]

The role of legal profession in international law making, development, implementation, and application in the Aral Sea basin also deserves consideration. International law is interpreted and applied in the legal offices at national levels. To perform this function, lawyers have to be knowledgeable in international law and competent in its application. This job requires skills beyond the identification of applicable law and includes understanding the underlying purpose of the treaty and its context, and even a more generalised set of expectations such as 'spirit of the treaty'.[815] To highlight this complicated and important function of international lawyers, Philip Allott states,

> International lawyers are not the servants of governments but of international society. As lawyers they are servants not of power but of justice. It is thus the duty of international lawyers, even lawyers employed by governments, to consider not merely what is in the interest of this or that state but what is in the long-term interest of international society. More

812 Wegerich and Olsson, 'Late developers and the inequity of "equitable utilization" and the harm of "do no harm"'.

813 Jacobson and Brown Weiss, 'Assessing the record and designing strategies to engage countries'.

814 Young, 'Political leadership and regime formation: On the development of institutions international society', Moravcsik, 'A new statecraft? Supranational entrepreneurs and international cooperation', Young, 'Comment on Andrew Moravcsik, "A new statecraft? Supranational entrepreneurs and international cooperation"' (differentiating three forms of leadership that regularly come into play in efforts to establish international institutions: structural leadership, entrepreneurial leadership, and intellectual leadership).

815 Jacobson and Brown Weiss, 'A Framework for analysis' at 4 ('preambles or initial articles in treaties place these specific obligations in a broad normative framework, which we refer to as the spirit of the treaty').

> than any other kind of lawyer, international lawyers have a universalizing function.[816]

In the context of transboundary waters, Wouters and Ziganshina similarly maintain that legal opinion and doctrine must be part of an integrated response to the global water crisis.[817] This aspects, illuminating a need for more active participation of legal profession in the construction of the legality, speaks directly to the third facet of international law, namely of legal consciousness.

With this appreciation, lawyers should be involved more actively in the process of international law making and development in the Aral Sea basin. Yet, as the discussion in Chapter 6 illustrates, a lack of local specialists qualified in international water law was detrimental to the process and outcomes of negotiations between Central Asian countries under the umbrella of the ADB technical assistance in 2005–2008. This hindered the opportunities to engage fully in legal deliberations and led to a situation where the discussion of complex technical issues overthrew the attention to the language and coherence of the draft agreements. The absence or sporadic attendance of legal experts from the sub-region in the work of the UNECE Conventions bodies is similarly discouraging (Chapter 6). Among other things, such non-participation leads to missed opportunities for the Aral Sea basin countries to become a part of 'epistemic communities', 'interpretive communities', 'legal thoughts', or 'communities of practice' that exert a powerful influence on the development and interpretation of international law (Chapter 2). Finally, the Aral Sea basin states should not neglect the need in more active engagement of academicians from the sub-region in the development of legal thoughts and understanding. As Fastenrath righty observes, 'Academic writings exert a huge but often underestimated influence on legal thought and understanding. In contrast to legal assertions by States, their power is based on persuasiveness'.[818] Nonetheless, academic writings on the issues of international water law in the sub-region are insignificant.

---

816 Philip Allott, 'State responsibility and the unmaking of international law' (1988) 29 Harvard International Law Journal 1–26 at 24.

817 Patricia Wouters and Dinara Ziganshina, 'Tackling the global water crisis: Unlocking international law as fundamental to the peaceful management of the world's shared transboundary waters – Introducing the H_2O paradigm' in Quentin Grafton and Karen Hussy (eds), *Water resources planning and management: Challenges and solutions* (Cambridge University Press 2011) at 200.

818 Fastenrath, 'A political theory of law: Escaping the aporia of the debate on the validity of legal argument in public international law' at 70.

Finally, the general public has an important role to play in contemporary international law. Non-state actors can influence the ability of states to comply with their legal obligations. However, the degree of participation in transboundary water interactions and inputs from these actors in the Aral Sea basin varies and is contingent to political and legal environment as well as the nature and scope of an issue at stake or activity under consideration. Currently, the public participation in transboundary water management in the sub-region is rather low.

To sum up, all these actors make for increasingly complicated interactions over transboundary water management in the sub-region. Certainly, broader participation can impose heavy costs on participants or stall processes, but building relationships and ultimately the construction of the legality in the Aral Sea basin can be reached only through active participation and mutual engagement of various actors. Individual experience has significant implications for the way norms and law in general matter.

7.1.5 *Enhance Legal Consciousness*

Legal norms exert social influence if they are formed through and/or become part of an individual consciousness. As was observed in Chapter 2, legal consciousness requires affirmative actions from individuals and collectivities to become active participants in on-going interactions about the law. Such on-going interaction help to build 'individual' understandings and to transform subjective experience with and understanding of law to intersubjective – commonly shared within a group of actors – meanings and understandings, which are essential for effective international law making and application.

Yet, misperceptions and misinterpretation of the norms of international water law are still present in the Aral Sea region. For instance, the provisions of the 1997 UN Watercourses Convention have been interpreted as giving preferential treatment to the interests of wealthy and powerful states, ignoring the situation in water-stress countries, leaving too much discretion on individual states to interpret its provisions on their own benefits, and being vague and imprecise in defining the rights and obligations imposed on riparian countries. The analysis in Chapters 4–5 helps to disperse these misunderstandings.

The degree of legal understanding in the sub-region can be increased, *inter alia*, through the on-going process of interactions in various forums such as treaty bodies, basin institutions and joint training and projects. As the studies on legal consciousness teach us, social learning through and about the law is not a passive process; rather, it involves active participation in the construction of legality. A process of social learning towards building normative consensus is especially powerful within treaty regimes. As was discussed above, the UNECE Conventions' institutional landscape supports such learning process for the CARs in a number of important ways. To reiterate, the construction of legality in the Aral Sea basin is a matter of building legal consciousness above all.

7.1.6 *Increase Transparency and Strengthen Linkages*

It is crucial to increase the degree of transparency about actors' behaviour and underlying norms and processes, if legal relationship on the basis of shared understanding and collective expectations are to be built and maintained. Norms and processes as well as reasons behind any decision or conduct in transboundary water interactions must be accessible, visible and understandable. This predetermines the acceptance of norms as legitimate. There exist a great potential to increase transparency of transboundary water governance in the Aral Sea region through adopting 'better' treaties in terms of norm stringency and determinacy and improving their legal design in terms of procedural and institutional systems. Further openness of decision-making, reporting, compliance review, information exchange and public participation are also desirable.

Increased linkages within various treaty regimes and between international and national domains also contribute to transparency, among other things. Interactions and networking between international, regional and domestic actors in various settings and scales constitute a significant component of the process of building shared understanding for norm formation and implementation.

7.1.7 *Transform Intergovernmental Bargaining into Deliberative Problem Solving*

The intersubjective nature of international law is defined by and relies upon processes through which actors interact. Interactions may include passive observance or active engagement in the form of deliberation or bargaining. Not denying the existence or usefulness of other forms of interactions, this book focused on deliberation (or even broadly discourse) because of its ability to enhance collective expectations and normatively shared meanings that form the very bases of legal ordering.

The discursive and deliberative aspect of interactions is still to be realised in the Aral Sea basin, which largely lacks a culture of reasoning and argumentation . The problems to be resolved in transboundary water management in the basin require stakeholders to work constantly in problem-solving and governance regimes. However, international interactions over shared waters in the sub-region largely take a form of strategic rather than communication action, failing short of developing shared understanding and intersubjective interpretation of the relevant legal norms such as equitable and reasonable use and no significant harm. Frequently, participation in actual discourse fails due to the fact that actors such as governmental officials chose to inform each other about their national points of view, rather than make endeavours to convince and persuade counterparts by legal arguments. For example, it is commonplace in the basin to make general reference to the principles of international water law in stating the country's position on certain issues; while more focused argumentation what these general norms imply in a particular situation is rather rare. Although years of interactions since gaining independence have established an 'institutional life-world' between the Central Asian countries where rational discourse possible, the lack of reasons given for decisions at each step of transboundary water governance remains a challenge. The structure and mandate of existing interstate institutions do not allow establishing a deliberative platform for joint decision-making based on reasoned consensus rather than political compromise. The laudable intentions calling for 'joint management' and 'joint consideration' can hardly be realised without the mechanisms for making 'joint' or 'collective' decisions, which would be acceptable by all actors who governed by them. To be deemed truly 'collective', a decision must be a product of reciprocal deliberative exchange and reasoned consensus.[819] Most importantly, the reasons for such decisions must be ongoingly made acceptable for and perceived legitimate by all participants.

More active and informed participation by the Aral Sea basin countries in deliberative forums under existing MEAs appears to be a useful exercise for building legal expertise, nourishing the capacity of strong legal argumentation and reaching shared understanding of the normative meaning of their rights and obligations. For example, experts and decision-makers from the countries have to be more active in the work of various treaty bodies that will allow them 'to bring home' and converge general discussion to more focused deliberation on how relevant legal norms can appropriately be related to the specific context of the case before them. The effective forum for collective deliberation and decision-making in the sub-region is also crucial to reach the intersubjective understanding of the meaning of equity and reasonableness as applied to transboundary waters in the basin. As was discussed above, indeterminacy of equitable and reasonable use principle does not make all things possible; and it just does not fix or predetermine possibilities. These possibilities arise, nourish and mature in discursive interactions, when different options are made 'relevant' by the participants themselves. Only then the principle of equitable

819 Risse, '"Let's argue!"'.

and reasonable use will serve as a legal constraint rather than a political manifestation.

7.1.8 *Build Normative Communities*

Ultimately, it can be argued that taken together and substantially centred on legal norms, the process features of inclusiveness, transparency, discursiveness, and coherence can contribute to forming normative communities. So far, a communitarian perspective as addressed in the field of international water law predominantly focused on the 'common' character of transboundary waters, reflecting on interdependencies, interconnectedness and common interests, drawing on the community of interest doctrine.[820] Recent studies on water security pushed the envelope further, arguing that 'common' character of shared freshwaters can be strengthened through the notion of 'hydro-solidarity', 'the regional common concern' and 'an emerging obligation *erga omnes* to ensure water for all'.[821] This book seeks to add to these developments and illuminates another dimension of 'community' that reflects at the level of a conception of international law itself rather than a concrete commonality of interests. Because interests are ever-changing, it is unsafe to build communities around interests.[822] Instead, as was suggested above, the law – where individual interests are moulded into collective understandings and expectations – can provide for a more stable ground for actors to connect and interact with each other.

The notion of normative community as used in this study implies therefore a sense of connection arising from transparent, discursive and integrative

820 *Case Relating to the Territorial Jurisdiction of the International Commission of the River Oder* (*United Kingdom, Czechoslovakia, Denmark, France, Germany, Sweden v. Poland*) PCIJ Series A No 23 (1929) 'The community of interest in a navigable river becomes the basis of a common legal right, the essential features of which are the perfect equality of all riparian States in the use of the whole course of the river and the exclusion of any preferential privilege of any one riparian State in relation to the others'. Nonetheless, the equitable and reasonable use rule embraces some ideas underlying the concept of the community of interest, whereas the doctrine as a whole remains rather aspirational.

821 Wouters, Vinogradov and Magsig, 'Water Security', Bjørn-Oliver Magsig, 'Overcoming state-centrism in international water law: "Regional common concern" as the normative foundation of water security' (2011) 3 Goettingen Journal of International Law 317–344, and Wouters and Tarlock, 'The third wave of normativity in global water law'.

822 Emile Durkheim, one of the founders of modern sociology stated: 'For if interest relates men, it is never from more than a few months [...] There is nothing less constant then interest. Today, it unites me to you; tomorrow, it will make me your enemy. Such a cause can only give rise to transient relations and passing associations'. See Emile Durkheim, *The division of labor in society* (Free Press 1997) at 203–204.

interactions between different actors within and across countries through and about the law. Requiring mutual engagement of actors in such interactions through the language of international law, the notion of normative community brings together normative, sociological and psychological facets of international law. It assigns a central role to legal norms, which provide the normative frame for any actions. It also demands changes in actors' behaviour, understanding, and perception in order to transform individual actions and understandings to collective ones. Within such normative communities, mutual learning, coordination of action and socialisation can be enhanced and power asymmetry among actors mitigated. Treaty-based institutionalisation has been seen by some observers as a fruitful way of cultivating normative communities, that otherwise remain elusive.[823]

Normative community formed in such a way thus becomes the expression of a collective consciousness, which gives rise to sustained legal relationships. In turn, legal relationship is ultimately what international law, as comprised of legal norms, legally relevant behaviour and legal consciousness, is to produce. In this framing, the real test for the peaceful and sustainable regulation of transboundary watercourses and their ecosystems in the Aral Sea basin consists not so much in the numbers of treaties, protocols, and declaration, but in building legal relationships across the spectrum of actors. Treaties are important, but they have to be part of system that works.

The Aral Sea basin countries are still some distance from acting as active members of normative communities at the global and regional levels, let alone cultivating their own normative community (Chapter 6). Linked by geography and the infrastructure system put in place in the Soviet time and in recognition of their common interests, these countries do have a common platform for transboundary interactions at the basin level. Such pragmatic commonality out of a functional need for cooperation can give rise to a community in a legal sense, but hardly can substitute it. Thinking in terms of normative community can open up new dimensions for improving legal and institutional environment in the Aral Sea region, focusing both on the countries and their identification with certain communities and on a broader circle of actors forming these communities on the basis of discursive interactions. Ultimately, what seems important is not formally belong to a community, but actively engage in its discursive practice or, in other words, in formulating itself as a rule community.

---

823 Jutta Brunnée, 'Common areas, common heritage, and common concern' in Daniel Bodansky, Jutta Brunnée and Ellen Hey (eds), *The Oxford Handbook of International Environmental Law* (Oxford University Press 2007) at 568.

7.2 Making Use of International (Water) Law: Broader Implications and Areas for Future Research

Beyond the Aral Sea basin, the findings of this book speak to the general debate about the role and workings of international (water) law.

First of all, conceptual and analytical frameworks developed in this research and applied to the Aral Sea basin situation can be tested in other transboundary basins around the globe. Such research may take the form of a comparative assessment, essentially highlighting the shortcomings, experiences and possibilities of the use of international law means in addressing transboundary water challenges in diverse political, economic, social and cultural settings.

Second, in contrast to dominant approaches to the assessment of the workings of international law that set norms against behaviour, a conceptual understanding of international law proposed in this study opens up analysis to constitutive, facilitative and enabling role of legal norms and processes. Viewing international law as a conglomerate of legal norms, legally relevant behaviour and legal consciousness, as this book suggests, can inform international law and international relations scholars concerned with an inquiry of how international law matters in a number of important ways.

Third, the study offers a legal insight to emerging research on transboundary water interactions that uses a combined reading of conflict and cooperation, when examining transboundary watercourse relations.[824] Its findings support the skeptical appraisals of research that diagnoses cooperation by the existence of treaties. The fact that treaties, by themselves, are insufficient is not news. This study argues, however, that it is legal relationships that international law seeks to build. By focusing on process properties of international legal interactions, this book opens up the possibility for legal and political science scholars to examine more carefully how legal processes influence transboundary water interactions and build legal relationships.

Fourth, the process features of international law outlined in this study may also provide inroads for inquires about the role of law in water diplomacy efforts around the globe. The contemporary understanding of water diplomacy has transformed and expanded from a peaceful method of interstate relations over shared waters to a general instrument of communication among

824 Mark Zeitoun and Naho Mirumachi, 'Transboundary water interaction I: Reconsidering conflict and cooperation' (2008) 8 International Environmental Agreements: Politics, Law and Economics 297–316. See also, Mark Zeitoun and Jeroen F. Warner, 'Hydro-hegemony – a framework for analysis of trans-boundary water conflicts' (2006) 8 Water policy 435–460.

globalised societies.[825] This new dimension suggesting the move beyond relationships solely between riparian states has been evidenced in the recent linking of water stress in Asia and Africa with the national security of North America and Europe. The 2011 United States Senate Report stressing that water plays an increasingly important role in US diplomatic and security interests outlines the country's possible involvement with respect to water scarcity and water management in Central and South Asia.[826] Similarly, in its recent conclusions on EU water diplomacy, the European Council notes that managing the effects of climate change and demographic and economic development, as well as reconciling different uses of water resources such as drinking water and sanitation, agriculture, food production, industry and energy, are major water security challenges and highlights the potential of water diplomacy to help safeguard security, development, prosperity and the human rights of water and sanitation.[827]

Thus, at the very least, the emerging notion of water diplomacy can be characterised by three distinctive elements: (i) the preventive nature of diplomacy in maintaining peace and security; (ii) the need for a dialogue in which traditional bilateral diplomacy is complimented by multilateral and multilevel diplomacy; and (iii) the notion of the collective responsibility of the international community.[828] Such developments on the ground justify the need for a more rigorous academic investigation of the concept of water diplomacy, especially given growing threats to national, regional, and global water security . The increased interest in water diplomacy has to be supported by its systematic analysis and further conceptual and theoretical undertakings to deepen understanding of the role and relevance of water diplomacy in the globalised world.

Similarly, the notion of normative community suggested in this book can feed into contemporary debate on hydro-solidarity and water security by adding a new dimension of 'community' that reflects at the level of a conception of international law itself rather than a concrete commonality of interests. The notion of normative community demonstrates that conceiving analysis in terms of state and non-state actors involvement is not enough; the underlying

---

825 Wilfried Bolewski, *Diplomacy and international law in globalized relations* (Berlin, Springer 2007).

826 Avoiding water wars.

827 European Union 'Council conclusions on EU water diplomacy' Foreign Affairs Council meeting (Brussels, 22 July 2013). Online <www.consilium.europa.eu/uedocs/cms_data/docs/pressdata/EN/foraff/138253.pdf> accessed 30 January 2014.

828 Wouters and Ziganshina, 'Tackling the global water crisis'.

perceptions and discursive network of relationships have to be examined more carefully to understand actor's conduct and expectations. One of the possible areas for further research on this line includes the study of legal consciousness nourished in different communities of practices operating in legal spheres: law making, interpretation, implementation, application, and adjudication.

Finally, despite the fact that the present book confined itself to study the workings of international law, its findings suggest that the link between international and national law is crucial. This is so because nation states are expected to give effect to international commitments in national legislation and actions at national level feeds back to the international domain. While linkages between international and national domains are typically nominated as important, there is little analysis how these connections can be strengthened in the context of the Aral Sea basin and beyond. The process feature of coherence sought to illustrate this point, which can be extended in further research.

Conclusions

This book has examined international water law in the Aral Sea basin shared by Afghanistan and five post-Soviet countries of Central Asia (Kazakhstan, Kyrgyzstan, Tajikistan, Turkmenistan and Uzbekistan) by posing the question, 'How does international law work in addressing transboundary water challenges in the Aral Sea basin?'

The underlying argument of the book is that the problems with the operation of international law are not so much in the law itself, but in the (mis) conception of international law, its potential and limits. A broad conceptual framework mapping the terrain of international law as comprised of legal norms (normative facet), legally relevant behaviour (sociological facet), and legal consciousness (psychological facet) was offered to facilitate understanding of this phenomenon. It was argued that international law works and gains its authority and power through the internal complexity and interconnection of its three facets. Conceived as a tripartite of its normative, sociological and psychological facets, international law operates through a system of norms and processes that generate, elaborate and refine shared understandings and collective expectations about the meaning and implementation of norms. Built on this conceptual understanding, the book has developed an analytical framework of norm and process properties by which to examine international law and its workings with due regards to its three facets. Two properties of legal norms (determinacy and stringency) and four properties of legal processes (inclusiveness, transparency, discursiveness, and coherence) have been proposed as entry points for such an inquiry.

Having used an analytical framework of norm and process properties to assess international water law in the Aral Sea Basin, the book concluded that the potential of international law to address transboundary water challenges through a sound system of legal norms and processes has not been fully realised in the region yet. This is so because international law is conceived only as comprised of legal norms, whereas legally relevant behaviour and legal consciousness are left aside. This omission makes it difficult to build and maintain legal relationships, which emerge and mature through practicing the law within normative communities. Requiring mutual engagement of actors in inclusive, transparent, discursive and integrative interactions through the language of international law, the notion of normative community brings together normative, sociological and psychological facets of international law. It assigns a central role to legal norms, which provide the normative frame for any actions. It also demands changes in actors' behaviour, understanding, and

 | DOI 10.1163/9789004274266_009

perception in order to transform individual actions and understandings to collective ones. Within such normative communities, mutual learning, coordination of action and socialisation can be enhanced and power asymmetry among actors mitigated. Normative communities formed in such a way then become the expression of a collective consciousness, which gives rise to sustained legal relationships. Because legal relationship is ultimately what international law is to produce, the real test for the peaceful and sustainable regulation of transboundary watercourses and their ecosystems in the Aral Sea basin consists not only in the quantitative and qualitative aspects of treaties, protocols, and declarations, but in building legal relationships across the spectrum of actors. By looking at international law in such a way, it is possible to better understand – and ultimately improve – its workings.

ANNEX 1

Treaty Law Governing Transboundary Waters in the Aral Sea Basin

I. Treaties at the global level	Afg	Kz	Kg	Tj	Tm	Uz
UN Convention on the Law of the Non-Navigational Uses of International Watercourses (1997, New York)	–	–	–	–	–	+
Convention on Wetlands of International Importance especially as Waterfowl Habitat (1971, Ramsar)	–	+	+	+	+	+
UN Convention on Biological Diversity (1992, Rio de Janeiro)	+	+	+	+	+	+
UN Framework Convention on Climate Change (1992, New York)	+	+	+	+	+	+
UN Convention to Combat Desertification in Those Countries Experiencing Serious Drought and/or Desertification, Particularly in Africa (1994, Paris)	+	+	+	+	+	+

II. Treaties at regional level	Afg	Kz	Kg	Tj	Tm	Uz
A. Commonwealth of Independent States (CIS)						
Charter of the CIS (1993, Minsk)	–	+	+	+	+	+
Agreement on Interaction in the Field of Ecology and Environmental Protection (1992, Moscow)	–	+	+	+	+	+
Agreement on the Main Principles of Interaction in the Field of Rational Use and Protection of the Transboundary Water Bodies (1998, Moscow)	–	s	–	+	–	–
Agreement on Informational Cooperation in the Field of Ecology and the Environmental Protection (1998, Moscow)	–	+	+	+	–	–
B. United Nations Economic Commission for Europe (UNECE)						
Convention on Environmental Impact Assessment in a Transboundary Context (1991, Espoo)		+	+	s	–	–

 | DOI 10.1163/9789004274266_010

B. United Nations Economic Commission for Europe (UNECE)						
Convention on the Protection and Use of Transboundary Watercourses and International Lakes (1992, Helsinki)	–	+	–	–	+	+
Convention on the Transboundary Effects of Industrial Accidents (1992, Helsinki)	–	+	–	–	–	–
Convention on Access to Information, Public Participation in Decision-Making and Access to Justice in Environmental Matters (1998, Aarhus)	–	+	+	+	+	–

III. Treaties at sub-regional level	Afg	Kz	Kg	Tj	Tm	Uz
A. Between Central Asian Republics						
Agreement on Cooperation in the Field of Joint Management of the Use and Conservation of Water Resources of Interstate Sources (1992, Almaty)	–	+	+	+	+	+
Agreement on Joint Actions for Addressing the Problems of the Aral Sea and its Coastal Area, Improving the Environment, and Ensuring the Social and Economic Development of the Aral Sea Region (1993, Kzyl-Orda)	–	+	+	+	+	+
Agreement on Cooperation over Water Management Issues (1996, Chardjev)	–	–	–	–	+	+
Agreement on the Use of Fuel and Water Resources, Construction and Operation of Gas Pipelines in Central Asian Region (1996, Tashkent)	–	+	+	–	–	+
Agreement on the Use of Water and Energy Resources of the Syrdarya Basin (1998, Bishkek)	–	+	+	+	–	+
Agreement on Cooperation in the Area of Environment and Rational Nature Use (1998, Bishkek)	–	+	+	–	–	+
Agreement on the Parallel Operation of the Energy Systems of Central Asian States (1999, Bishkek)	–	+	+	+	–	+
Agreement on Cooperation in the Sphere of Hydromet (1999, Bishkek)	–	+	+	+	–	+
Agreement about the status of IFAS and its organisations (1999, Ashgabad)	–	+	+	+	+	+

A. Between Central Asian Republics						
Framework Convention on Environmental Protection for Sustainable Development in Central Asia (2006, not in force, Ashgabad)	–	–	s	s	s	–
B. Selected agreements between the Soviet Union and Afghanistan						
Frontier Agreement (1946)(1946, Moscow)						
Treaty Concerning the Regime of the Soviet-Afghan State Frontier (1958, Moscow)						
Protocol on the Joint Execution of Works for the Integrated Utilization of the Water Resources in the Frontier Section of the Amudarya (1958, Kabul)						

Note: Afghanistan (Afg), Kazakhstan (Kz), Kyrgyzstan (Kg), Tajikistan (Tj), Turkmenistan (Tm) and Uzbekistan (Uz)

Bibliography

Abbott KO and others, 'The Concept of Legalization' (2000) 54 International Organization 401–419.

Abi-Saab G, 'Comment to M. Reisman "the Democratization of Contemporary International Law-Making Processes and the Differentiation of Their Application" in Wolfrum R and Röben V (eds), *Developments of International Law in Treaty Making* (Springer 2005).

Abseno M, 'How Can the Work of the General Assembly and the ILC on the Law of Non-Navigational Uses of International Watercourses Contributes Towards Basin-Wide Legal Framework for the Nile Basin?' (Unpublished, University of Dundee 2010).

ADB TA 6163-Reg: Improved Management of Shared Water Resources in Central Asia. Online: <http://cawater-info.net/reta/documents/index_e.htm> accessed 22 December 2011.

Adler E, *Communitarian International Relations: The Epistemic Foundations of International Relations* (New York, Routledge 2005).

Ahmad M and Mahwash W, *Water Resource Development in Northern Afghanistan and Its Implication for Amu Darya Basin* (Working Paper no 36, 2004).

Alderson K and Hurrell A (eds), *Hedley Bull on International Society* (Palgrave Macmillan 2000).

Allan JA, *WaterVirtual: A Long Term Solution for Water Short Middle Eastern Economies?* (SOAS Water Issues Study Group, School of Oriental and African Studies/King's College-London Occasional Paper 3, 1997).

Allott P, 'The Concept of International Law' (1999) 10 European Journal of International Law 31.

Allott P, 'State Responsibility and the Unmaking of International Law' (1988) 29 Harvard International Law Journal 1–26.

Amador FVC, 'Second Report on International Responsibility' (1957) 2 Yearbook of the International Law Commission 104.

Aust HP, 'The Normative Environment for Peace – on the Contribution of the ILC's Articles on State Responsibility' in Nolte G (ed), *Peace through International Law: The Role of the International Law Commission a Colloquium at the Occasion of Its Sixtieth Anniversary* (Springer 2009).

Austin JL, *How to Do Things with Words* (Oxford, Clarendon Press 1962).

Balkin JM, 'Understanding Legal Understanding: The Legal Subject and the Problem of Legal Coherence' (1993) 103 Yale Law Journal 105–176.

Ball C, 'What Is Transparency?' (2009) 11 Public Integrity 293–308.

Barnett M and Duvall R, 'Power in International Politics' (2005) 59 International Organization 39–75.

Barnett M and Finnemore M, 'The Politics, Power and Patologis of International Organisations' (Autumn 1999) 53 International Organization 699–732.

Barton D and Tusting K (eds), *Beyond Communities of Practice: Language, Power and Social Context* (Cambridge, Cambridge University Press 2005).

Bates BC and others (eds), *Climate Change and Water. Technical Paper of the Intergovernmental Panel on Climate Change* (IPCC Secretariat 2008).

Berman PS, 'From International Law to Law and Globalization' (2005) 43 Columbia Journal of Transnational Law 485.

Bernauer T and Siegfried T, 'Compliance and Performance in International Water Agreements: The Case of the Naryn/Syr Darya Basin' (2008) 14 Global Governance 479–501.

Beyerlin U, 'Different Types of Norms in International Environmental Law: Policies, Principles, and Rules' in Bodansky D, Brunnée J and Hey E (eds), *The Oxford Handbook of International Environmental Law* (Oxford University Press 2007).

Beyerlin U, Stoll P-T and Wolfrum R, 'Conclusions Drawn from the Conference on Ensuring Compliance with MEAs' in Beyerlin U, Stoll P-T and Wolfrum R (eds), *Ensuring Compliance with Multilateral Environmental Agreements: Academic Analysis and Views from Practice* (Koninklijke Brill NV 2006).

Beyerlin U, Stoll P-T and Wolfrum R (eds), *Ensuring Compliance with Multilateral Environmental Agreements: A Dialogue between Practitioners and Academia*, vol 2 (Martinus Nijhoff Publishers 2006).

Birnie P, Boyle A and Redgwell C, *International Law and the Environment* (Oxford, 3rd edn, Oxford University Press 2009).

Bodansky D, 'What's So Bad About Unilateral Action to Protect the Environment?' (2000) 11 European Journal of International Law 339–347.

Bodansky D, 'Rules Vs Standards in International Environmental Law' (2004) 98 American Society of International Law Proceedings 275–280.

Bodansky D, 'Legitimacy' in Bodansky D, Brunnée J and Hey E (eds), *The Oxford Handbook of International Environmental Law* (Oxford University Press 2007).

Bodansky D, *The Art and Craft of International Environmental Law* (Harvard University Press 2009).

Bohman J, *Public Deliberation: Pluralism, Complexity, and Democracy* (Cambridge, MA, MIT Press 2000).

Boisson De Chazournes L, Leb C and Tignino M, 'Environmental Protection and Access to Water: The Challenges Ahead' in Michael vd and Keenan P (eds), *The Right to Water and Water Rights in a Changing World. Colloquium Papers* (Delft, IHP-UNESCO 2011).

Bolewski W, *Diplomacy and International Law in Globalized Relations* (Berlin, Springer 2007).

Bourne C, 'Procedure in the Development of International Drainage Basins' (1972) 22 University of Toronto Law Journal 172–206.

Bourne C, 'Procedure in the Development of International Drainage Basins: The Duty to Consult and to Negotiate' (1972) 10 Canadian Yearbook of International Law 212–234.

Bourne CB, 'The International Law Commission's Draft Articles on the Law of International Watercourse: Principles and Planned Measures' (1992) 3 Colorado Journal of International Environmental Law and Policy 65–32.

Boyle A and Chinkin C, *The Making of International Law* (Oxford, Oxford University Press 2007).

Bradford WC, *International Legal Compliance: Surveying the Field* (SSRN 2004).

Brown Weiss E, 'International Law in a Kaleidoscopic World' (2010) Asian Journal of International Law 1–13.

Brown Weiss E and Jacobson H (eds), *Engaging Countries: Strengthening Compliance with International Environmental Accords* (MIT Press 1998).

Brunnée J, 'Wrap-up Plenary: What's Next in Implementation, Compliance and Effectiveness?' (1997) 91 American Society of International Law Proceedings 504–511.

Brunnée J and Toope SJ, 'International Law and Constructivism: Elements of an International Theory of International Law' (2000–2001) 39 Columbia Journal of Transnational Law 19–74.

Brunnée J, 'Coping with Consent: Law-Making under Multilateral Environmental Agreements' (2002) 15 Leiden Journal of International Law 1–52.

Brunnée J and Toope SJ, 'The Changing Nile Basin Regime: Does Law Matter?' (2002) 43 Harvard International Law Journal 105–159.

Brunnée J, 'International Legal Accountability through the Lens of the Law of State Responsibility' (2005) 36 Netherlands Yearbook of International Law 3–38.

Brunnée J, 'Reweaving the Fabric of International Law? Patterns of Consent in Environmental Framework Agreements' in Wolfrum R and Roben V (eds), *Developments of International Law in Treaty Making* (Berlin, Heidelberg, New York, Springer 2005).

Brunnée J, 'Common Areas, Common Heritage, and Common Concern' in Bodansky D, Brunnée J and Hey E (eds), *The Oxford Handbook of International Environmental Law* (Oxford University Press 2007).

Brunnée J and Toope SJ, *Legitimacy and Legality in International Law: An Interactional Account* (Cambridge, Cambridge University Press 2010).

Buchan R, 'A Clash of Normativities: International Society and International Community' (2008) 10 International Community Law Review 3–27.

Buzan B, 'From International System to International Society: Structural Realism and Regime Theory Meet the English School' (1993) 47 International Organization 327–352.

Cassese A, 'The Martens Clause: Half a Loaf or Simply Pie in the Sky?' (2000) 11 European Journal of International Law 187–216.

Cassese A and Weiler JHH (eds), *Change and Stability in International Law-Making* (Walter de Gruyter 1988).

Centre for Policy and Human Development, *Afghanistan Human Development Report 2011. The Forgotten Front: Water Security and the Crisis in Sanitation* (Kabul University 2011).

Chambers BW, *Interlinkages and the Effectiveness of Multilateral Environmental Agreements* (Tokyo, United Nations University Press 2008).

Chayes A and Chayes AH, *The New Sovereignty: Compliance with International Regulatory Agreements* (Cambridge, Harvard University Press 1995).

Checkel JT, 'Why Comply? Social Learning and European Identity Change' (2001) 55 International Organization 553–588.

Cheng B, *General Principles of Law as Applied by International Courts and Tribunals* (London Stevens and Sons 1953).

Cohen J, 'Procedure and Substance in Deliberative Democracy' in Bohman J and Rehg W (eds), *Deliberative Democracy: Essays on Reason and Politics* (MIT Press 2002).

Cotterrell RBM, *The Sociology of Law: An Introduction* (London, 2nd edn, Butterworths 1992).

Craick N, *The International Law of Environmental Impact Assessment: Process, Substance and Integration* (New York, Cambridge University Press 2008).

Crawford JR, 'Responsibility to the International Community as a Whole' (2001) 8 Indiana Journal of Global Legal Studies 303–322.

Curtin D and Nollkaemper A, 'Conceptualizing Accountability in International and European Law' (2005) 36 Netherlands Yearbook of International Law 3–20.

Deitelhoff N, 'The Discursive Construction of Legal Norms and Institutions: Law and Politics in Negotiations on the International Criminal Court' (SSRN 2007).

de Schutter J. and Dukhovny VA (eds), *South Prearalie – New Perspectives*. Project 'Science for Peace' (Ecotec Resource & SIC ICWC 2003).

Dickinson LA, 'Military Lawyers on the Battlefield: An Empirical Account of International Law Compliance' (2010) 104 American Journal of International Law 1–28.

Dictionaries, *"Consciousness." Oxford Dictionaries.* (Oxford University Press 2010).

Dictionaries, *"Intersubjective." Oxford Dictionaries.* (Oxford University Press 2010).

Dictionaries, *"Persuade." Oxford Dictionaries.* (Oxford University Press 2010).

Dinstein Y, 'The Interaction between Customary International Law and Treaties' (2006) 322 Receuil des cours 243–427.

Downs GW, Rocke DM and Barsoom PN, 'Is the Good News About Compliance Good News About Cooperation?' (1996) 50 International Organization 379–406.

Dryzek JS, *Deliberative Global Politics: Discourse and Democracy in a Divided World* (Cambridge, Polity Press 2006).

Dukhovny VA, 'Water and Globalization: Case Study of Central Asia' (2007) 56 Irrigation and Drainage 489–507.

Dukhovny VA and de Schutter J, *Water in Central Asia: Past, Present, Future* (Taylor & Francis Group 2011).

Dukhovny VA and Sokolov V, *Assessment of Water Resources in the Northern Afghanistan, Its Use and Impact on the Region of the Amudarya River Basin* (Scientific Information Center of Interstate Commission for Water Coordination in Central Asia, 2002).

Dukhovny VA and Sorokin A, *Assessment of the Impact of Rogun Reservoir on Amudarya River Water Regime. In Russian* (2007).

Dukhovny VA and Sokolov VA, *Lessons on Cooperation Building to Manage Water Conflicts in the Aral Sea Basin* (Paris, UNESCO-IHP 2003).

Durkheim E, *The Division of Labor in Society* (Free Press 1997).

Dworkin R, *Taking Rights Seriously* (Cambridge, Harvard University Press 1978).

Ehrenberg KM, 'Law Is Not (Best Considered) an Essentially Contested Concept' (2011) 7 International Journal of Law in Context 209–232.

European Commission Humanitarian Aid (ECHO), United Nations International Strategy for Disaster Reduction Secretariat – Central Asia and Caucasus (UNISDR – CA), *Disaster Risk Reduction in Central Asia, Building Partnerships to Secure Development Gains* (2009).

European Union 'Council conclusions on EU water diplomacy' Foreign Affairs Council meeting (Brussels, 22 July 2013).

Ewick P and Silbey SS, *The Common Place of Law: Stories from Everyday Life* (Chicago, University Chicago Press 1998).

Fastenrath U, 'A Political Theory of Law: Escaping the Aporia of the Debate on the Validity of Legal Argument in Public International Law' in Fastenrath U and others (eds), *From Bilateralism to Community Interest: Essays in Honour of Bruno Simma* (Oxford University Press 2011).

Feeley M, 'The Concept of Laws in Social Science: A Critique and Notes on an Expanded View' (1976) 10 Law and Society Review 501–528.

Feeley M, 'Three Voices of Socio-Legal Studies' (2001) 35 Israel Law Review 175.

Finnemore M, 'Are Legal Norms Distinctive?' (2000) 32 New York University Journal of International Law and Politics 699–706.

Finnemore M and Sikkink K, 'International Norm Dynamics and Political Change' (1998) 52 International Organization 887–917.

Finnemore M and Toope SJ, 'Alternatives to "Legalization": Richer Views of Law and Politics' (2001) 55 International Organization 743–758.

Fish S, *Is There a Text in This Class? The Authority of Interpretive Communities* (Cambridge, MA/London, Harvard University Press 1980).

Fish S, *Doing What Comes Naturally: Change, Rhetoric, and the Practice of Theory in Literary and Legal Studies* (Durham, NC, Duke University Press 1989).

Fitzmaurice G, 'The Law and Procedure of the International Court of Justice 1951–1954: Treaty Interpretation and Other Treaty Points' (1957) British Yearbook of International Law 203–293.

Fitzmaurice M, 'Finish-Swedish Frontier River Commission – Effective Water Co-Operation' (2003) 3 Non-State Actors and International Law 111–122.

Franck T, 'Legitimacy in the International System' (1988) 82 American Journal of International Law 705–759.

Franck T, *The Power of Legitimacy among Nations* (Oxford, Oxford University Press 1990).

Franck T, 'Fairness in the International Legal and Institutional System. General Course on Public International Law' in *Receuil Des Cours: Collected Courses of the Hague Academy of International Law 1993: Iii* (Martinus Nijhoff Publishers 1994).

Franck T, *Fairness in International Law and Institutions* (Oxford, Clarendon Press 1995).

Franck T, 'Dr. Pangloss Meets the Grinch: A Pessimistic Comment on Harold Koh's Optimism' (1998–1999) 35 Houston Law Review 683–698.

Franck T, 'The Power of Legitimacy and the Legitimacy of Power: International Law in an Age of Power Disequilibrium' (2006) 100 American Journal of International Law 88–106.

Fuller LL, *The Morality of Law* (New Haven, Conn., Yale University Press 1969).

Gehring T, 'Treaty-Making and Treaty Evolution' in Bodansky D, Brunnée J and Hey E (eds), *The Oxford Handbook of International Environmental Law* (Oxford University Press 2007).

Gerlak AK, Lautze J and Giordano M, 'Water Resources Data and Information Exchange in Transboundary Water Treaties' (2011) 11 International Environmental Agreements 179–199.

Goldstein JL and Martin L, 'Legalization,Trade Liberalization, and Domestic Politics: A Cautionary Note' (2000) 54 International Organization 603–632.

Goodman R and Jinks D, 'Toward Institutional Theory of Sovereignty' (2002–2003) 55 Stanford Law Review 1749–1788.

Goodman R and Jinks D, 'How to Influence States: Socialization and International Human Rights Law' (2004–2005) 54 Duke law journal 621–703.

Goodman R and Jinks D, 'Incomplete Internalization and Compliance with Human Rights Law' (2008) 19 European Journal of International Law 735–748.

Grant RW and Keohane RO, 'Accountability and Abuses of Power in World Politics' (2005) 99 American Political Science Review 29–43.

Granit J and others, *Regional Water Intelligence Report Central Asia* (SIWI 2010).

Haas P, 'Epistemic Communities' in Bodansky D, Brunnée J and Hey E (eds), *The Oxford Handbook of International Environmental Law* (Oxford University Press 2007).

Haas PM, 'Do Regimes Matter? Epistemic Communities and Mediterranean Pollution Control' (1989) 43 International Organization 377.

Habermas J, *The Theory of Communicative Action. Vol. 1. Reason and the Rationalization of Society* (Cambridge, Polity Press 1986).

Habermas J, *The Theory of Communicative Action. Vol.2 Lifeworld and System: A Critique of Functionalist Reason* (Cambridge, Polity Press 1987).

Habermas J, *Postmethaphisical Thinking: Philosophical Essays* (Polity Press 1992).

Habermas J, *Between Facts and Norms: Contribution to a Discourse Theory of Law and Democracy* (Cambridge MA,, MIT Press 1996).

Hafner G, *Risk Ensuing from Fragmentation of International Law* (Report of the International Law Commission on the work of its fifty-second session 2000).

Hafner-Burton EM, Victor DG and Lupu Y, 'Political Science Research on International Law: The State of the Field' (2011) Laboratory on International Law and Regulation Working Paper No 1.

Handl G, 'The Environment: International Rights and Responsibilities' (1980) 74 American Society of International Law Proceedings 223–242.

Handl G, 'Environmental Security and Global Change: The Challenge to International Law' in Lang W, Neuhold H and Zemanek K (eds), *Environmental Protection and International Law* (Graham & Trotman/Martinus Nijhoff 1991).

Handl G, 'Transboundary Impacts' in Bodansky D, Brunnée J and Hey E (eds), *The Oxford Handbook of International Environmental Law* (Oxford University Press 2007).

Hart HLA, *The Concept of Law* (Oxford 2nd ed. / with a postscript edited by Penelope A. Bulloch and Joseph Raz edn, Clarendon Press 1994).

Hathaway OA, 'Do Human Rights Treaties Make a Difference?' (2001–2002) 111 Yale Law Journal 1935–2042.

Hathaway OA, 'Between Power and Principle: An Integrated Theory of International Law' (2005) 72 University of Chicago Law Review 469–536.

Henkin L, *How Nations Behave: Law and Foreign Policy* (2nd edn, Columbia University Press 1979).

Hey E, 'International Institutions' in Bodansky D, Brunnée J and Hey E (eds), *The Oxford Handbook of International Environmental Law* (Oxford University Press 2007).

Higgins R, *Problems and Process: International Law and How We Use It* (Oxford Clarendon Press 1994).

Hoekstra AY and Chapagain AK, *Globalization of Water: Sharing the Planet's Freshwater Resources* (Oxford, Blackwell Publishing 2007).

Holder J and McGillivray D (eds), *Taking Stock of Environmental Assessment: Law, Policy and Practice* (Routledge-Cavendish 2007).

Howse R and Teitel R, 'Beyond Compliance: Rethinking Why International Law Really Matters' (2010) New York University School of Law Public Law & Legal Theory Research Paper Series Working Paper No 10-08.

Hunter DB, *The Emergence of Citizen Enforcement in International Organizations* (INECE 2005).

Ibatullin S, Yasinsky V and Mironenkov A, *Impact of Climate Change to Water Resources in Central Asia* (Sector Report No 6, 2009).

International Law Association (ILA), *Helsinki Rules on the Uses of the Water of International Rivers* (Helsinki 1966), Reprinted in S Bogdanovic, *International Law of Water Resources: Contribution of the International Law Association (1954–2000)* (Kluwer Law International, the Hague 2001).

ILA, *Berlin Rules on Water Resources* in Report of the Seventhy-First International Law Association Conference (Berlin 2004).

International Association of Lawyers Against Nuclear Arms, International Human Rights Clinic, Human Rights Program, Hravard Law School, *Good Faith Negotiations Leading to the Total Elimination of Nuclear Weapons. Request for an Advisory Opinion from the International Court of Justice.* Legal Memorandum (Cambridge, MA 2009).

International Monetary Fund, *Summary of Reports on the International Financial Architecture by the G22 Working Group on Transparency and Accountability, Working Group on Strengthening Financial Systems and Working Group on International Financial Crises* (1998).

Jacobson H and Brown Weiss E, 'A Framework for Analysis' in Brown Weiss E and Jacobson H (eds), *Engaging Countries: Strengthening Compliance with International Environmental Accords* (MIT Press 1998).

Jacobson H and Brown Weiss E, 'Assessing the Record and Designing Strategies to Engage Countries' in Brown Weiss E and Jacobson H (eds), *Engaging Countries: Strengthening Compliance with International Environmental Accords* (MIT Press 1998).

Jervis R, 'Realism and the Study of World Politics' (Autumn 1998) 52 International Organization 971–992.

Johnstone I, 'Security Council Deliberations: The Power of the Better Argument' (2003) 14 European Journal of International Law 437–480.

Johnstone I, 'Legislation and Adjudication in the UN Security Council: Bringing Down the Deliberative Deficit' (2008) 102 American Journal of International Law 275–308.

Kahler M, 'Conclusion: The Causes and Consequences of Legalization' (2000) 54 International Organization 661–683.

Kahler M, 'Legalization as Strategy: The Asia-Pacific Case' (2000) 54 International Organization 549–571.

Kemelova D and Zhalkubaev G, 'Water, Conflict, and Regional Security in Central Asia Revisited' (2003) 11 New York University Environmental Law Journal 479–502.

Kennedy D, 'Toward an Historical Understanding of Legal Consciousness: The Case of Classical Legal Thought in America, 1850-1940' (1980) 3 Research in Law and Sociology 3–24.

Keohane RO and Nye JS, 'Transgovernmental Relations and International Organizations' (1974) 27 World Politics 39–62.

Kingsbury B, 'The Concept of Compliance as a Function of Competing Conceptions of International Law' (1998) 19 Michigan Journal of International Law 345–372.

Kingsbury B, 'Global Environmental Governance as Administration: Implications for International Law' in Bodansky D, Brunnée J and Hey E (eds), *The Oxford Handbook of International Environmental Law* (Oxford University Press 2007).

Kipshakbaev N and Sokolov V, *Water Resources of the Aral Sea Basin-Formation, Distribution, Usage. Water Resources of Central Asia. In Russian* (2002).

Kirgis FL, *Prior Consultation in International Law: A Study of State Practice* (Univeristy Press of Virginia 1983).

Klabbers J, *The Concept of Treaty in International Law* (Leiden/Boston, Martinus Nijhoff Publishers 2006).

Klabbers J, 'The Meaning of Rules' (2006) 20 International Relations 295–301.

Klabbers J, 'Constitutionalism and the Making of International Law: Fuller's Procedural Natural Law' (April 2008) 5 NoFo 84–112.

Klemm W and Shobair SS, *The Afghan Part of Amu Darya Basin. Impact of Irrigation in Northern Afghanistan on Water Use in the Amu Darya Basin* (2010).

Klotz A, 'Norms Reconstituting Interests: Global Racial Equality and U.S. Sanctions against South Africa' (1995) 49 International Organization 451–478.

Knox JH, 'The Myth and Reality of Transboundary Environmental Impact Assessment' (2002) 96 American Journal of International Law 291–319.

Koh H, 'The 1994 Roscoe Pound Lecture: Transnational Legal Process' (1996) 75 Nebraska Law Review 181–207.

Koh H, 'Why Do Nations Obey International Law?' (1997) 106 Yale Law Journal 2599–2659.

Koh H, 'The 1998 Frankel Lecture: Bringing International Law Home' (1998–1999) 35 Houston Law Review 623–682.

Koh H, 'Internalization through Socialization' (2005) 54 Duke law journal 975–982.

Koskenniemi M, 'The Fate of Public International Law: Between Technique and Politics' (2007) 70 Modern Law Review 1–30.

Koskenniemi M, *The Gentle Civilizer of Nations. The Rise and Fall of International Law 1870–1960* (Cambridge, Cambridge University Press 2001).

Koyano M, 'Effective Implementation of International Environmental Agreements: Learning Lessons from the Danube Delta Conflict' in Komori T and Wellens K (eds),

Public Interest Rules of International Law: Towards Effective Implementation (Ashgate 2009).

Krasner SD, 'Structural Causes and Regime Consequences: Regimes as Intervening Variables' (1982) 36 International Organization 185–205.

Kratochwil F, *Rules, Norms, and Decisions: On the Conditions of Practical and Legal Reasoning in International Relations and Domestic Affairs* (Cambridge, Cambridge University Press 1995).

Kratochwil F, 'Thrasymmachos Revisited: On the Revelevance on Norms and the Study of Law for International Relations' (1984) 37 Journal of International Affairs 343–356.

Kravchenko S, 'The Aarhus Convention and Innovations in Compliance with Multilateral Environmental Agreements' (2007) 18 Colorado Journal of International Environmental Law and Policy 1.

Krisch N and Kingsbury B, 'Introduction: Global Governance and Global Administrative Law in the International Legal Order' (2006) 17 European Journal of International Law 1–13.

Kritsiotis D, 'Arguments of Mass Confusion' (2004) 15 European Journal of International Law 233–278.

Kritsiotis D, 'Imagining the International Community' (2002) 13 European Journal of International Law 961–992.

Lammers JG, 'International and European Community Law Aspects of Pollution of International Watercourses' in Lang W, Neuhold H and Zemanek K (eds), *Environmental Protection and International Law* (Graham & Trotman/Martinus Nijhoff 1991).

Lauterpacht H, *The Function of Law in the International Community* (Hamden, Conn., Archon Books 1966).

Lloyd D, *Introduction to Jurisprudence* (4th edn, Stevens and Sons 1979).

Luhmann N, 'Legal Argumentation: An Analysis of Its Form' (1995) 58 Modern Law Review 285.

Lukashuk II, 'The Law of the International Community' in *International Law on the Eve of the Twenty-First Century: Views from the International Law Commission* (United Nations 1997).

Luterbacher U and Wiegandt E, 'Cooperation or Confrontation: Sustainable Water Use in an International Context' in Brown Weiss E, Boisson de Chazournes L and Bernasconi-Osterwalder N (eds), *Fresh Water and International Economic Law* (Oxford University Press 2005).

MacCormick N, 'Coherence in Legal Justification' in Peczenik A (ed), *Theory of Legal Science* (Reidel 1984).

Magsig B-O, 'Overcoming State-Centrism in International Water Law: "Regional Common Concern" as the Normative Foundation of Water Security' (2011) 3 Goettingen Journal of International Law 317–344.

Malanczuk P, *Akehurst's Modern Introduction to International Law* (London, Routledge 1997).

March JG and Olsen JP, 'The Institutional Dynamics of International Political Orders' (1998) 52 International Organization 943–969.

March JG and Olsen JP, 'The Logic of Appropriateness' (2004) ARENA – Centre for European Studies, University of Oslo Working Papers WP 04/09 28.

McCaffrey SC, 'Convention on the Law of the Non-Navigational Uses of International Watercourses' (2008) United Nations Audiovisual Library of International Law. Online: <http://untreaty.un.org/cod/avl/pdf/ha/clnuiw/clnuiw_e.pdf> accessed 22 July 2010.

McCaffrey SC, 'Preliminary Report on the Law of the Non-Navigational Uses of International Watercourses' in *Yearbook of the International Law Commission, Vol Ii(1), Pp 87–96, UN Doc a/Cn4/393* (1985).

McCaffrey SC, 'The Contribution of the UN Convention on the law of the non-navigational uses of international watercourses' (2001) 1 International Journal of Global Environmental Issues 250–263.

McCaffrey SC, *The Law of International Watercourses – Non-Navigational Uses* (Oxford, 2nd edn, Oxford University Press 2007).

McIntyre O, 'The Proceduralisation and Growing Maturity of International Water Law. Case Concerning Pulp Mills on the River Uruguay (Argentina v Uruguay), International Court of Justice, 20 April 2010' (2010) 22 Journal of Environmental Law 475–497.

McLachlan C, 'The Principle of Systemic Integration and Article 31(3)(C) of the Vienna Convention' (2005) 54 International & Comparative Law Quarterly 279–320.

Meron T, 'The Martens Clause, Principles of Humanity, and Dictates of Public Conscience' (2000) 94 American Journal of International Law 78–89.

Micklin Ph, 'The Past, Present, and Future Aral Sea' (2010) 15 Lakes & Reservoirs: Research and Management 193–213.

Milly PCD and others, 'Stationarity Is Dead: Whither Water Management?' (2008) 319 Science 573–574.

Mitchell RB, *International Oil Pollution at Sea: Environmental Policy and Treaty Compliance* (Cambridge, MIT Press 1994).

Mitchell RB, 'Regime Design Matters: Intentional Oil Pollution and Treaty Compliance' (1994) 48 International Organization 425–458.

Mitchell RB, 'Sources of Transparency: Information Systems in International Regimes' (1998) 42 International Studies Quarterly 109–130.

Mitchell RB, 'Compliance Theory: Compliance, Effectiveness, and Behavior Change in International Environmental Law' in Brunnée J, Bodansky D and Hey E (eds), *Oxford Handbook of International Environmental Law* (Oxford University Press 2007).

Moravcsik A, 'A New Statecraft? Supranational Entrepreneurs and International Cooperation' (Spring 1999) 53 International Organization 267–306.

Morgenthau HJ, 'Positivism, Functionalism, and International Law' (1940) 34 American Journal of International Law 260–284.

Morrison J and Ront-Ariaza N, 'Private and Quasi-Private Standrad Setting' in Bodansky D, Brunnée J and Hey E (eds), *The Oxford Handbook of International Environmental Law* (Oxford University Press 2007).

Mukhamadiev B, 'Evolution of a Treaty-Based Law in the Aral Sea Basin: Relevance, Application and Impact of International Water Law' (2006) unpublished LLM thesis University of Dundee.

Mullerson R, *Ordering Anarchy: International Law in International Society* (Martinus Nijhoff Publishers 2000).

Nanni M, 'The Aral Sea Basin: Legal and Institutional Issues' (1996) 5 Review of European Community & International Environmental Law 130–137.

Nazari MM, 'The Transboundary EIA Convention in the Context of Private Sector Operations Co-Financed by an International Financial Institution: Two Case Studies from Azerbaijan and Turkmenistan' (2003) 23 Environmental Impact Assessment Review 441–451.

Nino CS, *The Constitution of Deliberative Democracy* (New Haven, Yale University Press 1998).

Nollkaemper A, *The Legal Regime for Transboundary Water Pollution: Between Discretion and Constraint* (Dordrecht Martinus Nijhoff 1993).

Nollkaemper A, 'The Power of Secondary Rules to Connect the International and National Legal Orders' in Shany Y and Broude T (eds), *Multi-Sourced Equivalent Norms in International Law* (Hart Publishing 2011).

O'Connell ME, *The Power and Purpose of International Law: Insights from the Theory and Practice of Enforcement* (Oxford, New York, Oxford University Press 2008).

Oberthür S, 'Clustering of Multilateral Environmental Agreements: Potentials and Limitations' in Chambers BW and Green JF (eds), *Reforming International Environmental Governance: From Institutional Limits to Innovative Reforms* (Tokyo, New York, Paris, United Nations University Press 2005).

Onuf N, 'Do Rules Say What They Do? From Ordinary Language to International Law' (1985) 26 Harvard International Law Journal 385–410.

Paddock L and others (eds), *Compliance and Enforcement in International Law: Towards More Effective Implementation* (Edward Elgar 2011).

Panhuys JHF, 'Relations and Interactions between International and National Scenes of Law' (1964) 112 Recueil des Cours 1–88.

Patterson D, 'Interpretation in Law' (2005) 42 San Diego Law Review 685–710.

Peczenik A, 'Juristic Definition of Law' (1968) 78 Ethics 255–268.

Pomerantz JR, 'Perception: Overview' in *Encyclopedia of Cognitive Science* (MacMillan/ Nature Publishing Group 2002).

Pulkowski D, 'Universal International Law's Grammar' in Fastenrath U and others (eds), *From Bilateralism to Community Interest: Essays in Honour of Bruno Simma* (Oxford University Press 2011).

Raustiala K, 'Compliance and Effectiveness in International Regulatory Cooperation' (2000) 32 Case Western Reserve Journal of International Law 387–440.

Raustiala K, *Reporting and Review Institutions in 10 Multilateral Environmental Agreements* (2001).

Raustiala K, 'Form and Substance in International Agreements' (2005) 99 American Journal of International Law 581–614.

Rawls J, 'The Idea of an Overlapping Consensus' (1987) 7 Oxford Journal of Legal Studies 1–25.

Rawls J, *A Theory of Justice* (Cambridge, MA/London, Belknap Press of Harvard University Press 2005).

Reisman MM, Wiessner S and Willard AR, 'The New Haven School: A Brief Introduction' (2001) 32 Yale Journal of International Law 575–582.

Reisman MW, 'The Democratization of Contemporary International Law-Making Processes and the Differentiation of Their Application' in Wolfrum R and Röben V (eds), *Developments of International Law in Treaty Making* (Springer 2005).

Reisman MW, 'The Enforcement of International Judgments' (1969) 63 American Journal of International Law 1.

Regional Environmental Centre, the European Communities, *Handbook on the Implementation of EC Environmental Legislation* (2008).

Renner M, *Water and Energy Dynamics in the Greater Himalayan Region: Opportunities for Environmental Peacebuilding* (Norwegian Peacebuilding Resource Centre Report, 2011).

Rieu-Clarke A, *A Fresh Approach to International Law in the Field of Sustainable Development: Lessons from the Law of International Watercourses* (London, IWA Publishing 2005).

Rieu-Clarke A, Wouters P and Loures F, 'The Role and Relevance of the UN Convention of the Law and of the Non-Navigational Uses of International Watercourses to the EU and Its Member States' (2008) Thematic and Regional Assessments of the Relevance and Applicability of the 1997 UN Convention on the Law of the Non-navigational Uses of International Watercourses.

Risse T, '"Let's Argue!": Communicative Action in World Politics' (2000) 54 International Organization 1–39.

Romano CPR, 'International Dispute Settlement' in Bodansky D, Brunnée J and Hey E (eds), *The Oxford Handbook of International Environmental Law* (Oxford University Press 2007).

Ruggie JG, 'What Makes the World Hang Together? Neo-Utilitarianism and the Social Constructivist Challenge' (1998) 52 International Organization 855–885.

Rycroft DW and Wegerich K, 'The Three Blind Spots of Afghanistan: Water Flow, Irrigation Development, and the Impact of Climate Change' (2009) 7 China and Eurasia Forum Quarterly 115–133.

Sadoff CW and Grey D, 'Beyond the River: The Benefits of Cooperation on International Rivers' (2002) 4 Water policy 389–403.

Salman MAS, 'The Helsinki Rules, the UN Watercourses Convention and the Berlin Rules: Perspectives on International Water Law' (2007) 23 International Journal of Water Resources Development 625–640.

Salman MAS, 'Downstream Riparians Can Also Harm Upstream Riparians: The Concept of Foreclosure of Future Uses' (2010) 35 Water International 350–364.

Sands P, *Principles of International Environmental Law* (Cambridge, 2nd edn, Cambridge University Press 2003).

Sands P, 'Water and International Law: Science and Evidence in International Litigation' (2010) 22 Environmental Law and Management 151–161.

Sarat A, 'Legal Effectiveness and Social Studies of Law: On the Unfortunate Persistance of a Research Tradition' (1985) 9 Legal Studies Forum 23–32.

Schachter O, 'Towards a Theory of International Obligation' in Schewbel SM (ed), *The Effectiveness of International Decisions* (Sijthoff 1971).

Schachter O, *International Law in Theory and Practice* (Dordrecht, Martinus Nijhoff Publishers 1991).

Schreiner B, Mtsweni A and Pegram G, *An Institutional Framework for Stakeholder Participation in Transboundary Basins* (2010).

Scott KN, 'International Environmental Governance: Managing Fragmentation through Institutional Connection' (2011) 12 Melbourne Journal of International Law 1–40.

Second Report on the Law of the Non-Navigational Uses of International Watercourses, by Mr. Stephen C. Mccaffrey, Special Rapporteur, [1986] 2(1) Y B Int'l L Comm'n, 87.

Severskiy I and others, *Global International Waters Assessment Aral Sea, GIWA Regional Assessment 24* (Kalmar, University of Kalmar on behalf of United Nations Environment Programme 2005).

Shaffer G and Ginsburg T, 'The Empirical Turn in International Legal Scholarship' (2011) University of Minnesota Law School Legal Studies Research Paper No 12–09.

Shaw MN, *International Law* (Cambridge, 6th edn, Cambridge University Press 2008).

Shelton D, 'Soft Law' in Armstrong D (ed), *Routledge Handbook to International Law* (Routledge 2009).

Silbey SS, 'After Legal Consciousness' (2005) 1 Annual Review of Law and Social Science 328–368.

Simma B, 'From Bilateralism to Community Interest in International Law' (1994) 250 Recueil des Cours 217.

Skrylnikov D, *A Review of the National Legislation of the Republic of Tajikistan on Environmental Impact Assessment in the Context of Implementation and Application of the Espoo Convention. In Russian* (Bureau of Environmental Investigation, 2010).

Slaughter A-M, 'International Law in a World of Liberal States' (1995) 6 European Journal of International Law 503–538.

Slaughter A-M, 'A Liberal Theory of International Law' (2000) 94 American Society of International Law Proceedings 240–249.

Slaughter A-M, *A New World Order* (Princeton, New Jersey, Princeton University Press 2004).

Speech by Mr. Nabiel, Ministry of Foreign Affairs, Afghanistan (UNECE Workshop on transboundary water management in Central Asia 2010).

Stamalaev A, 'Development of the Renewable Energy Sector in the Kyrgyz Republic (Ministry of Energy of the Kyrgyz Republic)' (International Energy Efficiency Forum and Workshop on Investments in Energy Efficiency and Renewable Energy Projects 28–30 September 2010 Astana, Kazakhstan).

Stec S and Casey-Lefkowitz S, *The Aarhus Convention: An Implementation Guide* (New York/ Geneva, United Nations 2002).

Steffek J, 'The Legitimation of International Governance: A Discourse Approach' (2003) 9 European Journal of International Relations 249–275.

Stokke OS and Vidas D (eds), *Governing the Antarctic: The Effectiveness and Legitimacy of the Antarctic Treaty System* (Cambridge University Press 1996).

'Strengthening the Institutional and Legal Frameworks of the International Fund for Saving the Aral Sea: Review and Proposals. Discussion Paper' (2010) Prepared under the project 'Regional Dialogue and Cooperation on Water Resources Management', implemented by the IFAS Executive Committee and the United Nations Economic Commission for Europe (UNECE), supported by Deutsche Gesellschaft für Technische Zusammenarbeit (GTZ) GmbH.

Summers R, *Instrumentalism and American Legal Thought* (Ithaca, Cornell University Press 1982).

Summers R, *LonL. Fuller: Jurists: Profiles in Legal Theory* (Twining W ed, Stanford University Press 1984).

Susskind L, *The Consensus Building Approach: Water Diplomacy* (2011).

Susskind L and Cruikshank J, *Breaking the Impasse: Consensual Approaches to Resolving Public Disputes* (New York, Basic Books 1987).

Susskind L, McKearnan S and Thomas-Larmer J, *The Consensus Building Handbook: A Comprehensive Guide to Reaching Agreement* (Thousand Oaks, CA, Sage 1999).

Tamanaha BZ, 'The Perils of Pervasive Legal Instrumentalism' (2005) 1 Montesquieu Lecture Series, Tilburg University.

Tanzi A, *The Relationship between the 1992 UNECE Convention on the Protection and Use of Transboundary Watercourses and International Lakes and the 1997 UN Convention on the Law of the Non Navigational Uses of International Watercourses* (Report of the UNECE Task Force on Legal and Administrative Aspects, 2000).

Tanzi A and Arcari M, *The United Nations Convention on the Law of International Watercourses: A Framework for Sharing* (Wouters P and Vinogradov S eds, The Hague, Kluwer Law International 2001).

Tanzi A, 'Reducing the Gap between International Water Law and Human Rights Law: The UNECE Protocol on Water and Health' (2010) 12 International Community Law Review 267–285.

Tarlock D and Wouters P, 'Are Shared Benefits of International Waters an Equitable Apportionment?' (2007) 18 Colorado Journal of International Environmental Law and Policy 523–536.

Ticehurst R, 'The Martens Clause and the Laws of Armed Conflict' (1997) 137 International Review of the Red Cross.

Trachtman JP, 'International Law and Domestic Political Coalitions: The Grand Theory of Compliance with International Law' (2010) 11 Chinese Journal of International Law 127–158.

Tremblay H, 'An Analytical Framework for Legal Regimes Applicable to Freshwater Ecosystems' (2009) 20 Journal of Water Law 152–164.

Treves T and others (eds), *Non-Compliance Procedures and Mechanisms and the Effectiveness of International Environmental Agreements* (T.M.C. Asser Press 2009).

Ulfstein G, 'Treaty Bodies' in Bodansky D, Brunnée J and Hey E (eds), *The Oxford Handbook of International Environmental Law* (Oxford University Press 2007).

UN Economic Commission for Europe (UNECE), *Guidelines on the Ecosystem Approach in Water Management* (1993) UN Doc ECE/ENVWA/31.

UNECE, *Recommendations on Payments for Ecosystem Services in Integrated Water Resources Management* (2006) Meeting of the Parties to the Convention on the Protection and Use of Transboundary Watercourses and International Lakes, 4th Session Bonn 10–12 November 2006 UN Doc ECE/MPWAT/22.

UNECE, *Dam Safety in Central Asia: Capacity-Building and Regional Cooperation* (Water Series No 5, 2007).

UNECE, *Our Waters: Joining Hands across Borders. First Assessment of Transboundary Rivers, Lakes and Groundwaters* (2007) Convention on the Protection and Use of Transboundary Watercourses and International Lakes.

UNECE, *Draft Guidelines on EIA in a Transboundary Context for Central Asian Countries* (2007) Meeting of The Parties to the Convention on Environmental Impact Assessment in a Transboundary Context Working Group on Environmental Impact Assessment, 10th Session Geneva 21–23 May 2007 Item 4(d) of the provisional agenda UN Doc ECE/MPEIA/WG1/2007/6.

UNECE, *Facilitating and Supporting Implementation and Compliance: A Needed Step in the Convention's Evolution*. Background Document (2009) Meeting of the Parties to Convention on the Protection and Use of Transboundary Watercourses and International Lakes 5th Session Geneva 10–12 November 2009 UN Doc ECE/MPWAT/2009/3.

UNECE, *Guidance on Water and Adaptation to Climate Change to Convention on the Protection and Use of Transboundary Watercourses and International Lakes* UN Doc ECE/MPWAT/30, 2009.

UNECE, *Guide to Implementing the Convention* (2009) Meeting of the Parties to the Convention on the Protection and Use of Transboundary Watercourses and International Lakes, 5th Session Geneva 10–12 November 2009 UN Doc ECE/MPWAT/2009/L2.

UNECE, *Environmental Performance Review of Uzbekistan: Second Review* (NewYork-Geneva 2010).

UNECE, *Finalization of the Second Assessment of Transboundary Rivers, Lakes and Groundwaters in the United Nations Economic Commission for Europe Region. Executive Summary of the Second Assessment* (2011) Convention on the Protection and Use of Transboundary Watercourses and International Lakes, Working Group on Integrated Water Resources Management Working Group on Integrated Water Resources Management 6th Meeting Geneva 4–5 May 2011 UN Doc ECE/MPWAT/WG2/2011/3-ECE/MPWAT/WG1/2011/3 para 89.

UNECE, *Finalization of the Second Assessment of Transboundary Rivers, Lakes and Groundwaters in the United Nations Economic Commission for Europe Region. Major Findings of the Assessment for Central Asia* (2011) Convention on the Protection and Use of Transboundary Watercourses and International Lakes, Working Group on Integrated Water Resources Management 6th Meeting Geneva 4–5 May 2011 UN Doc ECE/MPWAT/WG2/2011/4–ECE/MPWAT/WG1/2011/4.

UNECE, *Overview of Existing Reporting Requirements of Relevance for the UNECE Water Convention – Challenges and Advantages Related to the Introduction of Reporting under the Convention* (2011) Convention on the Protection and Use of Transboundary Watercourses and International Lakes, Legal Board 8th meeting Geneva 24–25 February 2011 Item 2 (c) of the provisional agenda UN Doc LB/2011/INF1.

UNECE, *Possible Drafting Language for a Mechanism to Facilitate and Support Implementation and Compliance* (2011) Convention on the Protection and Use of Transboundary Watercourses and International Lakes, Legal Board 9th meeting Geneva 1 and 2 September 2011 Item 2 (a) Mechanism to facilitate and support implementation and compliance: possible drafting language for a mechanism to facilitate and support implementation and compliance UN Doc ECE/MPWAT/AC4/2011/6.

UNECE, *Strengthening Water Management and Transboundary Water Cooperation in Central Asia: The Role of UNECE Envrionmental Conventions* (2011) United Nations, Geneva UN Doc ECE/MPWAT/35.

UN Environmental Programme (UNEP) Division of Environmental Law and Conventions,*Compliance Mechanism under Selected Multilateral Environmental Agreements* (2007).

UN Department of Economic and Social Affars, *The Millennium Development Goals Report 2008* (New York 2008).

UN Development Programme (UNDP), *Central Asian Human Development Report. Bringing Down Barriers: Regional Cooperation for Human Development and Human Security* (2005).

UNDP Regional Bureau for Europe and CIS, *Central Asia Regional Risk Assessment: Responding to Water, Energy, and Food Insecurity* (New York 2009).

UN International Law Commission (ILC), *Draft Articles on the Law of Non-Navigational Uses of International Watercourses*, Report of the ILC on the Work of Its Forty-Third Session, UN. Gaor, 46th Sess, Supp (No 10), UN Doc A/46/10 (1991), Reprinted in [1991] 2(2) YB. Int'l L Comm'n 1, at 66.

UN ILC, Commentary to *the Draft Articles on the Law of the Non-Navigational Uses of International Watercourses* in Report of the International Law Commission on the Work of Its Forty-Sixth Session, UN Doc 2(2) (1994) Y B Int'l L Comm'n at 222.

UN ILC, Commentary to *the Draft Articles on Prevention of Transboundary Harm from Hazardous Activities* in Report of the International Law Commission on the Work of Its Fifty-Third Session, UN Doc a/56/10 (2001).

UN ILC, *Fragmentation of International Law: Difficulties Arising from the Diversification and Expansion of International Law* (Report of the Study Group of the International Law Commission Finalized by Martti Koskenniemi UN Doc GAOR A/CN4/L682, 2006).

United Nations International Strategy for Disaster Reduction Secretariat – Central Asia and Caucasus (UNISDR – CA), *Sarez Lake: Latest Achievements and Unresolved Problems* (2007).

UNISDR, *Usoi Landslide Dam and Lake Sarez: An Assessment of Hazard and Risk in the Pamir Mountains, Tajikistan* (2000).

United States Senate, *Avoiding Water Wars: Water Scarcity and Central Asia's Growing Importance for Stability in Afghanistan and Pakistan.* A Majority Staff Report Prepared for the Use of the Committee on Foreign Relations (2011).

Utton AE and Utton J, 'The International Law of Minimum Stream Flows', (1999) 10 Colorado Journal of International Environmental Law and Policy 7.

van Dijk TA, 'Relevance in Text and Context: Discussion of Joseph E. Grimes' Preprint "Context Structure Patterns"' in Allen S (ed), *Text Processing* (Almqvist & Wiksell 1982).

van Genderen R and Rood R, 'Water Diplomacy: A Niche for the Netherlands?' (The Netherlands Ministry of Foreign Affairs and the Water Governance Centre, December 2011).

Victor DG, Raustiala K and Skolnikoff EB (eds), *The Implementation and Effectiveness of International Environmental Commitments: Theory and Practice* (MIT Press 1998).

Vinogradov S, 'Transboundary Water Resources in the Former Soviet Union: Between Conflict and Cooperation' (1996) 36 Natural Resources Journal 393–416.

Vinogradov S and Langford V, 'Managing Transboundary Water Resources in the Aral Sea Basin: In Search of a Solution' (2001) 1 International Journal of Global Environmental Issues 345–362.

Vinogradov S, Wouters P and Jones P, *Transforming Potential Conflict into Cooperation Potential: The Role of International Water Law* (Paris, UNESCO 2003).

Vinogradov S, 'Background Paper on the Legal Basis for Transboundary Water Cooperation (in Russian)' (2004) CWC project workshop on Legal Basis for Transboundary Water Cooperation.

Viotti PR and Kauppi MV, *International Relations Theory: Realism, Pluralism, Globalism and Beyond* (Boston, MA/London, 3rd edn, Allyn and Bacon 1999).

Watt I and Vinogradov S,*Transboundary Water Security in Central Asia: Addressing the Crisis* (Cairneagle Associates LLP, July 2011).

Weber M, *Economy and Society: An Outline of Interpretive Sociology* vol 1 (Roth G and Wittich C eds, Berkeley/London, University of California Press 1978).

Weeramantry CG, *Universalising International Law* (Leiden/Boston, Martinus Nijhoff Publishers 2004).

Wegerich K, 'Hydro-Hegemony in the Amu Darya Basin' (2008) 10 Water policy 71–88.

Wegerich K and Olsson O, 'Late Developers and the Inequity of "Equitable Utilization" and the Harm of "Do No Harm"' (2010) 35 Water International 707–717.

Weil P, 'Towards Relative Normativity in International Law?' (1983) 77 American Journal of International Law 413–442.

Weiler JHH, 'The Geology of International Law – Governance, Democracy and Legitimacy' (2004) 64 ZaöRV 547–562.

Wendt A, 'Anarchy Is What States Make of It: The Social Construction of Power Politics' (1992) 46 International Organization 391.

Wenger E, *Communities of Practice: Learning, Meaning and Identity* (Cambridge University Press 1998).

Werner WG, 'Responding to the Undesired. State Responsibility, Risk Management and Precaution' (2005) 30 Netherlands Yearbook of International Law 57–82.

Wessel RA and Wouters J, 'The Phenomenon of Multilevel Regulation: Interactions between Global, EU and National Regulatory Spheres' (2007) 4 International Organizations Law Review 259–291.

Wettestad J, 'Monitoring and Verification' in Bodansky D, Brunnée J and Hey E (eds), *The Oxford Handbook of International Environmental Law* (Oxford University Press 2007).

Wiener A, 'Constructivism: The Limits of Bridging the Gaps' (2003) 6 Journal of International Relations and Development 252.

Wiener A, 'The Dual Quality of Norms and Governance Beyond the State: Sociological and Normative Approaches to 'Interaction'' (2007) 10 Critical Review of International Social and Political Philosophy 47–69.

Wiener A and Puetter U, 'The Quality of Norms Is What Actors Make of It: Critical Constructivist Research on Norms' (2009) 5 Journal of International Law and International Relations 1–16.

Wiersema A, 'The New International Law-Makers? Conferences of the Parties to Multilateral Environmental Agreements' (2009–2010) 31 Michigan Journal of International Law 231–288.

Wilkins H, 'The Need for Subjectivity in EIA: Discourse as a Tool for Sustainable Development' (2003) 23 Environmental Impact Assessment Review 401–414.

Wolf AT, Yoffe SB and Giordano M, 'International Waters: Identifying Basins at Risk' (2003) 35 Water policy 29–60.

Wolfrum R and Röben V (eds), *Developments of International Law in Treaty Making* (Springer 2005).

Wood MC, 'The Interpretation of Security Council Resolutions' (1998) Max Planck Yearbook of United Nations Law 73–95.

World Bank, Environmental and Social Impact Assessment Study (ESIA) for the Rogun Hydroelectric Power Plant Construction Project. Terms of Reference (3 April 2010).

World Bank, Techno-Economic Assessment Study (TEAS) for the Rogun Hydroelectric Power Plant Construction Project. Terms of Reference (3 April 2010).

World Resources Institute, *Millennium Ecosystem Assessment Ecosystems and Human Well-Being: Wetlands and Water* (Washington, DC 2005).

Wouters P (ed) *International Water Law: Selected Writings of Professor Charles B. Bourne* (Kluwer Law International 1997).

Wouters P and Vinogradov S, 'Analysing the ECE Water Convention: What Lessons for the Regional Management of Transboudary Water Resources' in Stokke OS and Thommessen ØB (eds), *Yearbook of International Co-Operation on Environment and Development 2003/2004* (Earthscan Publications 2003–2004).

Wouters P, Vinogradov S and Magsig B-O, 'Water Security, Hydrosolidarity and International Law: A River Runs through It…' (2009) 19 Yearbook of International Environmental Law 97–134.

Wouters P and Ziganshina D, 'Tackling the Global Water Crisis: Unlocking International Law as Fundamental to the Peaceful Management of the World's Shared Transboundary Waters – Introducing the H_2O Paradigm' in Grafton Q and Hussy K (eds), *Water Resources Planning and Management: Challenges and Solutions* (Cambridge University Press 2011).

Wouters P and Tarlock D, 'The Third Wave of Normativity in Global Water Law – The Duty to Cooperate in the Peaceful Management of the World's Water Resources: An Emerging Obligation *erga omnes*?' (2013) 23 Water Law 51–65.

Young OR, 'Political Leadership and Regime Formation: On the Development of Institutions International Society' (1991) 45 International Organization 281–308.

Young OR, 'Comment on Andrew Moravcsik, "a New Statecraft? Supranational Entrepreneurs and International Cooperation"' (1999) 53 International Organization 805–809.

Young OR (ed) *The Effectiveness of International Environmental Regimes: Causal Connections and Behavioral Mechanisms* (MIT Press 1999).

Young OR, 'Building Regimes for Socioecological Systems: Institutional Diagnostics' in Young OR, King LA and Schroeder H (eds), *Institutions and Environmental Change: Principal Findings, Applications, and Research Frontiers* (MIT Press 2008).

Young OR, King LA and Schroeder H (eds), *Institutions and Environmental Change: Principal Findings, Applications, and Research Frontiers* (MIT Press 2008).

Zaelke D, Kaniaru D and Kružíková E (eds), *Making Law Work: Environmental Compliance and Sustainable Development*, vol I (Cameron May Ltd 2005).

Zeitoun M and Mirumachi N, 'Transboundary Water Interaction I: Reconsidering Conflict and Cooperation' (2008) 8 International Environmental Agreements: Politics, Law and Economics 297–316.

Zeitoun M and Warner JF, 'Hydro-Hegemony – a Framework for Analysis of Trans-Boundary Water Conflicts' (2006) 8 Water policy 435–460.

Ziganshina D, 'International Water Law in Central Asia: Commitments, Compliance and Beyond' (2009) 20 Journal of Water Law 96–107.

Ziganshina D, 'The Role and Relevance of the UN Watercourses Convention to the Countries of Central Asia and Afghanistan in the Aral Sea Basin' (2011) Thematic and Regional Assessments of the Relevance and Applicability of the 1997 UN Convention on the Law of the Non-navigational Uses of International Watercourses.

Ziganshina D, 'Transboundary Impact Assessment in the Aral Sea Basin: Interplay of International and Domestic Laws' (International Law: The Trickle Down Effect Symposium, 4–6 May 2011).

Ziganshina D, 'International Water Law in Central Asia: The Nature of Substantive Norms and What Flows From It' (2012) 2(1) Asian Journal of International Law 169–192.

Ziganshina D, 'Legal Framework Governing Transboundary Waters in the Aral Sea Basin: What is a Role for the UNWC?' in A. Rieu-Clarke, and F.R. Loures (eds.) *The UN Watercourses Convention in force: Strengthening International Law for Transboundary Water Management* (Earthscan, 2013).

Ziganshina D, 'Procedural system of transboundary water cooperation in the Aral Sea Basin' in A. Kibariglu et all (eds.) *Water Law and Cooperation in the Euphrates-Tigrus Region: A Comparative and Interdisciplinary Approach* (Martinus Nijhoff Publishers, 2013).

Zonn IS and others, *The Aral Sea Encyclopedia* (Springer, Verlag Berlin Heidelberg 2009).

Index

www.ingramcontent.com/pod-product-compliance
Lightning Source LLC
LaVergne TN
LVHW010625300926
849162LV00001B/67
9789004274235